THE IMPACT OF PRIVATISATION

Over the past decade economic policy in the UK and elsewhere has been guided by the belief that resources are used more efficiently in the private sector than under state ownership. Consequently, many formerly state-owned companies have been transferred to the private sector. After surveying the theoretical arguments for and against this hypothesis, this book examines the experience of eleven firms, including British Airways, Rolls-Royce and British Telecom. Various indicators are used to measure each firm's performance before and after privatisation to assess whether this policy has brought about improvements in efficiency.

The first four chapters provide background material for the empirical work that follows. Chapter 1 outlines the theoretical arguments for and against the idea that private ownership will be more efficient than state control. Chapter 2 provides brief histories of the eleven organisations studied and chapter 3 discusses how their performance can be measured. Chapter 4 reviews the literature on the relative efficiency of public and private ownership. Chapter 5 considers the impact of privatisation on each of the eleven firms' labour and total factor productivity growth. Chapter 6 performs a similar analysis using two standard accounting ratios (value-added and the rate of profit). Chapter 7 assesses the impact of privatisation on technical efficiency using data envelopment analysis. In chapter 8 the impact of ownership on employment, wage levels and the distribution of business income is considered. The penultimate chapter discusses the restructuring that has followed each company's move into the private sector, and the final chapter summarises the results.

Stephen Martin is Research Fellow in the Centre for Defence Economics, University of York. He has published several papers on privatisation in journals including *Fiscal Studies, Scottish Journal of Political Economy* and *Managerial and Decision Economics*. His current research interests include resource allocation in the National Health Service and the economics of defence procurement. He is the editor of a book entitled *The Economics of Offsets: Defence procurement and countertrade* (1996).

David Parker is Senior Lecturer in Managerial Economics and Co-director of the Research Centre for Industrial Strategy at the University of Birmingham. He has also published several papers on privatisation in leading economics and management journals. His current interests include corporate governance and the economics of regulation.

INDUSTRIAL ECONOMIC STRATEGIES FOR EUROPE
Series editors: Patrizio Bianchi, Keith Cowling and Roger Sugden

Europe is currently at a crucial stage in its economic, social and political development. This series addresses the challenges to European economic policy. It will explore the design of industrial economic strategies enabling European industries and regions to flourish and prosper as we begin the twenty-first century.

COMPETITIVENESS, SUBSIDIARITY AND INDUSTRIAL POLICY
Edited by Pat Devine, Yannis Katsoulacos and Roger Sugden

EUROPE'S ECONOMIC CHALLENGE
Analyses of Industrial Strategy and Agenda for the 1990s
Edited by Patrizio Bianchi, Keith Cowling and Roger Sugden

THE IMPACT OF PRIVATISATION

Ownership and corporate performance
in the UK

Stephen Martin and David Parker

London and New York

First published 1997
by Routledge
11 New Fetter Lane, London EC4P 4EE

Simultaneously published in the USA and Canada
by Routledge
29 West 35th Street, New York, NY 10001

© 1997 Stephen Martin and David Parker; Chapter 7
© Aziz Boussofiane, Stephen Martin and David Parker

Typeset in Times by Pure Tech India Ltd., Pondicherry
Printed and bound in Great Britain by
TJ International Ltd, Padstow, Cornwall

British Library Cataloguing in Publication Data
A catalogue record for this book is available from the British Library

Library of Congress Cataloging in Publication Data
Martin, Stephen, 1961–
The impact of privatisation: ownership and corporate performance in the UK /
Stephen Martin and David Parker.
p. cm. – (Industrial economic strategies for Europe)
Includes bibliographical references (p.) and index.
1. Privatisation – Great Britain. 2. Industrial productivity – Great Britain. I. Parker,
David, 1949 Sept. 28- II. Title. III. Series.
HD4145.M37 1997   96–25484
338.941—dc20
ISBN 0–415–14233–4

CONTENTS

v

CONTENTS

FIGURES

TABLES

PREFACE

Raising the efficiency with which resources are used has been a major goal of privatisation in the UK and elsewhere. John Moore, the Financial Secretary to the Treasury from 1983 to 1986 and responsible for planning a number of key privatisations in the UK, has claimed that the benefits from privatisation are widespread:

> Begun as a radical experiment, privatisation works so well that it has become a practical process by which a state-owned industry can join the free market with visible, often dramatic gains for the industry, its employees, its customers, and for the citizens who set it free by purchasing its shares.
>
> (Moore, 1992, pp. 115–16)

At the same time, however, earlier empirical work, by ourselves and others, detailed in chapter 4, has questioned whether there is any simple relationship between ownership form and performance.

This book is concerned with assessing the impact of privatisation on eleven major firms transferred to the private sector in the UK in the 1980s using a number of different performance measures. Various indicators were chosen to see how sensitive the results are to the precise measure used. The study identifies performance changes over particular time periods based on the final years in state ownership, the decision to privatise and the years following privatisation. The study also covers the performance of the firms over a complete business cycle, including the recession of 1989–92. A number of the firms were privatised in the mid-1980s at a time of economic expansion. It is of interest to consider their performance during not only these years but also the more difficult economic period from 1989. In this part of the study an attempt is made to control for the effects of the business cycle on performance.

Earlier versions of some of the empirical work reported in this book have been published in a number of journals, namely: *Scottish Journal of Political Economy, Managerial and Decision Economics, British Journal of Management, Public Money and Management, Review of Policy Issues* and

International Journal of Public Sector Management. We would like to thank the editors of these journals for permission to reproduce some of the material. The opportunity has been taken to correct a few minor errors in the original work and, importantly, to update the statistical series to 1994 or, where possible, to 1995. Some of the data for earlier years varied from that used in the published papers because of the recent availability of more accurate figures. Also, the Central Statistical Office has revised some of the national wage and productivity figures for the years we study and this has affected the relative enterprise to economy comparisons we report. Nevertheless, the conclusion remains that privatisation has had mixed results. In some enterprises productivity growth has risen since privatisation but in other cases the result has been more disappointing. The same is true for our other performance measures.

We would like to thank Anthony Dnes, Keith Hartley and Roger Sugden who read and commented helpfully on early drafts of some of the papers from which the book was written and participants at numerous conferences where we presented our findings. We also wish to acknowledge the advice given by anonymous reviewers of the published papers before they were accepted by the various journals. Aziz Bousoffiane at the University of Hertfordshire introduced us to the intricacies of data envelopment analysis and jointly authored chapter 7. Stephen Martin's contribution was funded by the ESRC under the second phase of its research programme on contracts and competition (L114251031) and under its single European market programme (L113251028). We would finally like to thank Val Nash and Roberta Blackburn for help with the laborious task of typing and our families and friends for accepting our long periods of bad-tempered writing with their usual understanding.

Stephen Martin, University of York, UK
David Parker, University of Birmingham, UK

March 1996

ABBREVIATIONS

ABP Associated British Ports
BA British Airways
BAA British Airports Authority
BNOC British National Oil Corporation
BSC British Steel Corporation
BT British Telecom
CSO Central Statistical Office (now the Office for National Statistics)
DEA Data Envelopment Analysis
DMU Decision Making Unit
ICC Industrial and Commercial Company
LP Labour Productivity
ME Mixed Enterprise
MMC Monopolies and Mergers Commission
MSB Marginal Social Benefit
MSC Marginal Social Cost
NEDO National Economic Development Office
NFC National Freight Corporation
PC Private Company
PSBR Public Sector Borrowing Requirement
RPI Retail Price Index
SIC Standard Industrial Classification
SOE State-owned Enterprise
TFP Total Factor Productivity
VA Value Added

1

PRIVATISATION

The conceptual framework

INTRODUCTION

In the last decade many countries have introduced privatisation programmes. In 1995 the value of state sell-offs is reported to have reached a
record figure of US$73bn with at least forty-five countries in the process of
privatising some industries (*Economist*, 13 January 1996, p. 5). This figure
may exaggerate the degree of true privatisation since some governments
choose to describe the sale to the private sector of only a small part of the
total shareholding as a privatisation. Nevertheless, there can be no doubting
the profound effect of world-wide privatisation on industrial organisation
both in the developed and the developing world.

Table 1.1 UK privatisation proceeds

Year	£mn at 1994–5 prices
1979–80	0.4
1980–1	0.2
1981–2	0.5
1982–3	0.5
1983–4	1.1
1984–5	2.0
1985–6	2.7
1986–7	4.5
1987–8	5.1
1988–9	7.1
1989–90	4.2
1990–1	5.3
1991–2	7.9
1992–3	8.2
1993–4	5.4
1994–5	6.4
1995–6	2.4
1996–7	4.0e
1997–8	2.5e
1998–9	1.5e

Source: H.M. Treasury, 1995.
Note: e = estimates.

This book is concerned with privatisation in the UK where, since 1979, over £60bn of UK business assets have been transferred from the state sector to the private sector. At first the annual value of sales was low but, as reflected in the figures in Table 1.1, since the mid-1980s sales have regularly exceeded £5bn per annum, reaching a figure of over £8bn in 1992–3. Table 1.2 provides a summary listing of the main industrial privatisations since 1979 in the UK. Whole industries, such as water, electricity and gas supply, have been affected, along with large sections of the transport, aerospace and telecommunications industries. Because of the size and scope of the privatisation programme, the UK is an obvious candidate for studying the economic effects of this policy. Also, sufficient time has now passed since the early privatisations to begin to assess their longer-term economic impact.

Table 1.2 Major privatisations in the UK

Organisation	Year of first share sale	Industry
British Petroleum	1979	Oil
National Enterprise Board Investments	1980	Various
British Aerospace	1981	Aerospace
Cable & Wireless	1981	Telecoms
Amersham International	1982	Scientific goods
National Freight Corporation	1982	Road transport
Britoil	1982	Oil
British Rail Hotels	1983	Hotels
Associated British Ports	1983	Ports
British Leyland (Rover)	1984	Car producer
British Telecom (BT)	1984	Telecoms
Enterprise Oil	1984	Oil
Sealink	1984	Sea transport
British Shipbuilders & Naval Dockyards	1985	Ship building
National Bus Company	1986	Transport
British Gas	1986	Gas
Rolls-Royce	1987	Aero-engines
British Airports Authority	1987	Airports
British Airways	1987	Airlines
Royal Ordnance Factories	1987	Armaments
British Steel	1988	Steel
Water	1989	Water
Electricity distribution	1990	Electricity
Electricity generation	1991	Electricity
Trust Ports	1992	Ports
Coal industry	1995	Coal
Railways	1995–7	Railways
Nuclear energy	1996	Electricity

In the UK, as in many other countries, the political pressure for privatisation came from a combination of disillusionment with the results of state ownership and from a belief that private ownership would bring substantial economic benefits. State-owned industries were viewed as highly inefficient, slow at developing and introducing new technologies, subject to over-frequent and damaging political intervention and dominated by powerful trade unions (Veljanovski, 1987). Privatisation seemed to offer a means of ridding the state of the financial burden of loss-making activities, while at the same time spreading share ownership and curtailing union power (Arbomeit, 1986). Moreover, privatisation sales offered a tempting source of state funding at a time when economic policy was geared to reducing the public sector borrowing requirement (PSBR).

From the beginning, government ministers have stuck tenaciously to the argument that the privatisation programme has been an outstanding success story, especially in terms of increasing efficiency. For example, John Moore, the Financial Secretary to the Treasury in charge of the privatisation programme in the mid-1980s, stated in a speech in November 1983 that:

> The privatisation programme is coherent, and well thought out. It holds substantial advantages for the management of the industries, their employees, the consumer and the taxpayer. And it also, of course, brings benefits to the PSBR and furthers our objectives of reducing the size of the public sector. But these important by-products are secondary to the main theme. Our main objective is to promote competition and improve efficiency.
>
> (Moore, 1983)

In a later statement he returned to the subject now certain that the source of performance gains lay in the nature of state ownership:

> To begin with, the priorities of elected politicians are different from and often in conflict with the priorities of effective business managers. Yet, in state-owned industries politicians are in charge, which means that whenever politicians cannot resist getting involved in what should be management decisions, political priorities take precedence over commercial ones. Politicians may overrule commercial judgements in order to build a new factory in an area where voters need jobs or they may refuse to close an uneconomical plant. They can become involved in policies affecting the hiring and the size of the workforce.
>
> (Moore, 1992, p. 117)

Inefficiency is, allegedly, the inevitable result. Similarly, Tim Eggar, Minister for Industry and Energy, felt able to summarise recently the certain and enormous economic benefits that had resulted from the government's privatisation programme as 'price reductions; the shake up of old management practices leading to large efficiency improvements and dramatically falling costs; and . . . improvements in standards of service' (Eggar, 1995, p. 7).

A more critical commentary, however, would note that the programme has been dogged from the outset by some incoherence. In particular, the government had a number of objectives for privatisation that are potentially contradictory. For example, the promotion of quick and successful asset sales sits uneasily alongside a desire to promote competition in industries previously supplied by state monopolies and to raise funds to reduce the PSBR. Monopolies with their more or less guaranteed profits fetch a higher price in the stock market than an identical firm facing intense competition in the product market. In addition, the promotion of small shareholdings, by favouring the small investor during flotation sales, may be inconsistent with the imposition of an effective capital market constraint on managerial behaviour. The government has based its case for privatisation largely on the benefits that it produces in terms of competition in the product market and the pressure private investors place on management to manage efficiently. However, a number of state-owned companies were already operating in competitive markets and others retained their monopoly at privatisation. Moreover, large share-holders are arguably more likely than small investors to manage their share portfolios actively to maximise income and capital gains; a point we return to later.

This book is concerned with the primary rationale for privatisation both in the UK and elsewhere and as evidenced in the above statements by government ministers, John Moore and Tim Eggar, that is to say, the impact of privatisation on efficiency. The remainder of this chapter is concerned with developing a conceptual framework for the analysis of privatisation and efficiency, in which some of the above contradictions will feature. The concern is with why ownership may matter from an economic point of view. Chapter 2 provides a brief history of each of the eleven organisations that are the subject of this study. In chapter 3 the principles and method of performance assessment are discussed, including the mean-ing of 'efficiency'. Chapter 4 is concerned with a review of earlier studies of public versus private efficiency and the effects of privatisation.[1] Chapters 5–8 provide a detailed investigation of pre- and post-privatisation perfor-mance for a selected group of eleven enterprises privatised in the UK in the 1980s. Performance is assessed using a variety of performance measures: labour and total factor productivity, value-added, the rate of profit, and an efficiency frontier method. Data are also provided on the distribution of business income, wage relativities and employment pre- and post-privatisa-tion. Chapter 9 looks at how privatisation has affected the internal organi-sation of the firms in this study. Chapter 10 provides conclusions and draws lessons for industrial policy in the UK and overseas, especially for other countries pursuing privatisation policies. The chapter also attempts to answer the central question: has privatisation been successful in improving efficiency?

PROPERTY RIGHTS, PUBLIC CHOICE AND INCOMPLETE CONTRACTS: AN AGENT–PRINCIPAL FRAMEWORK

In the privatisation literature state enterprises are said to be inefficient because:

a. state-owned industries suffer from excessive political intervention;
b. management in state industries have vague, fluctuating and often conflicting objectives. Political time frames are often incompatible with the longer time cycles that successful investment needs;
c. politicians and civil servants fail to monitor managerial behaviour as effectively as the private capital market and, amongst other things, this leads to over-investment (Rees, 1989; Pryke, 1981) and the trading of more output for lower profits (Pint, 1991);
d. trade unions in the public sector are able to succeed in obtaining above market wages, employment levels and conditions of work at the expense of consumers (so-called rent-seeking behaviour) (Windle, 1991);
e. bankruptcy is not a credible threat when there are seemingly unlimited taxpayers' funds to call upon;
f. managerial salaries in the public sector are politically determined and rarely compare well with the pay of equivalent jobs in the private sector. Consequently, the quality of management suffers;
g. there is a lack of performance related rewards in the public sector;
h. public sector firms are insufficiently consumer orientated when operating in monopoly markets; and
i. state ownership confuses the regulation of the activities of industry with the role of ownership so that state regulation is less effective.

Clearly, there are some difficulties with these arguments. For example, the suggestion that some labour groups (workers) receive an above market wage while others (managers) earn a below market rate seems slightly contradictory. Or if paying a below market rate to one group reduces their quality, then paying an above market rate to another group would presumably lead this part of the workforce to be of a better than average quality. Nevertheless, research suggests that the record of state ownership in the UK accords with a number of these weaknesses, including politically motivated pricing, distorted investment programmes and uneasy industrial relations (NEDO, 1976; and see chapter 4). In their influential study of privatisation Vickers and Yarrow conclude that:

> The history of the nationalized industries has shown that . . . a system of control that relies heavily upon agents' internalization of the public interest objectives is unlikely to produce good performance. In the event . . . the results of the policy failure have included widespread goal displacement, lack of clarity in corporate objectives, overlapping

responsibilities and excessive ministerial intervention in operational decisions. These in turn have had detrimental effects on the pricing, investment and internal efficiency performance of the nationalized industries.

(Vickers and Yarrow, 1988, p. 151)

Given these perceived failures of state ownership, Rees (1989, p. 108) predicts that privatisation will lead to 'higher prices, lower outputs, higher labour productivity, lower employment, and lower wage rates, since these are the consequences in the model of tightening the profit constraint'. Other results of privatisation are said to be: more commercial management; greater consumer focus and more imaginative marketing; improved capital usage; less damaging state interference; and more effective regulation of industries in the public interest (Veljanovski, 1987).

A useful starting point for the economic analysis of privatisation is agent–principal theory. Agency situations arise when one party (principals, such as shareholders) delegate to another party (agents, such as managers) decisions over the use of their property or property rights (Jensen and Meckling, 1976; Arrow, 1985; Fama and Jensen, 1983). This arrangement may be economically efficient from a specialisation or comparative advantage perspective, but agency relationships raise the prospect of divergent goals. The agenda of the agents may well not be the same as those of the principals, especially since agents can be expected to be self-interested. In particular, principals are at risk of slacking and other dysfunctional behaviour by agents that reduces the underlying value of the property rights.

This can be illustrated as follows: in both the public and private sectors managerial utility can be expressed as a function of profit (Π) and quantities of inputs. Hence $U = U(, I)$ where U (.) takes the usual shape and is a twice continuously differentiable concave function and I is a vector of inputs. The manager's utility will be related to profit if he or she owns shares, benefits from profit-related pay, gains prestige from high profit or where higher profit improves job security. Inputs enter the utility function because the manager's income may rise when there are more employees and a larger capacity to manage or extra employees may mean more free time. Profit is the product of costs deducted from revenue. The cost efficiency of the firm will be weaker the smaller the relationship between the manager's utility and profit, and the stronger the relationship between the manager's utility and the volume of discretionary inputs. Assuming that managers in the public and private sectors pursue either profits or output (or some combination of the two) expressed as Φ, and both require management effort, the management objective is to maximise $\Phi - (\lambda - 1)E$ where E is managerial effort and $\lambda > 1$ reflects the disutility of such effort.

The aim of principals wishing maximum profits must therefore be both to maximise E and to ensure that management effort is directed at maximising profit and not at maximising output and employing discretionary inputs. In practice, the agent knows the amount of useful effort he or she puts into the management of the business. The principal, however, knows the outcome but cannot monitor effort directly. Assuming that costs depend upon (a) environmental random variables that represent factors impacting on the performance of the firm that are outside the agent's control, such as the business cycle, M_i, and (b) the agent's effort at controlling and reducing production costs, E, then total costs, C_i, take the form $C_i = f(M_i, [\lambda - 1]E)$.

The principal monitors C_i but in a world of imperfect information cannot be certain whether an inflated C_i is the result of changes in M_i or E. To ensure that E is maximised the principals must write and enforce a contract with the agent to maximise effort. Given that E is known to the agent but not the principals, an incentive system must be designed to maximise E irrespective of the M_i states so that agent maximisation of effort becomes the dominant strategy. The differences between public and private ownership, therefore, can be reduced to the efficacy of the incentive mechanism.

This discussion suggests that if privatisation is to lead to more managerial effort leading to efficiency gains in the organisation, it must involve improved policing of agent behaviour or more constraints on managerial discretion. In other words, a change in ownership involves a new agent–principal relationship with new forms of information and incentive regimes in a world of incomplete contracts.

Ownership and competition

When a state-owned monopoly is privatised, the government might also introduce competition into the product market (that is, remove the company's monopoly). Economists have a predilection for competition. The first fundamental theorem in welfare economics states that, under certain conditions, a competitive equilibrium in a market economy is Pareto efficient since when this exists no one can be made better off through a resource re-allocation without making someone else worse off. The second fundamental theorem broadly states that most such Pareto-efficient outcomes can be achieved in a perfectly competitive economy, provided redistribution is dealt with first.

As with all theorems, certain assumptions have to be made if the theory is to hold. In particular, the first theorem assumes the absence of externalities in consumption or production, and the technical conditions required for the second are relatively onerous. But broadly speaking the two theorems together amount to saying that competition produces efficiency and, if the outcome is inequitable, this can be dealt with as a separate issue.

(Waterson, 1995, p. 132)

Empirical study of the effect of competition on productivity in manufacturing has borne out that it affects both the level and growth rate positively (Nickell, 1993). Competition sharpens the incentives for management to manage the firm's assets efficiently. Also, where there is competition, the firm's profits reflect and identify differences in managerial ability creating a link between the product and capital markets. At the same time, however, privatisation may have no effect on competition. Monopolies might be sold-off with their monopoly powers wholly or largely intact while many state-owned firms have traditionally operated in competitive markets. Thus conceptually, the impact of ownership and competition (in the product market) are quite distinct, and while the positive effect of competition on performance is a relatively uncontroversial one in economic theory, the impact of ownership *per se* is much less well determined. In this book, the primary focus is on the impact of ownership (although where competitive conditions change this is noted since the results may be influenced by the change in the product market).

If competition in the product market does not alter when privatisation occurs then the source of any performance improvement will lie in a change in the capital market, that is to say directly in the change of ownership. Privatisation subjects enterprises to the discipline of the competitive capital market, which many believe imposes a more effective constraint on managerial discretionary behaviour than political control (Crain and Zardkoohi, 1980; Pera, 1989, p. 181). The result, it is claimed, is higher efficiency even under similar product market conditions.

The argument is that in the private sector owners can trade their shares in the capital market and this constrains managerial behaviour. If management lose the confidence of their shareholders the share price falls, which may trigger a hostile takeover bid (Alchian, 1965; Jensen and Meckling, 1976; Fama, 1980). Alternatively, management may be deposed by large shareholders when performance disappoints at company annual general meetings (AGMs) or on other occasions (Aoki, 1983; Leech, 1987). In contrast, in the public sector there are no shares to trade and managerial appointments depend upon government decisions which may not be heavily weighted by economic results (Zeckhauser and Horn, 1989, p. 35).

The possible impact of both the product and capital markets on performance can be discussed with the aid of Figure 1.1. Position A represents a monopoly supplier in the public sector. With no or very limited product market competition and taxpayer funding, incentives for management to achieve high efficiency in their firms are poor. Hence the expectation is that efficiency will be low. By contrast, position D represents a competitive firm raising funding from the private capital market. Here the expectation is that there are high incentives for management to operate their firms efficiently. Both the product market (competition) and the capital market (tradeable

	Monopoly	Competition
Public ownership	A	B
Private ownership	C	D

Figure 1.1 Alternative ownership and competitive regimes

shares) constraints apply. B and C are in effect intermediate positions, they represent mid-way states in which either the product market or capital market constraints on behaviour are limited. The expectation would be that the performance of firms in positions B and C will be higher than firms in position A but not as high as those in position D. The expectation would be that maximum efficiency gains will arise when privatisation is combined with the introduction of competition in the product market; that is, where there is a move from point A to D. Smaller gains might be anticipated when the movement is from position A to C (privatising a monopolist) or from B to D (privatising a firm in a competitive market). Gains would also be anticipated when exposing a state-owned monopoly to competition (moving from A to B) or when exposing a privately owned monopoly to competition (moving from C to D).

Differences in behaviour under state and private ownership may be compounded by differences in objectives. In the private sector although profit may not always be pursued rigorously and consistently there is, nevertheless, a clear bottom line. If losses continue to be made ultimately the firm will fail. In the state sector, however, objectives are often vague and tend to change according to the political climate, leading to uncertainty about long-term strategy within the industries. Public enterprises pursue multiple and often blurred or ill-articulated objectives which may help to mask inefficiency. Privatisation should change and clarify the objectives of the enterprise as well as affecting managers' incentives to achieve these goals (Bös, 1991). At its most simple, profit maximisation will replace wider and less well articulated goals to do with welfare maximisation. But it is important to note that whether this actually translates into higher efficiency and how the efficiency gains are distributed in terms of profits and prices is complex. For example, De Fraja (1993) argues that because consumer surplus enters into the government's social welfare function, but not the shareholders' profit function, the government has more to gain from a given improvement in the firm's efficiency. Higher efficiency leading to lower prices benefits the consumer but not shareholders. If managers' utility enters the social welfare function then the government will pay the managers more, inducing a higher effort level. 'The results contained in the present paper considerably strengthen the hand of those favouring public ownership by showing that the latter is not only not necessarily less productively efficient, but in some circumstances more productively efficient...' (De Fraja, 1993, p. 24).

This result emphasises the dangers of drawing a set of conclusions about relative performance in the state and private sectors. Taking into account objectives, which can be expected to be different in the public and private sectors, complicates the analysis of performance and this is pursued in chapter 3. At the same time, De Fraja's analysis is only one possible outcome and differs from that of the public choice and property rights literatures detailed below. It also seems to conflict with the arguments of some economists, such as Bös and Peters (1989), who show that under certain conditions the monitoring of employees can be more effectively undertaken in private sector firms.

Property rights

Especially important in shaping attitudes towards public and private ownership have been the public choice and property rights literatures in economics. Although they developed separately, and have two distinct analytical traditions, they produce highly complementary conclusions. Lindblom defines property rights as follows:

> Property is a set of rights to control assets: to refuse use of them to others, to hold them intact, or to use them up. Property rights are consequently grants of authority made to persons and organizations, both public and private and acknowledged by other persons and organizations.
>
> (Lindblom, 1977, p. 26)

A standard property rights approach to public and private ownership acknowledges that there are agency problems in all forms of ownership, but that because ownership is transferable through a competitive capital market in the private sector, a better use of resources results. Monitoring by residual claimants is more efficient than monitoring through the political process. The literature lays heavy emphasis upon the attenuation of property rights where public ownership exists and, in turn, explores the consequences of attenuated property rights for efficiency.

Drawing upon seminal work by Coase (1937), the firm is perceived to be a 'nexus of contracts' between management, labour, suppliers, shareholders and other stakeholders (Jensen and Meckling, 1976; Fama, 1980; Aoki, 1983; Hart and Holmstrom, 1987; Aoki *et al.*, 1990). The boundary of the firm is determined by the relative costs of transacting for inputs in the market as against employment within the firm given: (a) information asymmetries between contractors; (b) an inability to write complete contracts covering all contingencies; and (c) the costs of monitoring contract compliance (Marschak and Radner, 1972; Arrow, 1974, 1987; Williamson, 1975; Holmstrom and Tirole, 1989). In certain circumstances it will be more cost efficient in terms of transaction costs to employ inputs directly, in other cases it will be more efficient to contract in the market. In terms of the privatisation debate, this analysis draws attention to the important role of contracting for inputs and of monitoring their performance within firms. If employment within firms is to be more efficient than contracting in the market then the inputs must be efficiently managed. Equally, the success of one firm compared to another derives from more efficient contracting leading to higher performance.

Alchian and Demsetz (1972) have argued that the firm is a team of factor suppliers with contracts established and monitored by management. It is the role of management to ensure that there is no free-riding or slacking in the team, but, since there are costs in terms of time and effort in devising an optimal monitoring-reward system, to perform this task well management need an incentive (also see Jensen and Meckling, 1976). In the property rights literature the incentive is profit (usually referred to in the property rights literature as 'the residual'). This leads to the expectation that private sector organisations in which rights to profits are clearly defined will perform better than those in the public sector where rights, it is claimed, are diffused and uncertain (Alchian, 1965, 1977; Furubotn and Pejovich, 1972 and 1974; De Alessi, 1980; McCormick and Meiners, 1988). Consequently, the monitoring of management by owners is likely to be much more effective in the private sector. In sum, the property rights literature is concerned with the *incentives* to monitor agent behaviour effectively under public and private ownership.

Public choice, incomplete contracts and agency relationships

In contrast, public choice theory is concerned more directly with actual *behaviour* in the public sector. At the core of this literature is the argument that politicians and state bureaucrats pursue their own utility rather than the public interest (Downs, 1967; Niskanen, 1971, 1987; Tullock, 1965; Buchanan, 1972, 1978; Blankart, 1983; Mitchell, 1988; Mueller, 1989; Aranson, 1990). Policies are arranged to maximise votes, thereby securing the careers of the politicians, and departmental budgets are expanded so that bureaucrats benefit from better jobs and higher salaries (Migue and Belanger, 1974; Orzechowski, 1977). It is also claimed that public monitoring of spending is inhibited in the state sector because bureaucrats will have more information than taxpayers about the consequences of budgetary changes (Olson, 1965; Kristensen, 1980; Breton and Wintrobe, 1982). Civil servants gather information and can lobby for their budgets as a matter of course in their jobs. By contrast, it will usually be quite rational behaviour for any individual member of the public not to seek out the information needed to monitor state spending adequately. For any individual, the costs of information gathering and lobbying (the political transaction costs) are likely to far exceed the benefits that would accrue directly from success in changing policy. This may not be true, however, for interest groups, such as trade unions representing employees in the public sector or major suppliers. In consequence, the public sector is fertile ground for rent-seeking activity. In particular, the argument suggests that trade unions will inflate wage demands and staffing levels and contractors will gather high profits (Tullock, 1976; Bhagwati, 1982). The expectation in the property rights literature is that this will be especially true in countries where state industries raise little or no capital on the open market (as, for example, in the UK) and hence are not open to the sanction of the private capital market.

Together the property rights and public choice literatures suggest that state-owned and privately-owned firms will differ in behaviour and hence performance because of differences in: (a) management's objective function; and (b) constraints. In effect, the fundamental differences between state and private enterprise reduce to a matter of incentives in the face of incomplete information leading to differences in behaviour (Hart and Holmstrom, 1987; Holmstrom and Tirole, 1989; Shapiro and Willig, 1990, p. 55). Hence, incompleteness of contract becomes the starting point for the theory of ownership. If contracts were complete ownership would not matter since managerial discretionary behaviour would be avoided through the contract (Grossman and Hart, 1986; Hart, 1993, pp. 140–1). It is the inability of principals to write complete contracts for their agents covering all possible contingencies and to perfectly monitor and enforce such contracts that leads to scope for managerial discretionary behaviour or agency problems (Hart, 1995).

Two types of information problem may exist where there are incomplete contracts: *adverse selection* (as a result of hidden information) and *moral hazard* (hidden action) (Jensen and Meckling, 1976; Arrow, 1985; Laffont, 1989). In both the public and private sectors there are agent–principal relationships which are characterised by asymmetric information leading potentially to adverse selection and moral hazard (Ross, 1973; Mitnick, 1980; Jackson, 1985; Rees, 1985; Bös and Peters, 1991). This necessitates the creation of efficiency incentive systems. In the economics literature, the solution to an agent–principal problem involves the development of an

12

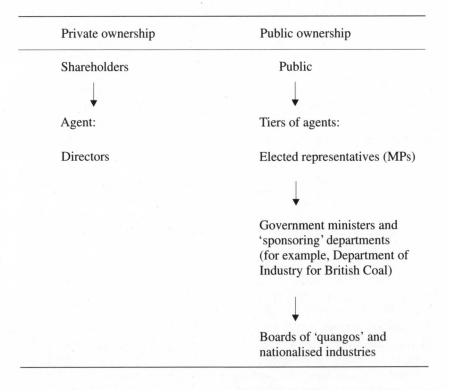

Private ownership	Public ownership
Shareholders	Public
↓	↓
Agent:	Tiers of agents:
Directors	Elected representatives (MPs)
	↓
	Government ministers and 'sponsoring' departments (for example, Department of Industry for British Coal)
	↓
	Boards of 'quangos' and nationalised industries

Figure 1.2 Flows of information between principals and agents in the public and private sectors

effective incentive package that binds the agents to follow the objectives of the principals.

In the private sector an important agency relationship exists between shareholders (principals) and directors (agents). At its simplest, the share-holders own the enterprise and appoint directors to manage it on their behalf. The implications of this relationship for efficiency in the private sector are explored below. In the public sector, by contrast, the agent–principal relationship is more complex because the ultimate owners of state assets, the principals, are the public. Between the public and the managers of the assets (the boards of state industries) exist layers of agencies (Aharoni, 1982). The greater complexity of the agency relationship is illustrated in Figure 1.2.

The existence of layers of agents seems to provide more scope for 'noise' to distort the information flow between principals and resource managers (Smith, 1990, p. 55). Hence privatisation can be viewed as changing the nature of the agent–principal relationship to reduce this noise and therefore facilitate the introduction of more effective incentive systems that bind agents to the principals' goals (Rees, 1985). The failure of the ballot box, especially in the face of rent seeking groups, to control agents in the public sector is well documented (see, for example, Crew and Rowley, 1988; Mitchell, 1988; Carroll, 1990). Arrow's impossibility theorem (1963) states that it is not possible for multiple principals to generate social choices that are consistent with transitivity, Pareto efficiency and independence of irrelevant alternatives in the absence of a dictator. Though the probabilistic voting literature can demonstrate that under certain circumstances political competition for votes may lead to socially efficient outcomes (Wintrobe, 1987; Mueller, 1989, p. 214; Peltzman, 1990, 1992), the more general view is that in practice the ballot box is much less reliable than market signals (Borcherding, 1977). In terms of Hirschman's (1970) terminology, 'voice' through the political process is a more inferior indicator of public demands than 'exit' (sale of shares) in the competitive capital market.

According to public choice theory, the result of the agent–principal relationship in the public sector is an over-expansion of state budgets leading to waste or inefficiency. Various models have been put forward leading broadly to this conclusion. For instance, Navajas (1984) assumes that state enterprises can be modelled according to a minister wishing to maximise the difference between the sum of total consumer surpluses plus profit, and managerial income. This occurs in an environment where there is asymmetric information and incompatible preferences. Rees (1984) uses a model that assumes managers want to maximise output, and hence income and utility, and workers want to maximise real wages and employment. More generally, models have been developed based on managerial utility maximisation (for a review see Lawson, 1994) but with different variables entering into the utility function.

In the words of a leading proponent of public choice theory, William A. Niskanen, government officials (bureaucrats) pursue their own utility which is held to be a function of 'salary, perquisites of the office, public regulation, power, patronage, output of the bureau, ease of making changes, and ease in managing the bureau' (Niskanen, 1971, p. 38). All but the last two relate to the size of the bureau and, therefore, the expectation is that public outputs will be over-supplied. Niskanen (1973, p. 33) concludes that the output of a monopoly government bureau will be twice as large as provision in competitive private markets (though for critical reviews of this conclusion see Jackson, 1982, pp. 131–5; Cullis and Jones, 1987, ch.6; and Dunleavy, 1991, pp. 156–62). Others have suggested that too low a rate of discount will be used when appraising investments and there will be excessive employment of labour (see, for example, Buchanan and Tullock, 1962; Buchanan, 1968, 1986; Tullock, 1976; Breton, 1974; Orzechowski, 1977; Breton and Wintrobe, 1975). Tullock (1979, p. 34) argues that as a result, and as a rough rule of thumb, public sector outputs will be twice as costly as they would be if privately supplied.

Whatever the precise outcome in terms of over-production and other inefficiencies, there can be no doubting the powerful effect of the property rights and public choice theories on the academic literature on privatisation since the 1970s. Together they have provided a formidable *a priori* argument in favour of reducing state budgets and, wherever possible, transferring state activities to the private sector.

CRITICISMS OF THE PROPERTY RIGHTS/PUBLIC CHOICE APPROACH

This literature, however, is not free from weakness. Drawing a sharp distinction between the public and private sectors may be misleading. Arguably ownership is best viewed as a continuum of organisational types. In the UK, these range from the archetypal government bureaucracy (for example, the Foreign Office) through various types of agencies (such as trading funds, 'next steps' agencies and public corporations), through to private sectors firms heavily dependent on government contracts (for example, construction and defence businesses), limited liability companies, and lastly the archetypal entrepreneurial small business (such as the corner grocery store) (Dahl and Lindblom, 1953; Rainey, Backoff and Levine, 1976; Bozeman, 1987; Dunsire *et al.*, 1988; Perry and Rainey, 1988; Rainey, 1991). At the same time *all* firms, whatever their legal ownership, are subject to *some* degree of state influence, namely through regulations, taxes and the impact of macroeconomic management on demand, prices and interest rates.

An emphasis upon ownership as a continuum always involving some state intervention suggests that it might be too simplistic to presume some readily identifiable public versus private split in organisational design and orientation. Public sector and private sector firms may have similarities that define their behaviour and performance more clearly than the presumed differences. Interestingly, two of the privatised firms whose performance is studied in detail in this book, Rolls-Royce and British Aerospace, have remained highly dependent upon state contracts, while a number of other firms have remained state regulated, as detailed later.

Two further criticisms can be made of the approach to ownership differences in the property rights and public choice literatures: first the attitude to motivation in the public sector; and second the supposed working of the capital market in the private sector.

At the heart of the public choice model is the neoclassical rational actor or maximising individual. Agents are considered to behave rationally in a self-regarding way and through the pursuit of self-interest they optimise their preferences in a consistent fashion. This is held to be as true of politicians and employees in the state sector as it is elsewhere in the

15

economy. The resulting perspective on motivation in the public sector contrasts markedly with the Weberian notion of disinterested officials pursuing the public interest which underpinned public ownership in the UK in the 1940s.[2] The chief architect of post-war nationalisation, the Labour minister Herbert Morrison, applied the phrase 'high custodians of the public interest' to the new boards of state industries.

Motivation

From its inherent assumptions about individual motivation based on rational self-seeking behaviour, public choice theory leads to the conclusion that state employees pursue their own interests even when they clearly conflict with the public interest. This may be a correct view of the public sector, but on the other hand it may seriously misrepresent how employees in the public sector actually behave. Certainly, the organisational behaviour literature for a long time has argued that the motivational needs of individuals in organisations are more complex than as represented by neoclassical utility-maximising man (Maslow, 1964; Herzberg, 1966). Maslow argued that individuals have a hierarchy of needs, which range from physiological needs at the lowest level (such as food and warmth), through safety needs, love needs, esteem needs, to self-actualisation at the highest level. Neoclassical economics tends to emphasise low level needs, whereas the concept of 'high custodians' is more commensurate with esteem and self-actualisation needs important to high income groups.

Since the management of public enterprises are often recruited from the private sector and have reputations to defend, and senior civil servants and politicians frequently come from higher social backgrounds, from a Maslow perspective we might expect attitudes and behaviour to be similar and concerned with a 'job well done'. Self-interest becomes inter-related with a wider group interest. From doing the job well peer group recognition results (Posner, 1984). In which case, utility maximisation will not necessarily lead to starkly different performance outcomes in the public and private sectors as implied in the public choice literature (for such a discussion of the role of group interest and public choice theory, see Lewin, 1991 and Udehn, 1996). The inclusion of esteem, pride or group respect in people's utility functions is compatible with Gary Becker's more inclusive notion of utility maximisation (Becker, 1976). Furthermore, Fama notes how the labour market for management may capitalise performance in managerial remuneration producing a direct incentive for managers to satisfy owners independent of the precise form of the ownership (Fama, 1980; also Frech, 1980). In its simplest terms, effective management has its own rewards in terms of salary and promotion prospects.

The work on bureaucracy by Downs (1957, 1967), which spawned a good deal of the later public choice literature, recognised that employees in the public sector could have broader motives than purely egotistical ones (such as loyalty to the bureau or nation, pride in the proficient performance of work, and even serving the public interest). Downs work also stands out because he recognised the importance of intra- and inter-bureau relationships. Much of the public choice literature takes a homogeneous view of the public sector. All state bureaucrats are assumed to act identically or, at least, differences in behaviour between officials is considered to be relatively unimportant. This simplification may result in a distorted view of the performance of bureaux and state industries, especially if contrasted with an idealised, entrepreneurial private sector. Downs (1967) reminds us that bureaucracy exists in the private sector too.

In any event the notion that public sector managers may wish to expand their bureaux, for example by using low discount rates when appraising investments, is not the same thing as saying they will be able to do so. Although there may be no private capital market, government employees face extensive political monitoring of their behaviour and performance, including media scrutiny and official audits and enquiries. Certainly the notion that politicians and public servants do pursue the public interest, at least some of the time, should not be entirely discounted (Fiorina and Noll, 1978). This may help to explain why budget maximising models of behaviour have been strikingly unconfirmed by empirical evidence. As Mueller concludes in his review of the public choice literature: 'systematic support for the bureaucracy–size relationship is sparse and contradictory' (Mueller, 1989, p. 339; for a similar view, see Green and Shapiro, 1994). Hood et al. (1984), after studying the manner in which the UK civil service reacted to changes in public spending budgets between the early 1970s and the early 1980s, concluded that: 'the link between budgetary increases and bureaucratic utility is neither clearly demonstrable nor universally applicable' (p. 163). There seemed to be no clear relationship between an increment in budget and an increase in bureaucratic benefits represented by changes in total staff and top staff within departments. Dunsire et al. (1989) also noted that in times of retrenchment there was no evidence that top civil servants unduly protected their own grades, as might be expected if the utility maximising model is a sufficient predictor of behaviour. Moreover, overall they found no evidence that the salaries of top civil servants had grown faster than the pay of junior staffs or pay in comparable private sector work. A study of changes in public spending in the USA came to a similar conclusion (Peters, 1989).

The fact that the biggest increases in public spending in the UK since the 1960s have occurred in the area of transfer expenditures and outside central government, notably in the NHS and local authorities, also fits uneasily into a public choice framework. If civil servants pursued their own utility and this was linked to the size of the budget, the expectation would be that Whitehall would have protected central government spending and concentrated cuts elsewhere. Moreover, it is difficult to explain the apparent lack of strong opposition within government to privatisation including contracting out, though Dunleavy (1986, 1991) explains this in terms of 'bureau reshaping', which is most costly for the lower grades. Similarly, if state ownership is more compatible with the pursuit of managerial utility than private ownership, the expectation would be that the management of state industries would have opposed privatisation. In fact, the opposite has been true. The top management of state industries have embraced privatisation enthusiastically as an opportunity to shake free from political control.

The private capital market

The second criticism of the public choice and property rights literatures is concerned with the operation of the private capital market. While the disincentive effects of the attenuation of property rights in the public sector are emphasised, a more sanguine attitude is adopted about arrangements in the private sector. In the sole proprietor business there is a clear and direct incentive to be efficient, for slacking and other such behaviour will affect the pecuniary income of the entrepreneur directly. In small partnerships and private companies there may be a slightly less direct but nevertheless still a significant relationship between an individual owner's efforts and his or her income (Farrell and Scotchmer, 1988). However, sole proprietor businesses, partnerships and small companies are not the obvious alternatives to state ownership. Public enterprises are usually replaced by public joint-stock companies (the main exceptions in the UK have been the management buy-outs during the sale of the National Freight Consortium and the break-up of the state-run bus industry).

Mitchell (1983, p. 89) reminds us that, in relation to state spending, 'nobody spends somebody else's money as carefully as he spends his own', but presumably this maxim also applies to the private sector. In public joint stock companies ownership and control are divorced, producing the agent–principal relationship introduced earlier. Capital is raised from the investing public in the shape of equity and the financial institutions in terms of equity and loans, while the control or management of assets is in the hands of professional managers (directors, mainly executive directors). The latter act as agents for the shareholders' interests. The utility of shareholders is advanced by maximising profits (or more precisely the net present value of the firm's current and future profits) as this increases dividends and promotes growth in share values.

Managerial activities which are not intended to increase the utility of the owners of resources are possible because of information asymmetries and incomplete contracts between the directors of boards and their shareholders. Shareholders lack the information to know whether profits are being maximised, and contracts which heavily constrained managerial dis-

18

cretionary behaviour would restrict the ability of management to react to unforeseeable contingencies on behalf of shareholders.

There is a respected literature in economics, dating especially from Berle and Means (1932), which highlights the existence of managerial discretionary behaviour in the private sector when ownership and control are divorced (Baumol, 1959; Marris, 1964; Williamson, 1964; Jensen and Meckling, 1976; Zahra and Pearce, 1989). A more traditional approach in economics has private sector managers maximising profits and retaining or distributing those earnings in the interests of shareholders. By contrast, managerial theories of the firm stress the importance of the separation of ownership and control in modern corporations, leading to discretionary (non-profit) behaviour by managers in the private sector. Interestingly, statements made about management motivation in large private corporations in this literature appear almost identical to those made by Niskanen *et al.* regarding the behaviour of state bureaucrats.

The public choice and property rights literatures concentrate upon the lack of incentive for management in the public sector to minimise inefficiency because public sector management have no rights to profit. But in the public joint stock company, while shareholders will be interested in high profit, directors may be more interested in their own utility. This may be better advanced by director perks, high salaries and bonuses or an 'easy life' rather than by generating more profit. Even though directors may hold shares in the company, and stock options and profit related bonuses schemes have proliferated in recent years, it is still the case that management are largely rewarded by salary. Figures from the British Institute of Management a few years ago, for instance, revealed that the percentage of managers owning shares in their companies was still only around 36 per cent (Mansfield and Poole, 1991). Also, unlike civil servants whose pay and conditions tend to conform to nationally agreed levels, private sector management appear to have considerably more discretion to raise their own pecuniary and non-pecuniary incomes.

In the public choice and property rights literatures the divorce of ownership and control is recognised. But the literature suggests that the capital market restricts managerial discretionary behaviour in the private sector better than political control in the public sector (Fama and Jensen, 1983; Jensen, 1983; Millward and Parker, 1983, pp. 215–17). Firstly, there is a bankruptcy constraint in the private sector. Private sector companies can go bankrupt, while loss making state industries are usually supported from taxpayers' funds.[3] In the UK, the coal and rail industries in particular have a long history of public subsidy and periodic capital write-offs.

Secondly, in the private sector shareholders can attend Annual General Meetings and call directors to account (there are no public AGMs for state enterprises) and more importantly shares can be traded. Most of the relevant literature emphasises selling shares when performance disappoints; a minority of economists have also emphasised the possibility that larger shareholders might depose management (Aoki, 1983; Leech, 1987). Shares will be sold in companies which produce disappointing profits leading to a fall in the share price and this, in turn, increases the likelihood of takeover by new management (this reasoning is similar to that in Marris's (1964) model of the firm, in which managerial utility is a function of the growth rate of the firm, which is limited by the negative effect on the share price of investing for growth). It is the ability to transfer property rights and the associated threat of takeover in the private sector which are emphasised in the property rights literature as the mechanism by which managerial beha-viour is constrained in the public joint stock company (Manne, 1965; Alchian, 1965; and, for more recent arguments along the same lines, see Madden, 1981; Coffee, 1986). By contrast, no such tradeable property rights tend to exist for public sector organisations except in 'mixed' public and private enterprises (Boardman and Vining, 1989). The inability to trade property rights in state industries also means that specialisation in owner-ship cannot occur. It is held that this further reduces effective monitoring of the management in state industries (De Alessi, 1980, pp. 27–8). In the private sector, individuals and perhaps more importantly the institutional investors can specialise and build up information on industries, leading to more effective monitoring of management.

In practice, however, though the private capital market is efficient, in the sense that prices appear to adjust to firm-specific information (Fama, 1991), there is considerable uncertainty as to whether it does distribute funds to areas of highest return to act as an effective constraint on managerial behaviour. A large number of studies of the market for corporate control now exist and suggest that it works imperfectly.

The capital market can act as a fully effective constraint on managerial discretionary behaviour only if there are insignificant information imperfec-tions and transactions costs. In practice, although specialist intermediaries assist, shareholders usually will not have sufficient information about com-pany performance to ensure perfect monitoring of management, except perhaps in small companies where the directors are the shareholders or are connected through family relationships. Under company law audited accounts and periodic reports have to be presented to shareholders, but statements can be disguised and important information omitted (Hindley, 1970; Salamon and Smith, 1979). The ability of shareholders to influence management has also been questioned even when they are adequately informed (Holmstrom and Tirole, 1989, p. 88). Inertia along with the transaction costs of trading shares, may mean that funds are not moved even when a higher return could be earned elsewhere. This will apply particularly to small shareholders, where the transaction costs of share dealing are likely to offset gains and where individual shareholders may free ride in the hope that others sell. By retaining their shares, they would hope to benefit subsequently from any improved performance (Grossman and Hart, 1980).

Firms with highly diffused shareholdings do not necessarily perform worse than those with highly concentrated shareholdings (Demsetz and Lehn, 1985), but nevertheless recent studies have argued that corporate control is likely to be more effective where there are large blocks of shares (Shleifer and Vishny, 1986; Caves, 1990; Leech and Leahy, 1991; Boycko *et al.*, 1996). In this literature, however, there is particular disagreement regarding the effect of large *managerial* shareholdings. On the one hand, managers personally benefit from higher profits which should encourage efficiency. On the other hand, their large shareholdings may mean protection from hostile takeover bids (Demsetz, 1983; Fama and Jensen, 1983). Empirical studies of the relationship between firm performance and the percentage of stock held by directors continue to produce mixed results (relevant studies up until the early 1980s are reviewed in Millward and Parker, 1983, p. 216; for more recent studies see Demsetz and Lehn, 1985; Lloyd *et al.*, 1986; Kesner, 1987; Kim *et al.*, 1988; Schellenger *et al.*, 1989; Oswald and Jahera, 1991). Empirical evidence suggests that managerial emoluments may be more closely correlated with firm size than with profitability (Scherer, 1980, pp. 29–41).

Where ownership is concentrated, the benefits to the individual from monitoring management behaviour and trading in shares are more likely to exceed the transaction costs of share trading, whereas where ownership is widely dispersed there may be no individual or group with the incentive or voting power to exercise control and ensure profit maximisation. In this sense it has been suggested that a single owner as in the public sector might improve agent monitoring (Estrin and Perotin, 1991, p. 67; Sappington and Stiglitz, 1987), though allowance needs to be made for the possibility that public officials pursue their own private agendas (Shapiro and Willig, 1990, p. 75). It has been suggested that privatised industries need dominant experienced shareholders 'to compensate for the weaknesses of managers never before exposed to best business practice' (McDonald, 1993, p. 49).

This conclusion, however, has unfavourable implications for the UK privatisation programme where there has been an emphasis upon encouraging small shareholdings. In so far as this impairs the capital market's monitoring of managerial discretionary behaviour, there is a potential conflict with the goal of the privatisation programme, raising efficiency. Also, recent research at the theoretical level has demonstrated that where a privatised firm does not operate in a perfectly competitive market, to enable the state to exert pressure on management to prevent monopoly pricing, it may be welfare optimal for the state not to sell all of its shares in the public firm (Bös, 1988). In the UK, however, privatisation has been associated with total disposals and the creation of an alternative regulatory structure (this issue is taken up below). The main exception has been where privatisation has occurred and the government has retained a golden share (Graham and Prosser, 1988). Currently eighteen privatised firms in the UK have golden shares. It is difficult, however, to reconcile the importance of the takeover threat to raising efficiency in privatised firms with the existence of such shares for they create uncertainty as to whether a takeover would be permitted, thus reducing the likelihood of a bid. Also, the golden share usually rules out a foreign takeover. The removal of the golden share which led to Ford's takeover of Jaguar in 1989 may be seen as a belated recognition of the contradiction in government thinking about the desirability of takeovers. The takeover threat also loses credibility when the government lays down the level of maximum individual shareholdings allowed in the company's articles of association, as in the cases of Rolls-Royce, BT and British Airways. For example, in the case of British Airways at privatisation no one person was allowed to hold more than 15 per cent of the issued shares and non-UK nationals were limited to a total holding of 25 per cent.

There also appears to be a contradiction between the high expectations of property rights theorists in the ability of the capital market to constrain managerial behaviour and the results of research into the effects of takeovers. Some studies suggest that the takeover threat produces short-termism, which penalises investment in, for example, training and research and development, leading to a long-term decline in competitiveness (Aoki, 1984; Dertouzos *et al.*, 1989, p. 144; Shleifer and Summers, 1991; Williamson, 1991; but, for an opposing view, see Ball, 1991). Compared with their UK counterparts, German and French managers have far more security from hostile takeovers because of the structure of shareholdings, the concentration of voting rights and the terms of management contracts (Berglof, 1990; Franks and Mayer, 1990). At the same time both the German and French economies have outperformed the UK economy since 1945, implying that the link between an active market in takeovers and economic efficiency is ambiguous.

Other studies have cast doubt on whether it is necessarily firms with flagging profits that attract the hostile takeover bid (Singh, 1971, 1975; Jenkinson and Mayer, 1994). Moreover, in recent years management have learnt to protect themselves from the personal costs of a bid through methods which either make successful takeovers more difficult or provide generous compensation for loss of office, such as 'poison pills', 'golden parachutes' and the like (Jacobs, 1991). Also, studies by Singh (1975), Meeks (1977) and Ravenscraft and Scherer (1987) have found that many acquisitions and mergers do not necessarily produce the expected profits. Indeed, around 50 per cent of acquisitions and mergers are said to fail, in the sense of not achieving the expected performance gains. This has led to suggestion that takeovers are a product of management empire building rather than a means of ensuring that management pursues shareholder welfare. Acquisitions increase the size of the firm and therefore the management's span of control. They can also improve management job security because making the firm bigger can reduce exposure both to particular market segments and the likelihood of a hostile takeover bid (Mueller, 1980; Roll, 1986; Hughes and Singh, 1987; Jarrel et al., 1988; Caves, 1989; Hughes, 1989; Morck et al., 1990). The finding that average returns to bidding shareholders from making acquisitions are at best only slightly positive (Jensen and Ruback, 1983; Franks and Harris, 1989) and in some studies significantly negative (Firth, 1979 and 1980; Bradley et al., 1988) conforms to the idea that takeovers are motivated by the pursuit of managerial rather than shareholder utility.

Lawriwsky (1984, p. 217) at the end of a detailed study of the relationship between private sector industries and the capital market concluded that the degree of control over management varies and is far from predictable and that a mixture of 'internal organisation and external constraints are important determinants of company performance'. He also found that the relationship between the external capital market constraint and conduct and performance varied according to a number of factors, including organisational form, control type and size. In the private sector large size was 'associated with freedom from stock market restraints – and this is what distinguishes large firms from small and medium-sized firms'. Studies by Kuehn (1975) and Singh (1975) suggest that as the ratio of the stock market value of the company to its book value (known as the valuation ratio) falls, the probability of takeover increases. This suggests some capital market constraint on managerial behaviour. But the larger the firm the smaller the threat seems to be and in any case the constraint does not work perfectly. This may suggest that large firms foster managerial discretionary behaviour irrespective of the type of ownership. This is an important conclusion in the light of the fact that a number of the privatised industries (such as BT and British Gas) are giants in the stock market.

The evidence suggests, therefore, that a capital market discipline exists but may operate far from perfectly. The takeover threat *may* encourage managers to minimise costs or achieve static efficiency gains but an undesirable consequence may be lower long-term investment or dynamic efficiency. The distinction between static and dynamic efficiency is explored at more length in chapter 3. As Jenkinson and Mayer comment:

> managers who constantly live under the threat of removal may discount the long-term future performance of the company at a higher rate than a manager with a more secure tenure. Why initiate long-term projects whose fruits may be enjoyed by others?
>
> (Jenkinson and Mayer, 1994, p. 52)

To make matters worse, long-term investment may reduce short-run profits provoking a hostile stock market response.

The above discussion should not be interpreted, however, as a complete dismissal of the capital market as a useful constraint on corporate behaviour. The threat of takeover *is* a constraint which clearly does not exist in the public sector. Also, large private sector firms can and occasionally do go bankrupt. Neither are the public choice and property rights theorists necessarily wrong about relative behaviour in the public and private sectors. Nevertheless, quite clearly privatisation involves a move from one intricate agent–principal relationship to another and the outcome is not entirely clear (Bös, 1991; Bös and Peters, 1991; Bös, 1993). The motivation of public sector employees may be more complex than portrayed in the public choice literature, especially in its more populist forms. Moreover, it is important not to fall into the trap of comparing a flawed state enterprise with an idealised image of the operation of firms in the private capital market. Gibbard and Varian (1978, p. 665) warn against the use of caricature models in economics which exaggerate or distort reality. Arguably, in recent years the public choice and property rights theories have taken on a semblance of caricatures to support the wholesale transfer of industries from the public to the private sectors.

In reality the effects of ownership on managerial behaviour and hence on organisational performance are likely to be complex (Gravelle, 1984; Rees, 1984; Bös and Peters, 1989; De Fraja, 1993). In so far as a convincing case for privatisation cannot be made by deduction alone, it is necessary to resort to empirical study of public versus private efficiency. This book is concerned primarily with such empirical study.

PRIVATISATION AND REGULATION

Often following privatisation the state retains an interest in the operations of an enterprise, once again reflecting the importance of seeing ownership as a continuum rather than as discrete public versus private sectors. This is particularly the case with firms that operate in industries with natural monopoly characteristics, that is to say, industries where cost conditions are such that it would be inefficient to have more than one or a very small number of suppliers; but it also applies to certain strategic industries, notably those in the defence sector. Natural monopolies tend to be found where the production technology requires a high (often durable and largely irreversible) fixed cost and a much smaller variable cost so that one firm can produce the industry's output more cheaply than a number of smaller firms. The distribution networks in the electricity, gas, telecommunications and water industries are examples of natural monopolies. Where the production technology precludes competition in the product market, the monopolist must be prevented from abusing its dominant position when it is transferred to the private sector. Consequently, a regulatory system is usually introduced and, in the UK, regulation has taken the form of legislation that lays down certain operational requirements. Typically, this includes: an operating licence for the company, which sets out its public service obligations in detail;

a pricing formula to determine maximum prices (and therefore indirectly maximum profits); and a regulatory office headed by a director general. The regulatory office polices the licence, regulates market entry and negotiates and monitors the pricing formula and service standards.

In the UK prices are mainly regulated under a RPI−X structure, in which prices are allowed to rise by the rate of inflation (as measured by the RPI) less an efficiency factor 'X'. The efficiency factor is set for each industry periodically (typically every five years) to reflect the scope for cost savings in the industry. For example, if the X factor was set at 3 per cent then overall prices in the industry would be permitted to rise by the RPI−3 per cent each year until the next price review.

The RPI−X price-cap system of regulation begins with negotiation over the appropriate level at which X should be set. At privatisation X has tended to be set at a relatively low level to ensure the success of the flotation and because government and the regulator have typically underestimated the scope for cost savings. But in subsequent price reviews the efficiency factor has been raised to much more demanding levels. Table 1.3 summarises the evolution of price regulation for British Gas, British Telecom and British Airports Authority – the three regulated enterprises included in the eleven organisations which are the main focus of the studies in this book. In all cases the price cap has become more demanding. Similar price regulation exists for the electricity, water and railway industries in the UK but is not discussed here as these industries are not included in our later studies.

Industries came into state ownership for a variety of political, social and economic reasons, but one reason, interestingly, was the failure of state regulation of privately-owned utilities such as gas and water (Millward and Singleton, 1995). A main difference between public and private ownership can be attributed to the transaction costs faced by government when attempting to intervene in production activities. The expectation might be that such intervention would be generally less costly under public ownership because the enterprises are directly owned by the state. Managerial behaviour in state firms would be directly monitored and controlled reducing the scope for managerial discretion. If this is the case then the expected result would be a fall in managerial effort after privatisation with continued regulation and a decline in operating efficiency.

Certainly privatisation involves a change in information, incentives and controls over enterprises, as discussed earlier, and it may reduce the amount of intimate information about an enterprise available to the government or regulator (Sappington and Stiglitz, 1987; Shapiro and Willig, 1990). At the same time, the disadvantages of state ownership have been rehearsed and relate to the *incentives* for principals to monitor their agents effectively. In general terms, state ownership will be a superior form of regulation when the monitoring-control costs are lower under state ownership and these cost

Table 1.3 The evolution of price regulation: BT, British Gas and BAA

Organisation	Main features of the price regulation	Comment
British Telecom (BT)	1984–9 RPI–3% 1989–91 RPI–4.5% 1991–3 RPI–6.25% 1993–7 RPI–7.5% Rentals for lines and connections limited to RPI+2%. Median user bill and leased lines have a cap of RPI–0%.	Applies to inland calls, line rentals, leased lines and international calls (since 1991). Apparatus supply, mobile services and value-added networks are unregulated.
British Gas	1987–92 RPI–2% 1992–4 RPI–5% 1994–7 RPI–4% Standing charge to rise by no more than the RPI.	Excludes gas input costs, which can be passed on to the consumer less a 1% efficiency factor (since 1992).Price regulation applies to small (<25,000 therm) users. Supply to large users is unregulated and competitive. Full competition in all markets to be permitted after 1998.
British Airports Authority (BAA)	1987–92 RPI–1% 1992–4 RPI–8% 1994–5 RPI–4% 1995–7 RPI–1%	Applies to landing charges, passenger fees and aircraft parking charges at Gatwick, Heathrow and Stansted. All other services (for example, parking fees and retail services) are unregulated but profits made on these are taken into account under the price cap.

Notes:1 The RPI–X price cap is an index applied either to a weighted basket of services provided by the company or to the company's average revenue. The basis of the price index is: BT – weighted quantities in previous year; British Gas – average revenue per therm; BAA – average revenue per passenger.
2 The above table is intended as a general guide only. The pricing rules are complex and subject to variation.

savings are not offset by any reduced operating efficiency in the state sector resulting from inferior agent-monitoring incentives. Another way of stating this is to say that the superiority of each form of ownership and regulation depends upon the *net* advantages from state intervention in managerial decision making. For example, we might expect there to be large net advantages from political control of an activity like defence.

In privatised but regulated industries, the regulator needs to take a view on the development of a number of key variables, notably operating expenditure, capital expenditure, asset valuation and the cost of capital, over the regulatory period to establish both fair prices to the consumer and fair profits for shareholders. At the same time, it will be in the interests of the management of the regulated firm to try to exaggerate all of these costs and values in an attempt to secure a slacker pricing regime in the form of a lower X factor. The role of the regulator is to collect and pass judgement on the information supplied by the regulated enterprise to ensure that cost reductions are pursued vigorously and that profits are not so low that necessary investment levels are damaged. If the regulator had perfect information then this regulatory activity would simply be a matter of routine. In practice, however, the regulator will have imperfect information, for example, on cost-reducing activities and the effect of exogenous factors (such as the business cycle) on performance (Sappington and Stiglitz, 1987).

Regulatory failure might occur under both state ownership with direct control and private ownership with regulatory structures like those created in the UK. But there is a substantial literature in economics which focuses on state regulation of private-sector firms and the nature of the potential resulting inefficiencies, which it is important to review, albeit briefly (for more details see, for example, Bailey, 1973; Laffont and Tirole, 1990, 1993; Foster, 1992; Armstrong *et al.*, 1994). Whereas state ownership has been associated with excessively labour-intensive production because of limits on external capital raising (Rees, 1984), both theoretical and empirical research suggest that private sector state-regulated firms spend revenues which cannot be turned into profits because of profit ceilings. While this could lead to managerial slack in the form of excessive management salaries and perks, other possible outcomes include either over-staffing or over-capitalisation of the business depending upon the precise circumstances. Over-capitalisation has been especially singled out as a problem of profit regulation (Averch and Johnson, 1962; Sappington and Stiglitz, 1987; Pint, 1991). Profit regulation can take the form of a ceiling on the permitted rate of return or cost of service regulation, where the regulator sanctions a profit mark-up on an agreed cost of providing the service, as in most US utilities. Either way, when the profit is controlled, directly or indirectly, there are disincentives for management to reduce costs. Instead management is likely to dissipate potential excess profits (for example, through higher management salaries and better perks) and exaggerate the true cost of service. Moreover, by expanding its asset base (the rate base) the company can increase its total profits without exceeding the rate of return ceiling.

The RPI−X pricing formula was established in the UK with a view to avoiding the efficiency disincentives associated with rate of return or cost of service regulation in the economics literature (Littlechild, 1983). Pure rate of return regulation is essentially a 'cost-plus' method of regulation with disincentives to cut costs. RPI−X regulation in its pure form would create incentives to reduce costs since any cost savings achieved above and beyond the X level will raise profits to shareholders. The X factor is set following negotiations over the capacity of the firm to reduce its real operating costs as a result of new technology, economies of scale and reductions in slacking. If management succeed in cutting costs by more than X then shareholders benefit through higher profits. This means, however, that over time the prices will deviate more and more from the costs of supply leading to allocative inefficiency (for an explanation of allocative efficiency see chapter 3). The purpose of the periodic price reviews is therefore to bring prices back closer to costs of supply. At the same time, the price reviews must not be too frequent otherwise shareholders could achieve little in the way of profit gains thus diminishing efficiency incentives. If the X factor was immediately adjusted when costs were reduced by a larger amount then effectively the price cap would become a rate of return or cost of service regulation and the incentive to reduce costs by more than X would be removed.

The incentive to seek out cost reductions depends, therefore, upon the length of time between the price reviews. The shorter the period, the smaller the incentive. Moreover, in so far as a forthcoming price review leads management to search for ways of dissipating excess profits so that the next price cap is less hostile, efficiency will suffer. Equally, those regulated privatised firms which face potential competition (including British Gas and BT) may aim to restrict profit growth with a view to deflecting the regulator's interest from encouraging new competition; while low profits signal to potential new entrants to the industry that there is apparently little scope for profit making in the industry. Turning to wages and employment, if efficiency incentives are dulled by regulation then we would expect there to be less managerial interest in reducing over-staffing and in removing labour rents in regulated firms. Similarly, there may be less incentive to reorganise the business, out-source and negotiate tougher contracts with suppliers.

In the UK the RPI–X regulatory control for pricing was designed so as not to reduce efficiency incentives, but in practice the X factor seems increasingly to be set with a view to achieving an agreed satisfactory profit level between the enterprise and the regulator. In so far as this is the case, UK price regulation moves closer to being a *de facto* profit regulation. Also, the constant threat that the regulator may choose to intervene and change the price cap even within the agreed review periods (as has occurred, most recently, in the UK electricity industry) increases the risk that high profits will not be permitted even when earned through efficiency gains (gains in efficiency above and beyond the X factor). The effects of such a breach of trust in the regulatory system are reduced incentives for management to cut costs and a rise in the cost of capital to the industry, as potential investors are driven away by the uncertainty, especially where the investment would be sunk (Helm and Thompson, 1991, p. 238). Michael Reidy, Executive

Director Corporate Affairs of PowerGen, one of the regulated power generating companies in the UK, has commented: 'From a regulatee's perspective, this uncertainty is significant. We have to commit resources to trying to guess what is around the next corner' (Reidy, 1995, p. 124).

The regulator needs to know the marginal costs (cost function) and demand function of the regulated enterprise to set prices optimally. He or she may look at best practice costs from other utilities in the UK (when they exist) or from elsewhere in the world, but such 'yardstick competition' has its problems in terms of obtaining relevant comparisons (Shleifer, 1985). Also, the regulator becomes responsible for managing the level of competition in the industry. The regulators have favoured more competition but have been aware of the need to make market entry attractive to newcomers, especially in the face of the dominant, privatised incumbent. By managing the competition the regulator has attempted to ensure a profit environment conducive to new entrants while still protecting the consumer. This is an uneasy balance. It has, in particular, necessitated the regulator setting interconnection or access charges so that new entrants can use the incumbent's monopoly system or network without discrimination. Too high an access charge would deter competition, while too low a charge would lead to an excessive expansion of the industry resulting in under-utilisation of capacity. The regulator has also had to be vigilant to prevent the incumbent operator cross-subsidising those parts of its business subject to competition from charges in those parts still retaining a high degree of monopoly. If such cross-subsidisation occurred then it would be difficult for competition to develop.

Regulation in the UK has, therefore, been associated with an unexpected gradual increase in regulatory involvement. For example, at BT this has included deciding restrictions on services that could be offered, technologies that could be used, market entry by new competitors, requirements on internal accounting systems and approval of budgets in BT's apparatus supply business. In other words, this is 'a degree of direct management intervention almost unprecedented even in BT's public sector days' (Souter, 1995, p. 109).

Given the potential inefficiencies associated with state regulation of private sector firms the expectation would be, everything else being equal, that regulated privatised firms will have performed less well since privatisation than their counterparts operating in more competitive environments. Certainly earlier empirical studies on the effect of ownership on managerial behaviour and performance, reviewed in chapter 4, have suggested that, especially where the private sector operator remains state regulated, production efficiency may be no higher than in the state sector. Vickers and Yarrow (1988, p. 3) conclude that 'it can be argued that the degree of product market competition and the effectiveness of regulatory policy typically have rather larger effects on performance than ownership *per se*'.

CONCLUSION

After reviewing various possible ways of regulating public sector firms, Gravelle concludes that none of the methods ensures efficiency, but he warns us that to draw from this the conclusion that the answer is to substitute private ownership is

> to commit the 'grass is greener' fallacy: if one of the alternative systems of property rights (public firms) produces inefficient results then the other system (private ownership) must be adopted. This is to ignore the theoretical and empirical evidence which indicates that privately owned firms must also be allocatively and X-inefficient.
>
> (Gravelle, 1982, p. 102)

In this chapter certain concepts and theories relating to incentives and behaviour in the public and private sectors have been presented. Agent–principal theory, public choice theory and the study of property rights can be invoked to mount a case against state ownership. At the same time such theories are not conclusive as they rely on a particular view of human motivation and the assumption that the private capital market acts as an efficient disciplinarian. Empirical support for public choice concepts is especially thin and more generally the notion that privatisation will improve economic performance remains an empirical question. Also, the possible impact of continued state regulation of privatised enterprises needs to be considered as regulation can introduce its own set of efficiency disincentives.

The following chapter provides some background information on the eleven UK privatised organisations whose performance is the main focus of this book.

NOTES

1 Throughout this book the word public, as in public ownership and public enterprises, is used interchangeably with the term state, for example state ownership and state enterprises. A public enterprise should not be confused with a public joint stock company in the UK which is a private sector company with publicly traded shares.

2 Weberian after Max Weber the German sociologist who studied the operation of ideal bureaucracies (Weber, 1912).

3 Although, of course, occasionally bankrupt private sector companies are also rescued by public funds.

2

BRIEF HISTORIES OF THE ORGANISATIONS STUDIED

INTRODUCTION

The research on privatisation and performance reported in this book is based on a study of eleven organisations that were privatised before 1989 in the UK. These organisations account for the largest part of the total asset sales undertaken before 1989, the year chosen as a cut-off date to allow for sufficient time after privatisation to comment usefully on its impact. Readers should note that the electricity and water utilities are therefore excluded from our study since their privatisation occurred between 1989 and 1991. The study does include, however, the telecommunications and gas industries and the British Airports Authority (BAA), which were privatised as regulated enterprises. British Airways (BA) is also in the eleven companies and BA remains regulated in terms of certain aspects of its services (but not profits) by the airlines regulator, the Civil Aviation Authority. The eleven enterprises studied are: BA, BAA, Britoil, British Gas, British Steel, British Aerospace, Jaguar, Rolls-Royce, National Freight Consortium (NFC), Associated British Ports (ABP) and British Telecom (BT). Table 2.1 provides the dates when each of the organisations was privatised. In all cases the date shown is that on which the first share issue occurred. In a number of cases the government sold the shares in tranches over time, though in all cases the govern-ment ceased to interfere in the management of the firms from the first sale date. That date can, therefore, be taken as the effective privatisation date.

Table 2.1 also provides a summary of any important changes in each firm's competitive environment. As discussed earlier, both the product market and the capital market can impact on performance. Where there have been important changes in the product market, any performance differences could result from competition rather than the change in ownership *per se*, and the reader should be alert to this. Some of the changes in the competitive environment are discussed in the following brief histories of each of the firms studied. Those readers who are familiar with the organisations may choose to move directly to chapter 3.

Table 2.1 The organisations studied, dates of sale and main changes in the competitive environment

Organisations and date of sale	Competition/Regulation
British Airways – February 1987	Liberalisation of routes – North Atlantic in 1977, UK in 1982 and EU from 1984. Acquisition of domestic rival British Caledonian.
British Airports Authority – July 1987	Continued state regulation.
Britoil – November 1982	Dwindling power of OPEC in the 1980s leading to excess oil supplies and lower prices.
British Gas – December 1986	Growing competition in industrial and commercial markets from 1992. Competition in the domestic market in April 1996. Stiffer regulation by Ofgas.
British Steel – December 1988	International competition – periodic excess supply of world steel. EC steel quotas from 1980 – gradual removal later.
British Aerospace – February 1981	More competition for defence contracts.
Jaguar – July 1984	No noticeable changes.
Rolls-Royce – May 1987	More competition for defence contracts.
National Freight Corporation – February 1982	More intense competition for long-term haulage and logistics contracts with major retailers and others after 1989.
Associated British Ports – February 1983	No noticeable changes.
British Telecom – November 1984	Growing competition and stiffer regulation by Oftel.

BRITISH AIRWAYS (BA)

BA was formed in April 1972 by the merger of two state-owned airlines, the British Overseas Airways Corporation (BOAC) and British European Airways (BEA). BOAC had been formed in 1940 and BEA in 1946. The merger proved to be difficult, however, because of different management cultures and problems faced in combining computer systems, staffing and management structures. Hence post-merger rationalisation continued for some years. BA was privatised in 1987, though a formal decision on the sale had been made some years earlier (in 1980). The delay was caused by a legal dispute in the US courts relating to the collapse of Laker Airways (British Airways along with PanAm and TWA were accused of anti-competitive practices). Also, after 1979 the finances of BA deteriorated sharply in the face of a world-wide traffic slump combined with, what was by then, an unenviable reputation for sloppy service and poor reliability.

The company was prepared for privatisation under a new chairman, Lord King, who was appointed in February 1981, and a new chief executive, Colin Marshall, who was appointed in 1983. Both came from outside BA. In September 1981, with the corporation now in grave financial difficulty, a survival plan was introduced which involved the sale of non-core assets and 9,000 redundancies. The recovery package plus a revival in international air travel reversed the financial haemorrhage and in the following years BA underwent a considerable transformation. By 1985 BA was winning industry awards for customer service.

BA, like other airlines, is regulated by national and international agreements, though the airline market has become more competitive over the last two decades. The routes on which BA operates were liberalised in the UK in 1982 and liberalisation has been gradually developing in Europe. The EU airlines market is to be deregulated by 1997 and the North Atlantic routes are already liberalised. In 1984 BA successfully fought off proposals to transfer a number of important route licenses to its main domestic rival, British Caledonian (BCal), a private sector company. In 1987 BA purchased the ailing BCal and in November 1992 took over another loss-making carrier, the charter airline Dan-Air.

BRITISH AIRPORTS AUTHORITY (BAA)

BAA was established in the mid-1960s as the public authority responsible for all state-owned airports. The government announced the forthcoming privatisation of BAA in June 1984 and the Airports Bill, containing the necessary legislation, completed its passage through the House of Commons in April 1986. In July 1987 all of the government's shareholding was sold except for a golden share, retained to prevent unwelcome takeover bids. At the time of privatisation the company operated seven major airports in England and Scotland: Heathrow, Gatwick, Stansted, Glasgow, Edinburgh, Prestwick and Aberdeen.

BAA's share price has risen four-fold since privatisation. The company has proved especially attractive to investors because of the virtually guaranteed return on capital allowed by its regulator, the Civil Aviation Authority (CAA). Most airports in the UK are subject to economic regulation under the Airports Act of 1986. This allows the CAA to protect against unreasonable conduct by the airport operator. Under BAA's regulatory structure, the Monopolies and Mergers Commission (MMC) is responsible for undertaking periodic reviews of the company's RPI−X price cap. Less than a third of the company's business is subject to price regulation, but when setting the value of X profits earned from the company's unregulated activities, such as car parks, restaurants and duty-free sales, are taken into account. This has meant that landing charges, notably at Heathrow, have been held down when on congestion grounds there are reasons for a large uplift. Heathrow's charges are about two-thirds of those at JFK airport New York and only around 40 per cent of those at Tokyo's Narita airport.

In 1991 the MMC expressed some dissatisfaction with the effectiveness of the regulation of BAA and concluded that it might be useful to consider the scope for introducing further competition. At the same time BAA management were successful in convincing the MMC that they were operating in a high risk business, and this led to what some saw as a generous price cap for airport charges between 1992 and 1997. The price cap was set to achieve an 8 per cent return on the current cost of the company's capital, a result which allows the company to continue to meet the costs of financing its airport investment programme from cash flow rather than by borrowing.

Since privatisation BAA has moved into retail property investment and, for a short-time but with less success, hotel development. Today, its revenues come from landing fees, other airport charges, airport shopping and catering receipts, and property investments. The company also markets its airport management skills outside the UK. BAA is one of the UK's largest commercial landlords with over 20mn square feet of accommodation, mostly located at airports. It operates in an expanding business with good prospects for further growth. Although airport passenger growth fell from 11 per cent per annum in the late 1980s to around 1 per cent between 1990 and 1992, the long-term expansion in passenger numbers was renewed between 1992 and 1994, when they rose by 15 per cent.

BRITOIL

In January 1982 the Secretary of State for Energy announced his intention to establish a private sector company to manage the government's interests in North Sea oil exploration and development work, at that time vested in the state-owned British National Oil Corporation (BNOC). BNOC had been formed in 1976 to control the state's interests in the North Sea fields. The flotation of Britoil in August 1982 involved the sale of 51 per cent of the company's issued share capital to the private sector under a sale by tender with some shares set aside for employees at preferential rates. The remainder of the shares, except for a golden share, were sold by the government in August 1985.

Britoil was badly hit by the collapse of world oil prices in 1986 and this made the company a tempting target for predators in the oil industry. In 1988 the government agreed to waive its golden share and permitted the company to be bought by the oil giant BP Plc. In the analysis undertaken for this book, the data for Britoil include figures from BNOC relating to those activities subsequently taken over by Britoil. Since the company was purchased by BP, separate data for Britoil's activities have not been available and therefore it has not been possible to comment on performance after 1987.

BRITISH GAS

The gas industry in the UK developed from the nineteenth century as a mixture of municipal and private utilities. In 1949 the industry was nationalised under a federal structure with a central Gas Council and area boards retaining considerable operational autonomy. At this time the bulk of gas supplies came from local town gas works producing gas from coal. The development of North Sea gas supplies from the 1960s led to a national conversion to natural gas and the closure of the local gas plants. The coming of natural gas also removed much of the rationale for local management of supplies. In 1972 the Gas Council and area boards were amalgamated into a single British Gas Corporation (later called British Gas).

The decision to privatise British Gas was announced in May 1985. Apart from a special share retained by the government and a small allocation of shares to employees, the remainder of the shares were sold in December 1986. Under the terms of the privatisation no single person was allowed to own 15 per cent or more of the company's voting shares.

The company was privatised with minimal restructuring, something discussed at length in chapter 9, and with its monopoly of domestic and commercial and industrial supplies more or less intact. Its services and prices were regulated by a new dedicated body, the Office of Gas Supply (Ofgas). Since August 1992, however, the company has been forced by Ofgas and the Secretary of State, advised by the Monopolies and Mergers Commission (MMC), to open up its contract market (that is those customers with an annual requirement in excess of 2,500 therms) to competitors. By 1994 there were forty-two independent gas marketing companies supplying contract customers in the commercial and industrial markets. Between 1990 and 1995 British Gas's share of these markets plunged from almost 100 per cent to 35 per cent, triggering redundancies and a large-scale restructuring of the business.

In 1992 British Gas sought and obtained a MMC enquiry into the industry following disagreement with the regulator on a fair rate of return from investment in pipelines. By this time relations between the company and Ofgas had become notoriously frosty with Ofgas accusing British Gas of a failure to supply adequate information for proper regulation. The subsequent MMC report in 1993 recommended the splitting up of the company into separate gas supply and gas transportation and distribution companies. With this structure potential competitors would be more assured of obtaining access to British Gas's storage and pipeline system (the natural monopoly part of the industry) and hence access to customers. In December 1993, however, the government decided against a formal break-up of the company and opted instead for a radical restructuring, in which a new transportation subsidiary, later called Transco, would take over transportation and distribution of gas supplies from British Gas and

35

competitors under contract. 'Chinese walls' would exist within British Gas to ensure that both the company's supply businesses and outside gas suppliers had access on equal terms to the pipelines. The government also opted for an accelerated growth in competition by removing the company's monopoly of domestic supplies by 1998 rather than 2002, as earlier agreed. Competition for domestic supplies is now to be phased in between 1996 and 1998 starting in the south-west of England. It is likely that competition, from independent gas suppliers (such as Amerada Hess), regional electricity companies and oil companies, will be intense. There are already signs that prices for domestic gas may fall by 15 per cent, which will further depress British Gas's profits.

Since privatisation real domestic gas prices have fallen by 23 per cent (ignoring the price rise imposed by the imposition of VAT on domestic fuel bills from 1 April 1994). The fall in industrial gas prices has been even more severe (by over 40 per cent). These reductions contrast sharply with the price rises in the six years before privatisation, when average domestic gas prices rose by nearly one-third in real terms. According to critics, this amounted to an artificial fattening up of British Gas ahead of its flotation. The rising tide of competition, which will continue to push down prices in what is essentially an homogeneous product industry, will in turn adversely affect the financial position of British Gas. Supplying domestic households is believed to have given the highest return of any part of the company's business. The company is reacting with even more restructuring, further staff cuts and management changes.

In October 1995 British Gas embarked on a large-scale reorganisation of its board with the departure of three executive directors, in what many see as a belated recognition of the need for high level management change, in part because of adverse publicity affecting the company. In 1994–5 a record level of customer complaints about services was parallelled, embarrassingly, with the company's chief executive, Cedric Brown, obtaining a 71 per cent rise in pay and benefits. In February 1996 Mr Brown announced his early retirement. At the same time, and in a reversal of the decision made by the government in 1993, British Gas also announced plans for the formal division of the organisation into two new companies (British Gas Energy and Transco).

The future for British Gas is now highly uncertain faced as it is with strict regulation and mounting competition. Also, it faces a serious problem with long-term gas supply contracts, entered into when gas prices were well above current levels. About 55 per cent of the gas the company receives is covered by contracts with gas fields that were entered into before privatisation and most of the rest is under contracts signed before the government announced in 1993 that it intended to advance the introduction of competition into the domestic gas market.

To date, British Gas has been obliged by its operating licence to purchase gas to meet the requirements of the entire UK gas market under the most demanding of weather conditions. Hence, to ensure adequate supplies and not foreseeing the current glut in the gas market, the company entered into so-called 'take or pay' contracts with gas producers under which it contracted to pay for supplies whether they were required or not. In late 1995 it was estimated that the company had outstanding contracts to buy £15.4bn worth of gas over the next five years. In the past resulting losses would have been more easily met by cross-subsidisation from elsewhere in the monopoly business, but the new competitive environment limits such a strategy. British Gas is therefore attempting to renegotiate the contracts. The total value of the contracts has been estimated at more than £40bn (though some of this sum is an internal transfer to the production and exploration division of British Gas which owns the large Morecambe Bay gas fields). To make matters even worse for British Gas, Transco, which now yields much of the company's earnings, faced a stringent price review by Ofgas early in 1996.

BRITISH STEEL (BSC)

The British Steel Corporation was established on 28 July 1967 when fourteen of the country's largest steel companies representing around 90 per cent of steel making capacity were nationalised. A 1973 White Paper, *British Steel Corporation: 10 Year Development Strategy*, advocated expansion of production, but the oil crisis from 1974 led to steeply rising production costs and large losses. In response to these developments, there were some output cuts but the major rationalisation of the corporation began in earnest following a further rise in energy prices in 1979–80 and the resulting economic recession of the early 1980s. The difficulties facing British Steel in 1980 were compounded both by a three-month strike over pay and overcapacity in the European steel making industry that led to the introduction of steel output quotas in what is now the EU. With low steel prices and excess capacity, losses totalled around £2.5bn between 1979 and 1985.

The financial renaissance of British Steel began under a new chairman, Ian MacGregor, appointed with a mandate from the government to introduce new commercial goals in what was widely recognised to be an ailing giant. The subsequent rationalisation of the corporation saw employment fall sharply (by around 60 per cent in five years). These job losses and an associated rationalisation of capacity, including plant closures, meant that by 1986 British Steel was back into profit. By the end of the decade British Steel was both financially sound and generally recognised to be one of the world's most efficient steel producers. The corporation was privatised in December 1988. The world recession of the early 1990s led to another fall in the demand for steel products. Turnover reached £5.1bn in the year to March 1990 after which sales and profits slumped with losses recorded in 1992 and 1993. This led to a further big cost-cutting programme.

BRITISH AEROSPACE

British Aerospace was created in 1977 on the nationalisation of the UK's two largest aerospace companies – the British Aircraft Corporation and Hawker Siddeley (Aviation and Dynamics) – and the smaller Scottish Aviation. The result was an aerospace company shorn of the wider engineering industry activities that had existed in the earlier parent companies of Hawker Siddeley engineering and GEC-Vickers, the co-owners of the BAC. Four years later the corporation was privatised when just over half (51.6 per cent) of the share capital was sold to the private sector, including a small allocation to employees (3.3 per cent). The remainder of the shares were sold in May 1985. Foreign ownership of the company was restricted to 15 per cent of the issued share capital and the government retained a golden share.

The company is the UK's sole producer of military aircraft and a major supplier of civilian aircraft and components. British Aerospace is also important as a producer of other military equipment including missile systems. But since privatisation the company has been profoundly unstable, unable to cope with its industrial scale and deep-seated financial weaknesses. The company has also suffered from disruptive changes in management. Sir Austin Pearce, the former head of Esso UK, was brought in by Mrs Thatcher to privatise the company. Sir Raymond Lygo, a former Royal Navy admiral who had joined the firm in 1978 in its missile division, Dynamics, became managing director, but he always had an uneasy relationship with Pearce. When Pearce stepped down in 1987, Lygo did not get the promotion to chairman that he expected; instead, Professor Roland Smith was imported. Smith was professor of marketing at the University of Manchester Institute of Science and Technology (UMIST) and was already chairman of a number of companies.

Smith argued that the solution to the company's problems was diversification. Lygo had already purchased the privatised Royal Ordnance group, suppliers of munitions, in April 1987. Smith chose to build on this acquisition by purchasing other cash generating businesses that might satisfy the need of the two cash-hungry activities, military and civil aircraft production. Consequently, British Aerospace acquired Rover cars in 1988 from the government, on what some saw as highly favourable terms (the government paid the company almost £470mn to take Rover off its hands), and Arlington Properties (a property company with expertise in business parks). Whatever the merits of the acquisitions in terms of manufacturing synergy, the acquisitions assisted Smith in undertaking a financial restructuring of the company. British Aerospace had been chronically under-capitalised since its formation in 1977. This is illustrated by the fact that by simply writing up Rover's asset value, Smith was able almost to double the group's capital base to £2.2bn.

In September 1989 the company's share price reached a high of £7.33. But the recession doomed Smith's strategy. Arlington Properties was purchased at the peak of the property boom and now the scope for developing surplus company property and selling it off for huge gains dissolved as the property market slumped. Car sales were also depressed. But the biggest immediate problem occurred in the regional aircraft and turbo-prop operations where both sales and, importantly, residual values collapsed. A large majority of British Aerospace's 146 regional jets and Jetstream turbo-props had been leased. The company was now faced with the prospect of the aircraft being sent back to the company at huge potential losses. To raise cash, in September 1991 the company was forced to make a £432mn rights issue and Smith was soon ousted.

The large losses of the early 1990s led to a major rationalisation of the company including plant closures, redundancies and the sale of the Rover car division to the German company, BMW, in January 1994. Since 1992 the company has been trying to integrate parts of the business where gains can be made by putting together business units to achieve management and scale economies. Throughout its period in the private sector the company has remained one of the UK government's preferred suppliers of military equipment, a business from which most of the company's profits are still generated.

JAGUAR

The Jaguar and Daimler marques are well-known around the world as executive saloons and sports models. However, by the early 1970s their production was controlled by the British motor conglomerate British Leyland which also produced the Austin, Morris, Triumph, MG and Rover car ranges, LandRovers, and Leyland commercial vehicles. With a lacklustre model range and poor industrial relations, productivity and build quality, it was perhaps not surprising that following the 1974 oil crisis the company should have faced a financial crisis. Fearing the impact on employment of the conglomerate's collapse, in 1976 it was taken into state ownership as British Leyland (later renamed BL).

The years of state ownership proved difficult because of continuing financial losses and a declining market share. During the 1980s BL effectively shrank back to two marques, Rover cars and LandRover, before its sale to British Aerospace in 1988. Other parts of the company were either closed (for example, Triumph and MG cars) or were sold off (such as the parts supplier Unipart and Jaguar and Leyland). The sale of Jaguar occurred in July 1984 when 99 per cent of the shares were sold to the public with the remainder offered to employees for purchase. The government retained a golden share.

At the time of its privatisation, Jaguar was benefiting in the important US market for luxury cars from a favourable dollar–sterling exchange rate.

The company prospered. By 1989, however, the weakening of the dollar against sterling had severely reduced profit margins and made Jaguar cars much less price competitive in the US market. Now the underlying weaknesses of Jaguar in terms of its model range and its production methods became apparent. Years of under-investment since the 1960s had left the company with an out-moded assembly line and resulting poor build quality. Surveys showed Jaguar to be well behind competitor firms such as Mercedes in terms of customer satisfaction with their purchases. In 1989 the company was close to failure and was in desperate need of a major cash injection.

Jaguar was purchased by the US motor giant, Ford, for £1.6bn in July 1989, with the government choosing to waive its golden share rather than risk the company's failure. After the Ford takeover, which coincided with a further collapse in sales, the main assembly line at Browns Lane, Coventry was labelled an industrial relic by leading Ford management and one of the worst assembly lines this side of the Iron Curtain. Following large-scale investment by Ford, the Brown Lane plant has been re-equipped and product quality has improved sharply. In the late 1980s sales hovered around 50,000 vehicles a year, but by 1992 hit a low of 22,000. By 1995 output had recovered to around 39,000 vehicles.

ROLLS-ROYCE

Like British Leyland, Rolls-Royce was taken into state ownership in 1971 as part of a financial rescue. The company had run-up crippling losses during the development of the RB 211 aero-engine. After 1971 the new state enterprise consisted of Rolls-Royce's aero and marine engine interests, while the manufacture of Rolls-Royce cars had been hived-off to the private sector.

In November 1985 the government announced its intention to return Rolls-Royce to the private sector during the current Parliament and in December 1986 confirmation was provided that the sale would occur in the second quarter of 1987. Complete privatisation occurred in May of that year with the government retaining only a golden share to ward off an unwelcome takeover bid for the UK's only aero-engine supplier. Also, foreign ownership was limited to 15 per cent of the shares and until 1 January 1989 there was an identical limit on single shareholdings.

Today Rolls-Royce is involved in the design, development and production of large gas turbine aero-engines used in military and civil aircraft, naval vessels and in industry. The company competes with the two much larger US aero-engine makers Pratt and Whitney and General Electric. Nevertheless the company has managed to improve its share of the world aero-engine market from 8 per cent in 1982 to 25 per cent in 1993. In 1988 Rolls-Royce purchased NEI, a company primarily involved in engineering and project management with an emphasis on power generation.

NATIONAL FREIGHT CORPORATION (NFC)

The origins of the National Freight Corporation (later Consortium) lay in the nationalisation of the road haulage industry by the Labour Government in 1948. The aim at the time was to create a unified and planned transport system. This was not achieved, however, and during the 1950s much of the industry was denationalised. The NFC was formed in the late 1960s to bring together the state's remaining interests in road freight and freight related transport and storage activities. Important businesses included some spun off from British Rail, for example British Rail Parcels which later became National Carriers and Roadline – these were eventually amalgamated in the mid-1980s as Lynx Express Delivery Services – and British Road Services (BRS) formerly the road service arm of British Rail, Pickfords Removals and Tank Freight.

The merger produced a seriously under-capitalised corporation with a number of loss-making activities. In the recession that followed the 1974 oil price rise, the company registered large losses, worsened by some unwise investments in continental Europe. A government funded capital restructuring, branch closures and managerial changes led to some recovery of fortune in the late 1970s before profits slipped away again in the recession of 1979–81.

In the 1979 General Election the Conservative Party Manifesto discussed the possibility of introducing some private capital into the NFC. But by 1981 the new Conservative government had warmed to the idea of complete privatisation of the corporation. Initial plans for a stock market flotation had to be abandoned, however, when the impact of the recession on the corporation's profits turned the City institutions against the idea of a public share issue. Instead, the government accepted an offer of a management-employee buy-out. The sale of the company was completed in February 1982.

Although margins in road transport and storage are generally low because of the high level of competition, by rationalising, and developing higher value-added activities and reducing its reliance on bulk haulage, the company thrived during the 1980s becoming a leading logistics as well as haulage company (logistics is third-party distribution, warehousing, packaging and inventory management). Given the large level of bank loans in the balance sheet, the company was initially very highly geared, though gearing was brought down during the 1980s through asset sales and higher profitability. The high level of debt along with manager and employee shareholdings may have provided the important incentive to pursue efficiency improvements. Also, given that a high proportion of the company's capital was serviced through fixed interest payments, improvements in efficiency passed smoothly through into large shareholder gains.

The percentage of employees with shares rose from 37.5 per cent in 1982 to 80 per cent by 1989. Those managers and workers who took the risk (against union advice) and bought shares in the company reaped large capital gains. In 1989 the company obtained a stock market listing, by which time the average employee shareholding of £600 in 1982 had become worth around £60,000. Since that time the percentage of shares held by the management and employees has fallen. In December 1993 a controversial £263mn rights issue further diluted the proportion of shares held by employees. Employee shareholders enjoy double voting rights provided that collectively they continue to own more than 10 per cent of the issued shares. This threshold has now almost been breached.

The 1990s has proved to be a much more difficult decade for the NFC than the 1980s and this has resulted in a sharp drop in the share price. For example, the share price fell by 38 per cent between the beginning of 1994 and February 1995. The recession has been one cause but a more worrying underlying reason has been intensified competition from other transport and logistics companies. This has enabled customers of NFC, such as the large food retailers, to renegotiate contracts at much lower prices. Hence, where the company has retained business it has generally been at much lower margins.

ASSOCIATED BRITISH PORTS (ABP)

Under state ownership the British Transport Docks Board reigned over a port business that was gradually losing out to newer and privately-owned ports. These ports were not so handicapped by restrictive working practices on the docks, as encapsulated in the Dock Labour Scheme. This agreement between employers and dockers and backed by government, guaranteed dockers employment irrespective of the amount of work on hand. Productivity was also restricted by rigid demarcation lines between stevedores and dockers.

The 1980 Transport Bill contained proposals for introducing private capital into the ports and privatisation was included in the Transport Act passed in the following year. Actual privatisation of the ports, now transferred to a new company called Associated British Ports Holdings (ABP), occurred in February 1983, when 51.5 per cent of the shares were subject to a share flotation (49 per cent to the public and 2.5 per cent to the employees). The remainder of the shares were sold by tender in April 1984.

ABP is the largest port operator in Britain, owning and operating at privatisation nineteen ports and primarily offering cargo handling, warehousing and storage facilities. In more recent years property development has taken on considerable importance, in some years accounting for a half of profits. ABP inherited from the British Transport Docks Board large amounts of land that could be developed for commercial and residential use.

Since privatisation ABP has slimmed down its workforce, assisted by the government's decision to abolish the Dock Labour Scheme in July 1989. Competition from other ports, and the fact that ABP has no golden share or individual shareholding limits to protect it from unwelcome takeover bids, has necessitated strenuous management efforts to improve performance. In the property market boom of the late 1980s ABP was a tempting takeover target because of its large property assets.

The company was affected adversely by the protracted coal industry strike in 1984, which for a short time spilled over into a dock strike. More recently it has been hit by the collapse of the commercial and residential property markets, which has curtailed some property developments and necessitated some asset write-downs. In the analysis of the company's performance before and after privatisation in later chapters, the data used include figures from the accounts of the former British Transport Docks Board.

BRITISH TELECOM (BT)

Until 1981 what later became British Telecom was the Post Office Tele-communications and therefore part of the Post Office corporation. In 1981 it was separated from the Post Office and became a free standing corpora-tion though still publicly owned. In November 1984 50.2 per cent of the share capital was sold through an offer for sale targeted at the small share-holder and with some shares set aside for employees. Under the terms of the sale no person was permitted to own more than 15 per cent of the share capital. The remainder of the company's shares were sold in two further tranches in 1991 and 1993.

The sale of BT was the first in the UK to involve a major public utility with natural monopoly characteristics. This necessitated a regulatory struc-ture, on the lines outlined earlier. The company has, however, faced a gradual growth in competition in both telecommunications services and equipment supplies. Competition in apparatus supplies and value-added services was permitted from 1981 and a new network competitor, Mercury Communications, was licensed in 1982. After a slow start, by the end of the decade, Mercury had begun to take large numbers of business customers from BT. In 1991 a review of the telecommunications market by the regulator, the Office of Telecommunications (Oftel) led to a further and extensive liberalisation of the UK telecoms market. Since the BT–Mercury duopoly ended in 1991, over sixty new operating licences have been issued by the government and Oftel, sixteen to public telecom operators competing directly with BT and Mercury. Also, there are now around 126 cable operators offering telecoms services to their subscribers. Finally, in the area of value-added services a large number of companies offer licensed services using BT or rival networks. As a consequence of this competition, BT has seen its share of the lucrative business and international calls market decline and in 1995 the company saw the number of its residential telephone customers fall for the first time. Although BT still controls about 90 per cent of the UK telecommunications market and has about 20mn subscribers (Mercury, the next biggest single operator, has only 375,000 customers), to retain its position the company is having to compete hard on both price and quality of service.

In addition to a more hostile competitive environment, BT has been affected by a gradual tightening of the regulatory constraint. Initially, about 50 per cent of the company's turnover was regulated by the RPI price cap. Today over 60 per cent of turnover is included and the X efficiency factor in the formula has been raised in stages for most of the regulated services: from an initial 3 per cent per annum to the far more demanding level of 7.5 per cent.[1] Under the price cap, sales have to rise by the same percentage as the X efficiency factor if revenue is not to fall in real terms. Hence, BT must raise its sales by 7.5 per cent each year merely to maintain its (regulated) sales in real terms. This is a daunting target when competition is eating away at market share. Call growth slowed from 10 per cent per annum for inland calls in 1990 to 1 per cent in 1992 and zero in 1993. If BT cannot improve performance by raising its revenue then it must look to cost savings to maintain or boost profits. In the first ten years in the private sector the company saw improvements, partly through rationalisation of operations and partly from technical innovation, in particular the substitution of digital for the old electro-mechanical exchanges. The number of digital exchanges expanded from around a fifth of all exchanges in the late 1980s to three-quarters today. Now the scope for such technological gains has narrowed and more attention therefore is having to be paid to other ways of improving the efficiency of operations. Since 1990 there have been large-scale redundancies and a major restructuring of the business.

CONCLUSION

The above is merely a brief account of each of the eleven organisations studied and is intended simply to provide some background to their privatisation. In chapter 9 much more detail is provided, specifically about the business restructuring that has occurred in each of the enterprises immediately before and since their transfer to the private sector.

The eleven organisations studied were selected primarily on the basis that there was sufficient data to undertake the intended statistical analyses. The organisations are strictly, therefore, neither a population nor a random sample and the performance results reported in later chapters must be qualified by this fact. However, there is no reason to believe that the organisations studied are in any sense unrepresentative of other UK privatisations. Also, three of the organisations studied, BAA, British Gas and

BT, operate in a regulated environment. Each has an operating licence and is restricted in terms of the prices that can be set. A fourth organisation, BA, operates in markets where competition is still restricted by route and revenue sharing agreements. The presence of these firms in the study facilitates a comparison of the performance of those companies which remain regulated after privatisation with those that are subject to no such regulation.

The efficiency studies in chapters 5 to 8 are intended to provide a useful addition to our understanding of the impact of privatisation on performance. As we have seen, the desire for greater economic efficiency has been a major rationale for privatisation in the UK and elsewhere. The public choice and property rights literatures, reviewed in chapter 1, provide powerful arguments against state ownership, but these theories are not without their critics. The impact of ownership on performance remains an empirical question. Before turning to the performance studies, however, it is necessary to discuss the meaning of efficiency (chapter 3) and to place our empirical work in context by reviewing the results of earlier work on ownership and economic performance (chapter 4).

NOTE

1 Since drafting this chapter, Oftel has announced BT's price cap for 1997–2001. This is RPI−4.5% applying only to around a quarter of BT's revenues, low- to medium-spending residential consumers. The other markets served by BT are now considered competitive. Oftel is adopting a tough approach to outlawing anti-competitive behaviour by BT.

3

ASSESSING PERFORMANCE
Principles and method

INTRODUCTION

The notion that privatisation leads to improved performance needs to be tested. The public choice and property rights literatures, reviewed in chapter 1, have provided an important critique of state ownership and have done much to change perceptions about the nature of the state both amongst academics and policy makers. As we have seen, however, these theories are not without their shortcomings and therefore we cannot conclude that state ownership is inferior to private ownership on *a priori* grounds alone. In other words, actual evidence is needed about the relative performance of state-owned and private-sector enterprises before we can conclude that private ownership is to be preferred, especially where the alternative to state ownership is privately-owned but state-regulated firms. There is a considerable literature in economics that suggests that state regulation introduces its own set of inefficiencies. In sum, the nature of public choice, property rights and similar theories is such that the impact of privatisation cannot be safely deduced but needs instead to be investigated empirically.

In later chapters we set out a detailed empirical analysis of the effects of privatisation using a number of different statistical techniques. Before doing so, however, it is useful to look at some general issues concerning the nature of performance assessment. The later chapters are essentially concerned with the measurement of changes in economic performance when firms transfer from state to private ownership, but assessing the economic performance of organisations is not unproblematic. In particular, there are various possible measures of economic efficiency. Assessing performance is complex and ultimately involves some kind of judgement about *which* performance measure or measures to report. The performance measure(s) selected will determine the particular aspects of performance that the researcher concentrates on and hence the nature of the research undertaken (Parker, 1991, p. 9). Also, the efficiency of the enterprise should be measured in relation to the enterprise's objectives. If the main objective is to raise the real income of the poor, the performance indicator used will need to reflect this if it is to measure the organisation's success in achieving its goal(s).

46

The following discussion is concerned with the nature of economic efficiency and performance measurement. It also includes some introductory discussion of the methods adopted in assessing performance pre- and post-privatisation, the results of which are reported in the later chapters.

ECONOMISTS AND PERFORMANCE MEASUREMENT

A starting point in the discussion of performance measurement is to consider how economists approach the concept of efficiency. In broad terms economists distinguish between two categories of efficiency, productive and allocative efficiency. *Productive* efficiency is concerned with the lowest cost method of producing output and can itself be divided into two parts – *static* and *dynamic* efficiency gains. *Static* efficiency relates to producing existing products more efficiently while using existing production processes. By contrast, *dynamic* efficiency is concerned with raising performance by improving products and processes over time. *Allocative* efficiency requires static productive efficiency and focuses on achieving the output which society regards as socially optimal.[1] In simple economic models, allocative efficiency is achieved when the prices of products supplied to the market are equal to their marginal (economic) costs of supply; a first-best result that would emerge, under certain conditions, in a perfectly competitive economy.

In an ideal world organisational performance would be measured in terms of both productive and allocative efficiency. In practice, however, allocative efficiency is difficult to evaluate. A lack of data on marginal costs usually means that the researcher is unable to say whether prices have been brought closer to marginal costs. Also, in a second-best world, where prices deviate from marginal costs elsewhere in the economy, the extent to which prices should be related to marginal costs in the enterprise under consideration may be in doubt (Lipsey and Lancaster, 1956; Baumol and Bradford, 1970). The researcher studying the impact of ownership change will, therefore, usually concentrate on changes in productive efficiency. This has certainly been true in UK privatisation studies, though the degree of actual or potential competition before and after privatisation has been suggested as a broad indicator of the direction of allocative efficiency gains (Hartley *et al.*, 1990, pp. 169–70). Because competition drives prices down to marginal costs, the higher the degree of competition (assuming it changes) after privatisation the more likely it is that prices will equate with marginal costs. The position is less clear where a firm is privatised as a state-regulated monopoly, however, as the outcome will depend upon the pricing regime under regulation. Over the longer term we might expect a state regulator to encourage a monopoly supplier to price closer to marginal cost thereby mimicking a competitive outcome, though given the possibility of regulatory distortions and regulatory capture this cannot be guaranteed.

In privatisation studies it has been usual practice to search for changes in productive efficiency without attributing the results specifically to static or dynamic factors. Research has been concerned simply with whether productive efficiency has increased or not. This is the approach we adopt too, though we remain mindful that any dynamic gains following privatisation will materialise only over time. Early studies of the privatisation process in the UK were mainly limited to investigating static efficiency gains because of the short period studied. The longer period since privatisation covered in this book means that both static and dynamic gains may be relevant, Indeed, as detailed in chapter 9, a number of the privatised firms have introduced new products and instituted major internal reorganisations with the aim of improving the production process.

Concentrating upon static productive efficiency, the concept can be divided into two parts – *price* efficiency and *technical* efficiency (Farrell, 1957; Kopp, 1981). Costs can be above their feasible minimum because either (a) inputs are being employed in the wrong proportions given their marginal productivity and prices – this is price inefficiency;[2] or (b) too little output is being produced from a given set of inputs – this is technical inefficiency.

The efficient input mix for any given output is that mix which minimises the cost of producing that level of output or, equivalently, the combination of inputs that for a fixed money outlay maximises the level of production. Figure 3.1 shows isoquant and isocost curves with two factor inputs x and y. The shape of the isoquants reflects the marginal rate of technical substitution between the two inputs. The slope of the isocost lines C_1, C_2 and C_3 is equal to the ratio of the two input prices, P_x, P_y, with each isocost line further from the origin representing a larger money outlay. For example, the efficient mix of inputs given the expenditure represented by isocost curve C_1 occurs at point C. This represents the point at which the highest output can be achieved with the given expenditure.

Normally isoquants are drawn so that each isoquant further from the origin represents a higher output level. But technical efficiency can be represented on this diagram if instead each isoquant further from the origin is taken to represent the *same* output but with differences in the efficiency with which inputs are transformed into outputs. Hence, the isoquants I_a and I_b are associated with the same level of output but the isoquant I_b is less efficient. More inputs are needed to produce the same output than at I_a.

If the organisation whose efficiency is being measured is at point A then it is neither technically efficient nor price efficient. Technical inefficiency can be represented by the ratio $1 - (0B/0A)$, that is, it is the proportion by which the cost of production could be reduced while holding the input ratio constant. Price inefficiency can be represented by the ratio $1 - (0D/0B)$ and represents the proportional increase in costs due to the failure to employ the most efficient input mix given marginal products and factor prices. Overall, efficiency is the product of both price and technical efficiency and is represented here by the ratio 0D/0A. Overall inefficiency is shown by the ratio $1 - (0D/0A)$ and represents the extent to which costs exceed their feasible minimum.[3]

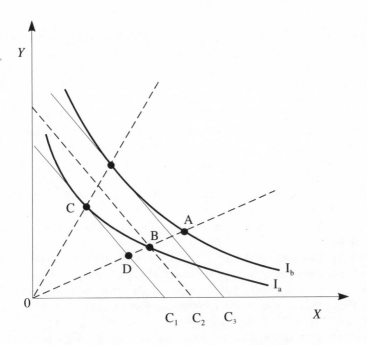

Figure 3.1 Identifying technical and price inefficiency

From Figure 3.1 the importance of efficiency improving technological change leading to dynamic gains can also be illustrated. A change in technology leading to higher technical efficiency will shift the isoquant inwards, that is the same output can now be produced with fewer inputs. In efficiency studies, to avoid confusing the effects of managerial efficiency improvements and the effect of new technology, it is usual either to assume no technological change or to include a separate independent variable to capture technology effects (this is the approach adopted in chapter 7).

When studying the productive efficiency of an organisation, the relevant isoquants could be derived and the firm's actual performance would be related to them (Førsund *et al.*, 1980). In practice, however, it is generally formidably problematic to estimate the most efficient isoquant for a particular enterprise. The nearest approximation will occur where there are a number of competing organisations in an industry so that an industry efficiency frontier can be estimated (Farrell, 1957). The efficiency frontier is represented by the firms with the most efficient input–output combinations. Hence, the estimated frontier is a *relative* concept reflecting best practice. In other words, those firms operating on the estimated frontier have the highest relative productive efficiency in the data set. But this does not guarantee that they are operating at maximum achievable efficiency, that is to say on the theoretically achievable efficiency frontier, which remains unknown.

In the statistical work presented in chapters 5 and 6, performance is gauged simply in terms of changes in a performance series, such as the trend in productivity for each of the privatised organisations studied. This makes the analysis much simpler because it means that we do not need to take a view about the overall scope for efficiency gains, the theoretical frontier, or for that matter the firm's position *relative* to an efficiency frontier before and after privatisation. At the same time, the results shed useful light on any changes in productive efficiency over time. Nevertheless, it was felt that it would be interesting to consider privatisation in terms of an efficiency frontier despite the fact that such an analysis makes considerable demands on the nature of the data set used. Therefore, in chapter 7 performance is assessed in the privatised companies using a technique called *data envelopment analysis* (DEA) which is a form of linear programming.

In each part of the analysis presented later, a decision had to be taken as to *which* particular performance indicator(s) to use. As mentioned earlier, arguably performance should be assessed in terms of the objectives set for the organisation. This is sound in principle since results should be considered in the light of the goals the organisation attempts to achieve. For the public sector the measurement of performance in terms of goals is difficult, however, because public sector organisations are usually expected to pursue a multitude of goals, often conflicting and poorly articulated (Aharoni, 1986, pp. 161–72; Nove, 1973; Milward and Rainey, 1983; Marchand *et al.*, 1984; Powell, 1987, p. 56; Pestieau, 1989; Smith, 1990, 1993). Looking specifically at UK nationalised industries, they were required under their founding legislation to meet an overriding financial objective – to ensure that revenues are not less than sufficient to meet all outgoings chargeable to the revenue account, taking one year with another. If profits were earned they were usually to remain in the industries to improve services and working conditions. In 1961 a White Paper on nationalised industries added to this requirement by laying down a target rate of return or similar financial goal (Cmnd 1337, 1961). But the industries were also given a 'public purpose' relating to the products or services they supplied. For example, the coal industry was expected to make:

> supplies of coal available, of such qualities and sizes, in such quantities and at such prices, as may seem to them best calculated to further the public interest in all respects, including the avoidance of

any undue or unreasonable preference or advantage.

(Coal Industry Nationalisation Act, 1946)

To confuse matters further, the industries were usually required to pursue good labour practices, including collective bargaining with recognised trade unions, while pursuing the interests of the consumer. On top of this, there could be other economic and social objectives, along with periodic political intervention in pricing, output and investment policies to meet short-term political goals. Rarely did the financial criteria act as binding constraints on decision making in the industries.

The change in social welfare $(\Delta\Psi)$ resulting from a change in the behaviour of a firm following privatisation can be divided into its effects on consumers and inputs. In a firm that uses only labour and capital inputs this would reduce to a change in consumer surplus (ΔC), a change in the rents to labour inputs (ΔR) and a change in the firm's profitability $(\Delta\Pi)$ such that $\Delta\Psi = \Delta C + \Delta R + \Delta\Pi$. In so far as privatisation leads to lower prices there will be a positive gain in consumer surplus and if, say, wages fall then labour rents will decline. Lower input costs need to be balanced against lower prices, but we might expect profits to rise. What is evident is the complexity of the welfare change which depends upon the outcomes in terms of prices, labour (and other non-capital input rents) and profits, along with the social weightings placed on the gains and losses. Are gains for consumers more important to social welfare than either lost rents to inputs or smaller profits?

Although there is no satisfactory normative theory regarding the appropriate role of government in a mixed economy, it is usually argued that the public sector should be concerned with *all* of the 'four Es': *effectiveness, efficiency, economy* and *equity*. Effectiveness is the extent to which objectives are met; efficiency is concerned with the ratio of output to input; economy is concerned with the difference between the actual and planned input to produce a given output; while equity centres on the fairness of both the distribution and financing of public sector outputs. State ownership is usually associated with a 'public purpose', a term which suggests the pursuit of goals other than merely profit. For example, it implies that keeping open loss-making rail lines for social reasons is a legitimate goal of a state enterprise. State enterprises might be making financial losses but be meeting important social objectives (Baumol, 1980, pp. 300–1). Recognition of all of the 'four Es' makes the measurement of public-sector performance highly complex for success in relation to one of the 'Es' does not guarantee a high overall performance. For example, a state-owned firm could be producing at minimum cost, hence it is efficient in cost terms, while it is not producing the outputs the public desires, and so it is ineffective. This may be relevant where outputs are not sold in competitive markets.

It is important not to lose sight of the fact that any reorganisation of service delivery will tend to have distributional consequences even when the intention is simply to raise efficiency (Pack, 1987, p. 532; Vernon, 1989). Tariff rebalancing, for instance, following privatisation usually involves losers as well as gainers (for a recent example from the UK gas industry see Hancock and Price, 1995; also see Burns et al., 1995). In this sense, privatisation will not be Pareto optimal since the Pareto rule in welfare economics states that welfare is maximised when through a resource reallocation a person cannot be made better off without making another person worse off. In some formulations this is amended to a less restrictive rule in which reallocation would be welfare improving if the gainers could compensate the losers. This is controversial, however, and some economists are more happy with a rule under which such compensation is *actually paid*. Whatever Pareto formulation is favoured, the Pareto principle has not been integrated into the privatisation debate. This is despite the fact that privatisation can be expected to lead to losers as well as gainers, that losers are not obviously compensated, and that it is also extremely difficult to know whether the gainers could compensate the losers and remain better off.

In so far as the objective function which the organisation pursues includes equity variables under state ownership, a trade-off of efficiency for equity gains cannot be interpreted necessarily as lowering performance (Okun, 1975; Schotter, 1985). Higher wages and better working conditions leading to higher staffing, for example, may be an objective of state ownership. Presumably the industries were not taken into state ownership simply to operate like private sector firms. By similar reasoning, higher efficiency at the cost of less equity following privatisation cannot be treated automatically as superior performance.

In principle, equity could be subsumed in some wider concept of marginal social benefit (MSB) and the output of enterprises following privatisation determined to make MSB = MSC (marginal social cost), thereby maximising social welfare. But in the absence of a ready means to quantify such benefits (for example, a market for such benefits) and sometimes some uncertainty as to the true economic costs of provision (including any externalities that should be included in marginal social cost), there is no way for public sector managers or policy makers to establish the equality.[4]

The nature of public sector outputs and, in particular, the intractable nature of the equity–efficiency trade-off leads economists studying privatisation to concentrate upon a much narrower, less sophisticated but more quantifiable range of performance measures. These measures are concerned primarily with efficiency and economy in the 'four Es' and reflect the difficulty in assessing effectiveness in the absence of a clear objective function and the traditional discomfort in the economics discipline with equity matters. This does limit the scope of the analysis.

The statistical work reported in later chapters concentrates upon the relationship between outputs and inputs. Something is said about profits, employment levels and wages and therefore the equity dimension to performance is not entirely omitted, but they are not emphasised to the same degree as efficiency and economy. It must be conceded, therefore, that the results may not accurately reflect the multi-dimensional nature of organisational performance.

MEASURING PERFORMANCE

Three commonly used measures of organisational performance are profits, productivity and costs of production (Millward and Parker, 1983; Vickers and Yarrow, 1988, p. 39). All three are concerned with productive efficiency. It is important to bear in mind that even where such efficiency is achieved, allocative inefficiency may still exist.

Profitability

In the private sector generally performance is measured by profitability (usually expressed as a rate of return on capital employed or some derivation, such as earnings per share). Even in the private sector, however, immediate profit may not be an ideal performance measure. Firms might pursue other objectives such as market share, perhaps with a view to increasing profits in the longer run. Also, studies of the goals of firms in the private sector where ownership and control are divorced highlight the possibility that short-run profit is a *constraint* on managerial discretionary behaviour rather than a goal (Baumol, 1959; Marris, 1964; Williamson, 1964, 1970).

More pertinent, generally profit will be an inadequate measure of public sector performance, especially where outputs and inputs are not traded in competitive markets. Profitability may vary between firms because of: (a) differences in the degree of importance attached to the profit objective; (b) differences in productivity; (c) differences in input price efficiency (choosing the input combinations which minimise costs); and (d) differences in the volume and range of products produced and prices charged. For example, a public firm could have high productivity and be cost efficient yet, because its objective is to set low prices, have low profits. Equally, a monopolist with low productive efficiency could have large profits because of high prices. A monopsony buyer of labour could increase its profits by paying wages below the marginal revenue product of labour. Moreover, low profitability in a state sector firm could result from the pursuit of a social objective that requires the paying of high remuneration or large pension contributions, and not from inefficiency in the use of factor inputs (Wood, 1975).

Where social and private returns diverge, the most efficient performance will not be the most profitable. Also, profitability is affected by accounting practice and usually accounting rates of return are not equivalent to an economic rate of return (Fisher and McGowan, 1983; Long and Ravenscraft, 1984; Davis and Kay, 1990). This results from differences in the measurement of depreciation and the timing of profits and capital expenditure.[5] Also, normally private sector firms finance part of their capital through equity, on which dividends are paid out of profit, whereas usually public enterprises are financed mainly or wholly by loan capital on which interest is charged before profits are calculated. This problem can be overcome, however, by comparing profits before dividends and interest. This is the method generally adopted in chapters 6 and 8 when pre- and post-privatisation profitability are specifically discussed.

The main alternatives to profit as a measure of efficiency are themselves not free from difficulty, though they are usually open to less serious criticism when used to compare the performance of public and private sector organisations. The main two alternatives are the related indices of productivity and costs of production.

Productivity

Productivity is concerned with the volume of inputs required to produce a given volume of output or outputs and is usually represented as a growth rate or index. Output per employee or employee-hour is the simplest measure and is an example of *partial factor productivity* – partial because it relates to only one of the factor inputs (labour). It is used on the understanding that the other factors of production, notably the capital stock, and technology do not change or do not change in a way that has an appreciable effect on the volume of output in the period studied. The growth in labour productivity is calculated as $((Q_t/N_t) - (Q_{t-1}/N_{t-1}))/(Q_{t-1}/N_{t-1})$ where Q is the level of output, N is employment expressed in total hours worked and t represents the time periods compared.

Since inputs other than labour will rarely remain unchanged, especially over longer periods of time, it is intuitively more appealing to measure productivity growth taking into account changes in the volumes of all factors of production, that is to calculate *total factor productivity* (TFP) growth. Adopting similar notation as used for labour productivity, TFP growth can be calculated as $((Q_t/X_t) - (Q_{t-1}/X_{t-1}))/(Q_{t-1}/X_{t-1})$ where X is a vector of factor inputs.

Though more satisfactory, there are considerable problems to overcome in measuring changes in these factor inputs, especially in measuring changes in the capital stock. Under certain conditions TFP growth can be represented as the rate of growth of output minus a weighted average of the input growth rates, where the weights for outputs in a multi-product firm are the product shares in total revenue and the weights for inputs are the shares of each input in total costs (Millward and Parker, 1983; Muellbauer, 1986). In other words, TFP can be calculated as (weighted index of outputs)/(total expenditure on inputs/weighted index of input prices).

This is the approach to TFP measurement adopted in chapter 5. The circumstances in which this is an unbiased measure of actual TFP are explored in that chapter. In the absence of physical output data, productivity may be estimated by using the value of output deflated into real terms by the use of an appropriate price deflator (or an appropriate composite price deflator where there are multi-products). It is important to use an accurate price deflator, otherwise the productivity figures could reflect changes in the price of the product in addition to changes in the volume of output.

Costs of production

In principle, study of the costs of production offers interesting possibilities for public–private comparisons. Unlike the measurement of productivity, the effect of differing prices of inputs can be directly reflected. But cost comparisons require a modelling of organisations' cost functions and this is not free from difficulty.[6] Cost functions are dependent upon the production function of the enterprise, which defines the maximum output possible for some specified level of inputs. Cost functions define the minimum cost of producing a specified level of output, given input prices and existing technology. However, whilst variations in cost can be due to the level of production, input prices and technology, they can also reflect technical and price inefficiencies. In such cases the firm's costs will not indicate opportunity costs. The use of a *cost frontier* (Schmidt and Lovell, 1979; Barrow and Wagstaff, 1989), which defines the limit to a range of possible observed cost levels, identifies the extent to which a particular firm lies beyond the frontier and hence can be used as a measure of inefficiency. The cost frontier incorporates the neoclassical idea of minimising the costs of producing a given output given certain input prices and the notion that production may be technically inefficient (hence the production function constraint is non-binding) and/or price inefficient (the selection of a sub-optimal input combination given relative factor prices). Estimates of a stochastic cost function would identify the efficient envelope of costs for a specified level of operations. This approach is related to the earlier discussion of an efficiency frontier and to the method used to measure performance in chapter 7, data envelopment analysis.

Whatever the precise method adopted, errors in cost studies can arise because of the misspecification of cost characteristics, including a failure to allow adequately for differences in scales of production. In addition, costs of production are affected by changes in the *quality* of output and this can be important, especially when evaluating state-sector outputs. For instance, services might be provided more cheaply following privatisation but less reliably. The problems of controlling for quality differences and of deciding how to treat differences in input prices are also relevant where profitability and productivity measures are calculated. On the one hand, higher state sector wages or lower costs of capital might be seen as signs of inefficiency. On the other hand, it could be argued that management of state enterprises should not be criticised if they react perfectly correctly to exogenously determined, albeit non-market, input prices. The rates of return or 'hurdle rates' under which state enterprises appraise investments, the interest rates at which funds are borrowed, and the wages paid to employees may all be determined (or heavily influenced) by the state and are therefore not controlled by management. This makes the interpretation of price inefficiency in public enterprises particularly problematic, though it does not affect the desirability of achieving technical efficiency.

Another difficulty with cost studies is that the accounting data used will typically not accurately represent the economic or social opportunity costs of supply. This is a particular consideration where supply is associated with appreciable external costs or external benefits (Bös, 1986b). A failure to account for external effects can seriously distort public versus private comparisons. If the costs of state ownership can arise from the relative neglect of enterprise, social costs of private enterprise can arise from the relative neglect of externalities. The criticism applies not only to costs such as pollution but to decisions on outputs and inputs that have wider, macroeconomic effects. For example, an awareness of the effect of outputs and inputs on unemployment, inflation, regional economies and the balance of payments could lead a state-owned industry pursuing a public purpose to have lower prices, more capacity, larger outputs and more employment than a comparable privately-owned firm. Once again, however, passing judgment on such outcomes requires taking a view on social benefits and social costs, which we are unable to do in any precise way because of an absence of information.

Normally, studies in the UK and elsewhere of privatisation must use more limited measures of efficiency because of the obvious quantification problems in accounting for full social opportunity costs. In other words, studies are undertaken in a *partial* rather than a *general* equilibrium framework. The study of privatisation and performance will then ignore the efficiency impacts on firms other than the one directly affected (for an insight into this problem see De Fraja, 1991).

TESTING FOR THE IMPORTANCE OF OWNERSHIP

Given the difficulties surrounding performance assessment and the limited nature of the analysis that can usually be undertaken, whatever performance measure is used the results should be interpreted with care. Barrow and Wagstaff (1989, p. 91) warn in their survey of performance measurement that we 'ought to be wary about accepting at face value the results of efficiency studies that are based on one estimation method'. An estimation method may be concerned, say, with labour productivity while study of, say, profitability could paint a different picture of efficiency changes.

In the research into privatisation conducted for this book, this issue has been addressed by using a number of different performance measures. The use of different performance measures is intended to act as a check on measurement bias, that is the possibility that performance could have improved using one indicator but not using another. The various performance measurements include: (a) labour and total factor productivity – the results are reported in chapter 5; (b) value-added per employee and the rate of profit – the results are reported in chapter 6; (c) data envelopment analysis – this is discussed in chapter 7; and (d) data on the distribution of each firm's income and on relative wage trends – reported in chapter 8.

The precise nature of the performance measures is explained in detail in the relevant chapter. The decision to assess performance using different measures permits a cross-check on the results, conducted in chapter 10. Where all of the results are consistent there should be more confidence in them. Performance measures based on stock market data such as earnings per share, which are widely used when assessing private sector performance, could not be used to make pre- and post-privatisation comparisons since state-owned industries were not quoted on the stock market. Stock market prices are used, however, in chapter 6 in a discussion of the market's expectation of future profitability.

The research was designed to test the central hypothesis derived from the public choice and property rights literatures presented in chapter 1: *that privatisation will lead to improvements in productive efficiency*. The study is concerned primarily with identifying changes in productive efficiency and not with wider economic and social welfare effects. In addition, because none of the organisations studied provides sufficiently consistent and comprehensive information to assess the quality of services before and after privatisation, no attempt was made to test whether economic performance improvements occurred at the expense of service levels. We have no reason, however, to believe that performance improvements have been at the cost of reduced output quality. The fact that a number of the organisations sell into competitive markets and that those that do not have their quality of service state regulated will have restricted management's ability to reduce the quality of output.

The studies in this book contribute to the literature on public versus private efficiency by measuring the impact of privatisation on eleven firms which were transferred from the state to the private sector in the UK in the 1980s. Brief histories of each of the firms studied were presented in chapter 2. One of these enterprises (British Aerospace) was first nationalised in 1977 only to be privatised in 1981. It therefore spent a very short period under state control. Some of the other enterprises studied, such as BT, had a much longer history of continuous state ownership while the British Steel Corporation has been in and out of state ownership in the post-war years. Details of the periods of state ownership are summarised in Table 3.1.

Table 3.1 The organisations studied and periods of state ownership

Firm	Details of state ownership
British Airways	Its origins can be traced back to just before World War II. British Airways was formed in 1973 from a merger of two state-owned airlines established in the 1940s, BOAC and BEA (British Overseas Airways Corporation and British European Airways).
BAA	Formally established in 1965, but state ownership of airports has a longer history.
Britoil	Origins in the state-owned British National Oil Corporation (BNOC) set up in 1975 to acquire North Sea oil interests and to undertake oil exploration and production. In 1982 the production assets of BNOC were transferred to Britoil.
British Gas	Established as a public corporation in 1949, though public ownership has its origins in nineteenth century municipally-owned enterprises.
British Steel	The UK iron and steel industry was first nationalised in 1951 but then subsequently denationalised in the early 1950s. The industry was re-nationalised in 1965 under the British Steel Corporation.
British Aerospace	Nationalised in 1977 as a merger of three private-sector companies.
Jaguar	Came under state ownership during the state rescue of the motor-manufacturing giant British Leyland in 1975.
Rolls-Royce	State ownership from 1971 following financial failure in the private sector.
NFC	Established in 1969 but has its origins in the state takeover of various freight companies after 1947.
ABP	Origins in the state-owned British Transport Docks Board formed in 1948.
British Telecom	Formerly part of the Post Office from which it separated in 1981. State ownership of telecommunications developed from the late nineteenth century.

As we saw in chapter 1, economic theory suggests that both ownership and competition will affect efficiency. Competition leads to greater allocative efficiency, since prices are related more closely to marginal costs, and provides incentives for management to minimise waste and maximise productive efficiency. In very competitive markets only the efficient can survive. In monopolistic markets the costs of waste can be passed on to consumers in higher prices. In this sense, the impact of competition on economic efficiency is independent of ownership (although it needs to be recognised that wherever state ownership exists, governments may have an incentive to restrict competition and introduce subsidies to protect their industries).

George Yarrow concludes that in choosing between product market competition and ownership, 'competition and regulatory policies are more important determinants of economic performance *per se*' (Yarrow, 1986, p. 235). A similar view has been voiced elsewhere (for example by Kay and Thompson, 1986), but totally separating the effects on performance of competition and ownership is problematical. Accurate analysis would require considerable data on market structures and their impact on organisational behaviour, which usually do not exist. This was true for our studies and therefore if there were significant changes in the product market at or around the time of the ownership change, the empirical results could reflect the aggregate effect of both competition and ownership.

Fortunately, for many of the firms studied, changes in the product market were not obviously significant and a summary of the main changes has already been provided in Table 2.1 above. But in more detail, this was true particularly of Jaguar, NFC, ABP, Britoil and BAA. Jaguar, NFC and ABP faced competition from other suppliers before privatisation and this did not change afterwards. Britoil operated in a competitive oil market until it was purchased by the oil multinational BP plc in 1988. The company's performance is studied up to this time. In the case of BAA, which operates a number of the UK's main airports, including the important Heathrow, Gatwick and Stansted airports for London, the organisation was regulated both before and after privatisation.

Both BA and British Steel did face some changes in competition in the 1980s resulting from a gradual liberalisation of air routes and changes in the EU's steel industry policy respectively. These changes occurred independently of privatisation but at around the same time as privatisation was being planned and implemented. Similarly, British Aerospace and Rolls-Royce, which have always faced fierce international competition, found a more hostile environment for domestic defence contracts in the 1980s. This resulted mainly from the Ministry of Defence moving away from cost-plus contracts for defence work and introducing more competition into contract tendering. In the cases of British Gas and BT, where competition has been gradually introduced into what was a monopoly supply arrangement, the changes in the competitive environment can be related to privatisation but have largely occurred in the 1990s. Today BT faces competition from over seventy suppliers of telecom services in the UK and is having to fight hard to retain its dominant market share, even in the domestic market. Five years after privatisation British Gas began to suffer from considerable competition in the contract (large-user) market (over 2,500 therms per annum) and this has accelerated in more recent years, as detailed in chapter 2. In addition, both British Gas and BT are supervised by regulatory bodies (Oftel and Ofgas). Both regulatory offices have increased their pressure on the companies to improve their economic performance.

Of the eleven firms studied, therefore, three were heavily state-regulated after privatisation (BT, British Gas and BAA) and two of these (BT and British Gas) faced major competition for the first time following privatisation (although significant competitive pressures for both companies largely date from the early 1990s). Four of the companies, Britoil, Jaguar, NFC and ABP operated in competitive markets before and after privatisation and seem to have suffered no important changes in competition. In the cases of four of the enterprises, BA, British Steel, British Aerospace and Rolls-Royce, there is some evidence of competitive changes which might well have impacted on performance, though in these cases it does not seem that the competitive environment changed fundamentally.

Since an independent effect of competition on performance cannot be entirely ruled out, such a possibility should be borne in mind when interpreting the results reported below. However, there is no reason to believe that the effects of changes in the product market will have swamped the effects of ownership change, except perhaps in the cases of BT and British Gas (and, in the case of British Gas, only since the early 1990s). Moreover, in both of these cases state regulation will have affected performance but with consequences that are not easy to predict. The goal of a regulator is to ensure that the enterprises operate efficiently, but at the same time the act of regulation can reduce managerial incentives to operate the business efficiently, as discussed in chapter 1. If state regulation does reduce efficiency incentives, this should show up in the performance figures as a less noticeable improvement in performance after privatisation compared with privatised firms which are not regulated.

THE COUNTERFACTUAL PROBLEM AND THE DATA SET

Unravelling the impact of privatisation on performance from other factors is always going to be problematic. Leaving aside the impact of competition and regulation, there is always a danger of attributing to privatisation performance changes which in fact result from other (exogenous) factors. For example, identified performance improvements in privatised enterprises may simply reflect the stage of the business cycle or general improvements throughout manufacturing industry in the same period. In an attempt to overcome the effect on performance of such exogenous factors, it is necessary to assess the performance changes found for each of the organisations against wider factors affecting the whole economy. To this end certain adjustments were made to the performance measures and these are detailed in the chapters below. It is recognised that the adjustments may not capture all exogenous effects, which by their nature may be multitudinous. The adjustments are best interpreted as an attempt to capture general changes in macroeconomic performance affecting either the whole economy or the manufacturing sector. The limitations of the adjustments are discussed in the relevant chapters (chapters 5, 6 and 7).

The data used in the performance assessment are detailed in the book's appendix. They included, for each of the organisations studied, relevant input and output figures from the annual reports and accounts. These figures were supplemented where necessary by further information supplied by the enterprises. Account figures are subject to changes in accounting practices, notably asset revaluations, changes in depreciation policy and debt write-offs. However, the reported figures were adjusted with the aim of providing a consistent set of data so that year to year comparisons could be made. In two cases, those of ABP and BAA, either asset transfers or frequent property revaluations occurred. These proved particularly difficult to adjust for accurately and without risking the introduction of significant error. It was therefore decided to use the published figures, while recognising that the resulting profit measure (rate of return on net assets) would be inflated or depressed. The property value is reflected in the denominator, net assets. National data (for example on output, employment and prices) were obtained from national income accounts and other publications of the Central Statistical Office.

To identify as precisely as possible the effect of privatisation, various specific time periods are usually compared. The data envelopment analysis (DEA) in chapter 7 did not lend itself to this approach and therefore annual performance details are reported. The specific time periods include periods before and after privatisation, and before and after the announcement of privatisation. The latter period is intended to capture improvements in performance in the immediate run-up to privatisation, that is, anticipation effects. By adopting this approach, the aim was to isolate more clearly the effect of privatisation on performance than has been the case in other studies of UK privatisation. The analysis below also examines a longer period after privatisation than was possible in earlier studies, including results for each of the enterprises up to December 1994 or March 1995, depending upon the latest data available at the time of writing (late 1995). In so far as the dynamic effects of privatisation on performance will emerge over time, the longer the post-privatisation period, arguably the more useful the results (Byatt, 1985). By taking a longer period the research also guards against a Hawthorne effect. In seminal studies of organisational responses in the 1920s and early 1930s, researchers found that performance often improved temporarily during changes in working practices and conditions, irrespective of the precise nature of the changes.[7] In a similar fashion, privatisation may have a short-term beneficial effect on static efficiency resulting from the attention given to the enterprise in the run-up to its sale. Such performance improvements might not be maintained thereafter.

As Hemming and Mansoor have commented, the relationship between privatisation and performance should be determined by following a privatised enterprise through a complete business cycle (Hemming and Mansoor, 1988, p. 8). By taking a period that includes the years from 1988–9 to 1991–2, it is possible to study how well the privatised enterprises performed during the recession conditions in the UK at this time, as well as the more favourable conditions earlier in the 1980s. Many of the enterprises were privatised in the mid-1980s at a time of relative economic prosperity. Therefore assessing their performance in these years may serve only to flatter their true, secular performance under private ownership. At the same time, managerial behaviour in terms of searching for cost savings is likely to intensify during a recession.

More specifically, and except for the DEA analysis in chapter 7, changes in performance were measured across six distinct periods: (a) a nationalisation period; (b) a pre-privatisation period; (c) a period following the public announcement of the intention to privatise; (d) a post-privatisation period; (e) a recession period from 1988 to 1992; and (f) a latest period, from 1992 to 1994–5, which captures performance in the most recent period.

In general, and with the exception of the post-announcement and the latest stages, each period covered four years and the figure reported is a four-year annual average. The main exception involved BA, which had a peculiarly long run-up to privatisation because of a combination of a recession in the airline industry and legal difficulties relating to the collapse of Laker airlines.[8] The decision to take four-year averages was determined by the desire to smooth out atypical performance in a particular year, while at the same time avoiding longer periods when performance changes could be affected by factors other than privatisation. The length of the post-announcement period was determined by the time between the first ministerial announcement of the decision to privatise and the date of the first offer of shares for sale. This varied from organisation to organisation. Of course, the public announcement of privatisation may well occur long after the management of the industry became aware that privatisation was being planned. The pre-privatisation period was designed to capture performance changes which pre-date the formal announcement.

In summary, for each organisation the following periods were identified. First, a nationalisation period to reflect performance when the organisation was in state ownership and before its privatisation was publicly announced. Second, a pre-privatisation period which comes immediately after the nationalisation period and which is designed to identify performance immediately before the firm moves into the private sector. Third, a post-announcement period to capture performance after the intention to privatise was publicly announced but before it actually took place. Fourth, a post-privatisation period to reflect the immediate impact of the change in ownership. Fifth, a four-year period to 1992 to capture performance under

Table 3.2 Periods studied

Firm	Nationalisation period	Pre-privatisation period	Post-announcement period	Post-privatisation period	Recession period	Latest period
British Airways	01. 4.1977–31. 3.1981	01. 4.1981–31. 3.1985	01. 4.1981–31. 3.1987	01. 4.1987–31. 3.1991	01. 4.1988–31. 3.1992	01. 4.1992–31. 3.1995
British Airports Authority	01. 4.1979–31. 3.1983	01. 4.1983–31. 3 1987	01. 4.1984–31. 3.1987	01. 4.1987–31. 3.1991	01. 4.1988–31. 3.1992	01. 4.1992–31. 3.1995
Britoil[3]	01. 1.1980–31.12.1981	01. 1.1980–31.12.1982	01. 1.1982–31.12.1982	01. 1.1983–31.12.1986	n/a[1]	n/a
British Gas	01. 4.1979–31. 3.1983	01. 4.1984–31. 3.1987	01. 4.1985–31. 3.1987	01. 4.1987–31. 3.1991	01. 4.1988–31.12.1992	01. 1.1993–31.12.1994
British Steel	01. 4.1981–31. 3.1985	01. 4.1985–31. 3.1989	01. 4.1987–31. 3.1989	01. 4.1989–31. 3.1993	01. 4.1988–31. 3.1992	01. 4.1992–31. 3.1995
British Aerospace[2]	01. 1.1978–31.12.1980	01. 1.1978–31.12.1980	01. 1.1979–31.12.1980	01. 1.1981–31.12.1984	01. 1.1989–31.12.1992	01. 1.1993–31.12.1994
Jaguar[4]	01. 1.1981–31.12.1983	01. 1.1981–31.12.1984	01. 1.1984–31.12.1984	01. 1.1985–31.12.1988	01. 1.1989–31.12.1991	n/a
Rolls-Royce	01. 1.1979–31.12.1982	01. 1.1983–31.12.1986	01. 1.1986–31.12.1986	01. 1.1987–31.12.1990	01. 1.1989–31.12.1992	01. 1.1993–31.12.1994
National Freight	01.10.1973–30. 9.1977	01.10.1977–30. 9.1981	01.10.1979–30. 9.1981	01.10.1981–30. 9.1985	01.10.1988–30. 9.1992	01.10.1992–30. 9.1994
Associated British Ports	01. 1.1975–31.12.1978	01. 1.1979–31.12.1982	01. 1.1981–31.12.1982	01. 1.1983–31.12.1986	01. 1.1989–31.12.1992	01. 1.1993–31.12.1994
British Telecom	01. 4.1977–31. 3.1981	01. 4.1981–31. 3.1985	01. 4.1983–31. 3.1985	01. 4.1985–31. 3.1989	01. 4.1988–31. 3.1992	01. 4.1992–31. 3.1995

Notes: 1 n/a = not available.
2 British Aerospace was nationalised for a short period only and hence the nationalisation period and the pre-privatisation period are identical.
3 For Britoil there were no reliable data before 1980 to compute productivity and value-added series. Therefore a two year nationalisation period and a three year pre-privatisation period were adopted in the analysis reported in chapters 5 and 6. These periods overlap. In the income distribution analysis in chapter 8, figures for a longer nationalisation period could be computed, 1978–81, leading to less overlap between the periods.
4 For Jaguar there were no reliable data before 1980 and therefore the nationalisation period consists of only three years. Since 1991 accounts for Jaguar have not been released and therefore the recession period terminates at 31 December 1991.

private ownership in a recession. And finally, a period from 1992 to 1994–5, to capture the firm's most recent performance.

The date of the announcement of privatisation and the date of the actual sale never coincided with the accounting dates of the firms studied. The relevant periods were therefore defined according to whether the relevant event, namely announcement or sale, occurred more closely to the start or the end of a firm's financial year. For instance, if an organisation's accounting year ran to 31 December and sale occurred after 30 June, that year's economic and financial results were treated as falling in the pre-privatisation period. By contrast, if the sale occurred on or before 30 June, that year's results were treated as forming the results for the first year of privatisation. The relevant periods for each organisation are detailed in Table 3.2.

CONCLUSION

This chapter has been concerned, firstly, with looking at the thorny issue of performance measurement and, secondly, with providing some introductory details of the approaches to performance measurement adopted in later chapters. Measuring performance is not straight forward. In particular, by their very nature all performance measures capture effects only in terms of the particular dimensions of the firm's overall performance that they address. At the same time, the scope of empirical study is necessarily limited by the availability of data and by the researcher's time and resources. Typically, therefore, privatisation studies are concerned only with the productive efficiency of the privatised firm itself, for example as measured by either profitability, productivity or costs of production. Study of the consequences of privatisation in terms of effectiveness and equity has been very limited, partly because of data problems and partly because traditionally economists do not feel particularly qualified to comment on equity issues. Study is generally of a partial equilibrium nature, therefore ignoring any wider effects of privatisation on the economy, including competitors and suppliers.

The empirical work reported in the following chapters shares the shortcomings of earlier studies in being concerned primarily with productive efficiency in the privatised enterprises. Nevertheless, the research adds to our knowledge of the impact of privatisation in the UK because it relates the measured performance results much more closely to the act of privatisation than was the case in earlier published work. Also, it uses a number of performance measures with the aim of overcoming any measurement bias. Lastly, it looks at a much longer period since privatisation, so taking into account both the possibility that the act of privatisation may have led to one-off but unsustained efficiency gains and the opposite possibility that the dynamic gains from privatisation will show up only over time.

NOTES

1 Allocative efficiency requires productive efficiency, in the sense that the marginal costs should be minimised for any given output. A firm can, however, be productively efficient while pricing its outputs in such a way that allocative efficiency is not achieved.

2 In some studies price efficiency is referred to as allocative efficiency since it involves the optimal employment of inputs given their prices. To avoid confusion with output allocative efficiency, in this study the term allocative efficiency is restricted to the pricing of the firm's outputs.

3 To be absolutely correct, overall inefficiency is the sum of $1 - OB/OA$ and $1 - OD/(OB + AB)$ and the latter is only approximately equal to price efficiency; see Barrow and Wagstaff, 1989, pp. 75–6 from which the above explanation is drawn. Hence, the inefficiency decomposes only roughly into the sum of price and technical inefficiency.

4 Externalities are costs not internalised in the production process and therefore included in production costs (for example, the effects of noise and other pollution).

5 Other problems relate to accounting for bad debts, realised gains and losses on investments and other assets, and the treatment of R&D expenditure. Despite the drawbacks, however, profitability is used as a performance measure in numerous studies such as Bain, 1951; Cowling and Waterson, 1976; and Boardman and Vining, 1989. Some research has suggested that accounting rates of return and economic rates of return may be correlated; see Kay, 1976 and Kay and Mayer, 1986. However, Fisher and McGowan (1983) show persuasively that accounting rates of return may not allow us to infer anything about the economic rate of return.

6 Lynk (1991, p.379) has pointed to the paucity of econometric analysis of production and cost functions for privatised industries.

7 The Hawthorne experiments involved varying the working conditions of groups of workers at the Western Electric Company at various times in the 1920s and early 1930s. Many of the experiments were performed at the Hawthorne plant near Chicago. The results showed no clear pattern between conditions (for example lighting levels) and performance. Researchers from Harvard concluded that employees would work harder if they felt that the management and supervisors were concerned about their welfare and paid attention to them. They speculated that productivity gains may even have resulted from the special attention paid to the workforce by the researchers themselves (Roethlisberger and Dickson, 1939).

8 Laker airlines, headed by the flamboyant entrepreneur Freddy Laker, collapsed in February 1982 following intense competition on North Atlantic routes from BA and a number of US operators. These airlines were sued in the US courts for alleged unfair trading practices. The case was eventually settled by way of an out-of-court settlement.

4

COMPARATIVE EFFICIENCY AND PRIVATISATION

The evidence so far

INTRODUCTION

The idea that under private ownership resources are used more efficiently has been employed as a central argument for privatisation (Littlechild, 1981; Beesley and Littlechild, 1983; Kay and Thompson, 1986; Vickers and Yarrow, 1988; Moore, 1992, p. 117). Later in the book we provide further evidence on the impact of privatisation in the UK. But in this chapter we review earlier studies of public versus private sector efficiency to place the later studies in context. There have been many such studies, including some on the effects of privatisation, and it is not possible to review all of them. The aim is to provide a broad overview of the approaches adopted to measuring performance and the results.

As we saw in the previous chapter, economists recognise two broad types of efficiency: allocative efficiency and productive efficiency. Also, productive efficiency can be divided into static gains and dynamic gains. Static efficiency is broadly concerned with producing a given output at lowest cost. By contrast, dynamic efficiency, as the name implies, is concerned with innovation and structural change. If privatisation leads to a more rapid and successful rate of innovation and structural change over the longer term then it will lead to performance improvements that will not necessarily be reflected in static efficiency in the short-term. Given the relatively short period of time since privatisation, not surprisingly the empirical research reviewed here has been mainly concerned with static efficiency effects. This may, however, under-estimate the longer-term impact of privatisation.

In the previous chapter it was also recognised that privatisation can have wider consequences extending well beyond the firm in question. Changes in a privatised firm's inputs and outputs may impact on the wider macroeconomy and on other firms that are competitors or suppliers. In addition, computation of efficiency changes following privatisation can be complicated by any related income redistribution (Jones et al., 1991). Any reorganisation of service delivery usually has distributional consequences for consumers and those employed in the affected industries, even when the intention is simply to

66

raise efficiency (Vernon, 1989). The privatisation studies reviewed below have, in general, tended to be concerned with efficiency rather than equity issues.

The review of recent empirical studies of public versus private ownership are separated below into a review of: (a) international studies; (b) studies of public versus private sector performance in the UK; and (c) studies concerned specifically with the results of UK privatisation. The performance measures used in these studies have varied, though most have involved measuring either profitability, productivity or costs of production. A few have considered other variables such as employment, pricing and the use of working and fixed capital. Generally the studies have concentrated upon productive efficiency rather than allocative efficiency. As was observed in the previous chapter, measuring changes in allocative efficiency is particularly difficult because it necessitates discovering whether new outputs and prices have improved resource allocation.

For reasons that follow from public choice, property rights and related arguments (detailed in chapter 1), the expectation would be that state-owned firms have lower allocative and productive efficiency with the latter made up of technical and price inefficiencies. In other words, state firms may be expected to price outputs to meet political and social objectives (allocative inefficiency), make less efficient use of inputs (technical inefficiency) and employ inputs at sub-optimal levels given their prices (price inefficiency). Allocative and productive efficiency is likely to be especially at risk where there is rent-seeking behaviour by employees and their unions, the industries' managements and government officials, and where politicians put short-term political gains ahead of longer-term economic outcomes. More specifically, and from the arguments in chapter 1, the expectation is that costs of production will be higher and productivity and profitability lower under state ownership.

INTERNATIONAL STUDIES

There have now been a very large number of studies of public and private sector firms both where they operate side by side in the same industry and where there has been some privatisation. Table 4.1 provides a summary of many (though by no means all) of them from various parts of the world and other reviews can be found elsewhere (for example, Borcherding *et al.*, 1982, Millward and Parker, 1983; Parker, 1985; Vickers and Yarrow, 1988; Bös, 1991). What is evident is the degree of variation in the conclusions with some studies clearly finding that private ownership leads to improved performance, while others have found no statistically significant difference. It does seem that state and mixed-ownership (state and private) corporations are generally less profitable than private enterprises, but, as discussed in chapter 3, profit is not necessarily an appropriate efficiency gauge, especially when firms operate in uncompetitive markets. High profit may

Table 4.1 Summary of empirical studies of public versus private efficiency

Study and country	Industry(s)	Main performance measure(s) used	Findings
(a) UK			
Ashworth and Forsyth (1984)	Civil aviation	Mainly total factor productivity	State-owned British Airways performed poorly compared with other carriers
Hamilton (1971)	Nationalised sector versus private industry	Mainly profitability in 1960s	Lower profits in public sector
Polanyi (1968) Polanyi and Polanyi (1972, 1974)	Nationalised sector versus private industry	Profitability in 1960s	Yield on investment in nationalised industry only around a quarter of that in the private sector.
Pryke (1971)	Nationalised sector versus private manufacturing	Productivity, mainly labour productivity, 1948–68	Nationalised industries had faster growth of output per man hour (e.g., 1958–68 increased at an average of 5.3 per cent compared with only 3.7 per cent in the private sector. Also finds faster growth in total factor productivity but the method of measurement is suspect, see Millward and Parker, 1983, pp. 240–1.
Rowley and Yarrow (1981)	Steel industry 1957–75	Various including productivity	Found that nationalisation of the UK steel industry in 1967 led to a general downturn in performance but 'with some ambiguity concerning the highly important productivity variable'.
Pryke (1981)	Nationalised sector versus private manufacturing	Labour productivity and profitability, 1968–78.	Nationalised industries performed on the whole much worse than private industry. Major cause identified is poor management leading to over-staffing.

Study and country	Industry(s)	Main performance measure(s) used	Findings
Pryke (1982)	Civil aviation, cross-channel ferry and hovercraft services, sale of gas and electricity appliances and gas and electricity contracting	Market share, profitability and labour productivity, mainly 1970s.	Public sector operator performed worse than private sector counterpart.
Foreman-Peck and Waterson (1984)	Electricity generation between the wars	Costs of production	Private generators tended to perform better but 'the best municipal undertakings are on a par in static efficiency terms with the best companies'.
Millward and Ward (1987)	Nineteenth century town gas	Costs of production	No evidence of a private sector cost advantage.
Monopolies and Mergers Commission (various dates)	Various state-owned industries in the 1980s e.g., coal (1983), Post Office (1980), electricity (1981).	Various including service quality	Severe criticism of certain operating characteristics and service, e.g., inefficient use of labour and capital.
Millward (1990, 1991)	Gas, electricity, water, mining, and transport and communications compared with UK private manufacturing and similar industries in the USA	Labour and total factor productivity	Higher labour and total factor productivity growth in UK public enterprises. UK public enterprise performance also compares well with similar and mainly privately-owned firms.
Molyneux and Thompson (1987)	Nationalised industries versus private manufacturing	Labour and total factor productivity	Productivity growth faster in the nationalised sector 1978 to 1985.
Bacon et al. (1991)	Steel industry in UK compared with West Germany	Restructuring	When restructuring in the 1980s to improve efficiency, ownership may not have been a critical factor.

Study and country	Industry(s)	Main performance measure(s) used	Findings
Lynk (1993)	UK private sector statutory water companies and the state-owned regional water authorities before their privatisation in 1989	Costs of production	The state-owned authorities operated at higher cost efficiency than the 28 statutory water companies.
(b) USA			
Atkinson and Halvorsen (1986)	Electricity industry	Allocative efficiency	No significant differences between publicly and privately-owned utilities.
Bruggink (1982)	Water industry	Costs of production	Operating costs on average 24 per cent lower in the public sector.
Clarkson (1972)	Hospitals: proprietary and non-proprietary	Various	Non-proprietary hospitals (state and private non-profit) had more formal and bureaucratic procedures.
De Alessi (1974b, 1977)	Electricity industry	Pricing policy and profits	Public sector electric utilities are less likely to set 'economic' prices and have more variable rates of return. They also have higher operating costs.
Crain and Zardkoohi (1978)	Water industry	Costs of production	Lower operating costs in the private sector.
Di Lorenzo and Robinson (1982)	Electricity industry	Costs of production	No significant difference in public and private efficiency.
Feigenbaum and Teeples (1983)	Water industry	Costs of production	No real difference overall in public and private sector utilities' costs.
Färe et al. (1985)	Electricity industry	Various (six measures)	Public utilities had better ratings in terms of technical efficiency; the private utilities performed better in terms of congestion and scale efficiency measures. Overall, no significant difference in cost efficiency.
Mann and Mikesell (1976)	Water industry	Costs of production	Lower operating costs in public sector.

Study and country	Industry(s)	Main performance measure(s) used	Findings
Meyer (1975)	Electricity generating, transmitting and distribution in the late 1960s	Costs of production	Generating and certain other costs, including administration, were lower in the public sector.
Moore (1970)	Electricity industry	Various	No significant differences between public and private sector costs of building plant and labour per plant.
Neuberg (1977)	Electricity industry	Costs of production	Costs on average 10 per cent lower in publicly-owned utilities.
Peltzman (1971)	Electricity industry	Pricing policy and profits	Public sector utilities and liquor stores are less likely to seek profit maximising prices.
Pescatrice and Trapani (1980)	Electricity industry	Costs of production	Costs up to 25 per cent lower in the public sector largely due to higher levels of technology.
Wallace and Junk (1970)	Electricity generation	Costs of production	Costs lower in the private sector.
Yunker (1975)	Electricity industry	Costs of production	No evidence of superior operating cost efficiency in the private sector.
Windle (1991)	US versus non-US airlines	Productivity and unit costs	European airlines (mainly state-owned) have 10.5 per cent higher costs.
Pollitt (1994, 1995)	129 US electricity transmission utilities and 145 electricity distribution systems, plus a few UK electricity firms	Cost efficiency and frontier analysis	The null hypothesis that publicly-owned and privately-owned electricity utilities had no significant differences in terms of technical or cost efficiency could not be rejected.
(c) Other countries			
Caves and Christensen (1980)	Railways in Canada	Total factor productivity 1950s, 1960s	Total factor productivity grew faster in the public sector.
Davies (1971, 1977, 1980)	Civil airlines in Australia	Productivity	Higher productivity in the private airline.
Davies (1981)	Australian banking	Productivity	Private sector more efficient.

Study and country	Industry(s)	Main performance measure(s) used	Findings
Forsyth and Hocking (1980)	Civil airlines in Australia	Productivity	Little difference in productivity between the public and private airline when allowance is made for route differences.
Finsinger (1986)	Insurance companies in West Germany	Premium levels	Public enterprises charge lower premiums and return a larger proportion of those premiums to the insured because of lower costs.
Forsyth et al. (1986)	Civil aviation	Productivity, 1983	Compared with sixteen other airlines, British Airways performed poorly. However, two of the top performers, Air Canada and Lufthansa, were state owned too.
Oelert (1976)	Bus services in West German cities	Costs of provision	Costs of provision up to 160 per cent per kilometre higher where services publicly provided.
Funkhouser and MacAvoy (1979)	Diverse range of industries in Java, Sumatra and Bali	Profitability and costs of production, 1971	Higher costs and lower profitability in the public sector. But no evidence that public sector firms are less cost efficient than private sector firms of the same size.
Tyler (1979)	Publicly-owned, privately-owned and multinational subsidiaries in Brazil	Technical efficiency	No statistically significant difference between the different forms of ownership.
Kim (1981)	Public and private sectors in Tanzania	Various	Higher efficiency in the private sector.
Palmer et al. (1983)	Canadian coach services	Various	Public sector less efficient.
Gantt and Dutto (1968)	Public enterprises in LDCs	Profitability	Average loss of 16 per cent recorded for the state sector.

Study and country	Industry(s)	Main performance measure(s) used	Findings
Monsen and Walters (1983)	Comparison of 25 largest industrial state-owned firms and 25 largest industrial private sector firms in Western Europe	Profitability, 1972–81	In each year the average return for state firms was negative and the average return for private sector firms was positive.
Boardman et al. (1986)	Acquisition of a private Canadian corporation, Domtar, by two Quebec Crown corporations	Stock market prices – abnormal returns to shareholders	The market value of Domtar dropped sharply leading to cumulative abnormal returns of minus 25 per cent. Between 8 and 19 percentage points of this was attributed to government control and the anticipated pursuit of non-profit objectives.
Foreman-Peck (1985)	International study of telecommunications	Variables relating to the expansion of telecommunications	State ownership had a positive impact on telecommunications in the early stages of development but continued government ownership tended to retard development.
Millward (1988)	Developing economies	Technical efficiency	No statistically significant evidence of a lower level of technical efficiency in state-owned firms.
Picot and Kaulmann (1989)	Public and private-sector companies, 1975–84, in largely unregulated markets and subject to competition. Six countries namely Britain France, Germany, Canada, Italy and Sweden, and 15 industries	Profitability and productivity	Government-owned corporations show lower levels of productivity, lower rates of return and a lower ratio of shareholders' equity to total assets than privately-owned corporations.
Boardman and Vining (1989)	500 largest non-US industrial firms	Profitability, productivity	Private corporations had higher profitability; productivity results more mixed.

Study and country	Industry(s)	Main performance measure(s) used	Findings
Sampson (1995)	Privatisation of banking in Jamaica	Various	Mixed results.
Vining and Boardman (1990)	500 largest Canadian corporations	Profitability, productivity	State-owned enterprises and enterprises with some state shareholding had lower profitability.
Duch (1991)	International telecommunications (OECD countries)	Density of telephone subscribers; revenue per employee	No evidence that private firms outperform public ones. But his 'private firms' could include some state ownership.
Perelman and Pestieau (1987)	International comparison of railways and postal services	Total factor productivity	All state owned – wide variations in performance.
Holmes (1990)	Electricity in Europe	Supply and prices	Overall, there does not appear to be any simple relationship between comparative performance and industrial or ownership structures.
Adhikari and Kirkpatrick (1990)	Developing economies	Various	Some evidence of poorer performance in state firms but causes may be more complex than simply a matter of ownership.
Lutter (1992)	23 airlines in 18 countries between 1973 and 1983	Allocative efficiency	State enterprises did not act to maximise welfare by reducing the deadweight loss resulting from imperfect competition.
Hjalmasson and Veiderpass (1992)	Swedish electricity distribution utilities, 1970s and 1980s	Productivity	No evidence of a correlation between ownership and performance.
Galal et al. (1992)	Privatisation of 4 airlines, 3 telecom firms, 2 electricity utilities, a road transport organisation, a container port, and a lottery business in Britain, Chile, Malaysia and Mexico	Economic gains and losses to employees, taxpayers and customers	In 11 of the 12 privatisations there was a net increase in wealth. Gains due to higher investment, managerial innovation, better pricing and changes in employment. But consumers were net gainers in only 4 of the cases.

Study and country	Industry(s)	Main performance measure(s) used	Findings
Plane (1992)	Public enterprise sector in 45 countries	Neoclassical production function and value-added by the state sector. Impact on the economic growth rate	Hypotheses derived from the theories of property rights, bureaucracy and X-inefficiency cannot be rejected.
Enderwick (1994)	Selected industries in Latin America and Asia	Profitability	Lower profitability in the state sector.
Megginson et al. (1994)	61 companies from 18 countries (6 developing and 12 industrialised) and 32 industries that experienced full or partial privatisation between 1961 and 1990	Mainly financial indicators	Following privatisation sales, profits, investment and operating efficiency typically increased.
Bhaskar and Khan (1995)	62 mills in the Bangladesh jute industry	Various	Reduced employment following privatisation.
World Bank (1995)	Analysis of 12 developing economies	Various	Labour productivity in privatised telecommunications rose by over 60 per cent in Argentina. In Chilean telecommunications the total gain for consumers, shareholders, workers and the government was 155 per cent of annual sales in the year before privatisation.

Note: This summary excludes studies mainly concerned with local authority services which are subject to competitive tendering or contracting-out. In general, these show that the introduction of competition leads to considerable cost savings from contracting; for a review of some of these studies see, for example, Parker (1990).

result from over-charging consumers rather than from reducing costs of production. Also, profit figures are affected by accounting conventions and financing methods. The studies that have used costs of production or productivity as the performance measure have generally provided more mixed results across sectors, though perhaps with still some slight leaning towards higher private-sector efficiency.

The expectation that state-owned firms will have higher costs and lower productivity and profitability seems most likely to be supported where firms operate in a competitive environment. Where monopoly conditions exist, particularly in water supply and in gas and electricity transmission and distribution, state regulation may dull efficiency incentives in the private sector. This may help to explain why performance differences between private sector and state-owned firms in these industries are less pronounced. The following studies are discussed here in more detail: Boardman and Vining (1989), Vining and Boardman (1990), Picot and Kaulman (1989), Megginson *et al.* (1994), Duch (1991), Pollitt (1994), Hjalmarsson and Veiderpass (1992), Ashworth and Forsyth (1984), Bhaskar and Khan (1995), Enderwick (1994), Adhikari and Kirkpatrick (1990) and Millward (1988) and Sampson (1995). These studies were selected because they provide an overview of the different approaches and perspectives adopted, both in the study of the industrialised and less developed economies (LDCs).

Consider first the frequently cited study by Boardman and Vining (1989). They used data from *Fortune 500* in 1983 to compare the performance of private corporations, state-owned enterprises and mixed enterprises among the largest non-US industrial firms: 409 were private corporations (PCs), 57 state-owned enterprises (SOEs) and 23 were mixed enterprises (MEs) having a mixture of public and private capital. For dependent variables they used four profitability measures (return on equity, return on assets, return on sales, and net income), two productivity measures (sales per employee and sales per asset) and a capital ratio (assets per employee). Independent variables included assets, sales, the number of employees to reflect size and therefore possible scale effects, and dummy variables[1] were introduced to reflect market concentration, industry, country differences and ownership form. In a series of calculations they concluded that the average rate of return on equity was 4.3 per cent for PCs, minus 10 per cent for SOEs and minus 14 per cent for MEs. They found less difference in the results for the return on assets and return on sales with PCs having the highest average sales per asset and SOEs slightly higher sales per employee.

Boardman and Vining claimed that their results confirm superior private sector performance. But as with all such studies certain reservations apply. In particular, the SOEs they included in their data set were mainly from the petroleum, metal manufacture and transportation industries. Although an attempt to capture industry effects was made, it may be that the results are still affected by differences in the samples of firms from the public and private sectors. Also, the results are surprising in so far as the market share variable did not seem to have an effect on profitability in their regressions, while industry concentration had a zero or negative effect. This is contrary to expectation and may imply other problems with their equations. Furthermore, the MEs appear to perform on balance worse than the SOEs, yet the theory on capital ownership reviewed in chapter 1 suggests that we might expect to find better performance where state ownership is combined with some traded shares compared with cases where the firm is wholly state-owned. Boardman and Vining explain the ME results in terms of inefficiencies introduced by conflicts between private and public shareholders, which leads to a high degree of managerial 'cognitive dissonance' (p. 26). But while this is possible, it does not stand easily alongside claims that managerial disillusionment is endemic in state-owned firms because of confused and conflicting objectives and political intervention.

Also, Boardman and Vining's study should be assessed in the light of the objections to profit as an efficiency measure. State-owned firms may have objective functions that include non-profit goals, such as maintaining employment, low prices, maximising output and no price discrimination – goals which are commensurate with a wider public purpose. Turning to the measurement of productivity, figures based on sales could reflect outputs and prices that may differ between public and private firms because of differences in goals, as well as because of differences in production efficiency. Moreover, it is difficult to know what to make of the assets per employee productivity measure which appears to be there as a kind of capital productivity indicator. It is not clear on *a priori* grounds whether a high or low ratio is desirable. For instance, a high ratio may indicate either high and beneficial investment or over-investment and waste. Perhaps aware of its crudity, Boardman and Vining barely report the results for this performance measure.

In a slightly later published paper Boardman and Vining used the same approach and measures as in their earlier study, but used data for 1986 on the 500 largest Canadian corporations. Their conclusion, once again, was higher performance in the private sector. SOEs and MEs had lower profitability than PCs, though the difference in sales per employee was not statistically significant (Vining and Boardman, 1990). The same weaknesses as highlighted for the previous study apply equally to this one. In particular, the results may be biased by the sample. This time the SOEs were disproportionately represented in mining. Recognising this Boardman and Vining argue that the results for MEs may be a better guide to the effects of state ownership, but this is once again problematic given the uncertainty about the optimal shareholding to maximise incentives for management to pursue efficiency. The argument also needs to be set against their findings when comparing MEs and SOEs in their previous study, where in general SOEs performed better than the MEs.

Turning to the study by Picot and Kaulman (1989), they used the same source of data as Boardman and Vining in their 1989 study, figures from *Fortune 500*, but extracted data for six countries (Britain, Canada, France, Germany, Italy and Sweden) and fifteen industries, all operating in competitive markets in the period 1975–84. Also, like Boardman and Vining, they regressed a range of performance measures derived from financial data against ownership, country and industry variables. Their conclusion, which is similar to Boardman and Vining's, is that government-owned corporations had lower levels of productivity, lower rates of return and a lower ratio of shareholders' equity to total assets than privately-owned corporations. But the same possible problem as in the Boardman and Vining studies, relating to whether like with like comparisons are being made, applies. In particular, it is not surprising that the shareholders' equity to loans ratio is lower in state-owned firms since they tend to be more dependent on loan capital. In addition, a low equity ratio is not unquestionably disadvantageous (Jensen, 1986).

More recently Megginson *et al.* (1994) compared the financial and operating performance of sixty-one companies from eighteen countries (six developing and twelve industrialised) and thirty-two industries that experienced full or partial privatisation between 1961 and 1990. A range of mainly financial indicators were used, including profitability, sales levels, operating efficiency, capital investment, leverage (gearing) ratios and dividend pay-out figures. They found that following privatisation firms typically increased sales, became more profitable, increased investment and improved their operating efficiency (measured by sales per employee and net income per employee). Interestingly, they also found that on average employment did not decrease after privatisation, as might have been expected, but actually rose.

This study looked, however, only at very short periods around the time of the public share offerings, plus or minus three years. This is too short to capture the full consequences of ownership change, especially any dynamic gains. Interestingly, they did find some suggestion that the best performance results were related to privatisation where there were large changes in senior management or control structure. This places the emphasis on internal reorganisation rather than privatisation *per se*, an issue we return to in chapter 9. A further study of privatisation, by Galal *et al.* (1992), looked at twelve companies (mostly airlines and regulated utilities) in Mexico, Chile, Malaysia and the UK. Unusually, they looked not only at changes in production efficiency but at how the costs and benefits of the ownership changes were allocated. Like Megginson *et al.*, they reported favourably on gains in production efficiency following privatisation and went on to record net welfare gains in eleven of the twelve cases. They calculated that on average the present value of these gains equalled 26 per cent of the firm's pre-divestiture sales revenue. They also concluded that in none of the cases were the workers made worse off and indeed in three cases they were made significantly better off.

While all of these studies are favourable to privatisation as a policy for raising performance and the Galal *et al.* paper suggests that welfare gains may be widespread, a number of other studies have questioned the importance of ownership. For example, Duch in a book length study of the international telecommunications industry in OECD countries measured performance by the density of telephone subscribers and revenues per employee. The conclusion of his study is that the results 'offer little support for the traditional argument that privately owned firms outperform those that are government-owned' (Duch, 1991, p. 77). As with the earlier studies, however, it is possible to raise objections, in this case most particularly with regard to the measures of performance. Public sector organisations are more likely to pursue market penetration as part of a social policy of increasing geographical coverage and this will be reflected in the density of telephone subscribers, one of Duch's performance measures. Also, the other performance series, sales per employee, may be a poor indicator of efficiency in what are monopoly industries. Typically, telecommunications companies in OECD countries are monopoly providers. Under monopoly the sales figure will be inflated by monopoly prices as well as by a rising volume of calls. In addition, objection can be raised to the method of aggregation adopted by Duch. His private ownership group includes all cases where there was some private capital and therefore includes utilities where the state remained the dominant owner. Private sector performance may be depressed by the inclusion of what are predominantly state-owned enterprises.

Pollitt's study is more careful in the way that performance is measured and in clearly delineating the public and private sectors (Pollitt, 1994, 1995). However, the industry he chose to study, electricity, is heavily state-regulated and this may well have affected his results. This comment also applies to the other US utility studies (electricity and water), summarised in Table 4.1, and which provide conflicting views about efficiency under public and private ownership. However, if ownership does affect performance (as the property rights literature reviewed in chapter 1 suggests) then we might still expect a privately-owned yet regulated firm to perform better than a state-owned company. Pollitt collected data for 129 US electricity transmission utilities and 145 electricity distribution systems. The latter were mainly made up of US utilities but the sample also included UK firms. Using both data envelopment analysis, a form of linear programming to measure production efficiency (DEA is used and explained in detail in chapter 7), along with a regression analysis of cost efficiency, he found that the null hypothesis, that publicly-owned and privately-owned electricity transmission and distribution systems had no significant difference in terms of technical or cost efficiency, could not be rejected. The regression analysis looked at cost efficiency and the DEA at technical efficiency and Pollitt concluded that: 'If anything the regression analysis suggested that publicly owned firms have lower costs than privately owned firms once environmental factors are taken into account' (p. 24). In a similar vein, Hjalmarsson and Veiderpass (1992) looked at productivity in the Swedish electricity distribution utilities in the 1970s and 1980s, a sector with both privately-owned and publicly-owned operators. They found no evidence of a correlation between ownership type and performance.

Other studies that have produced results that are difficult to square with the expectations from the public choice and property rights literatures are those by Ashworth and Forsyth (1984) and a number of the papers on the US electricity and water industries, whose findings are summarised in Table 4.1.[2] Ashworth and Forsyth studied the performance of the major international airlines in the late 1970s and while they were uncomplimentary about state-owned British Airways, they concluded that Air Canada, also a state-owned enterprise, was the most efficient.

All of the above studies were concerned with the industrialised economies, but there have been a number of studies of state ownership in the LDCs. For example, Bhaskar and Khan (1995) studied sixty-two mills in the Bangladesh jute industry, half of which were privatised in the early 1980s. The firms were selected for privatisation according to whether they were owned by Bangladeshi nationals at the time of nationalisation. Those firms previously owned by West Pakistanis remained nationalised. Hence, they felt able to argue that there was no evidence of selection for privatisation according to financial strength which might bias their results. The study concluded that privatisation had reduced employment without a statistically significant fall in output. There had, however, been a change in the composition of the workforce with more casual workers employed and large job losses amongst white collar staff. Bhaskar and Khan attribute this result to political favouritism leading to excessive bureaucracy under state ownership.

In a review of studies of profitability in state-owned industries in Latin American and Asian economies, Enderwick (1994) concluded that there was clear evidence of much lower profitability in the state sector. It was such findings along with other evidence of waste in developing economies that led both the IMF and World Bank in the 1980s to promote privatisation as a key part of structural adjustment programmes. Adhikari and Kirkpatrick (1990) reviewing an even larger number of studies of developing economies similarly concluded that state enterprises had suffered from conflicting objectives, protected markets, a lack of fiscal restraints and excessive government involvement in management, leading in many cases to public enterprises failing to cover their production costs. Overall, in the state sector profitability was low and productivity levels (though not necessarily growth rates) were found to be worse than in private sector firms. They went on, however, to point out that such comparisons were complex because state firms could be pursuing wider objectives than profitability and productivity and that state enterprises tended to be concentrated in basic industries with slower growth rates. They echoed a 1983 World Bank report which concluded that the quality of management rather than ownership *per se* may be what matters: 'the key factor determining the efficiency of an enterprise is not whether it is publicly or privately owned, but how it is managed' (World Bank, 1983, p. 50). By so doing they appeared to argue for more managerial autonomy from political control but, as we noted in chapter 1, agent autonomy from the control of a principal is not necessarily desirable and may lead to waste. Put simply, management freed from outside controls may pursue their own utility, especially where markets remain protected, as is the case in many LDCs.

In a further review of public and private enterprises in the developing economies Millward (1988, p. 157) reaches a more sympathetic conclusion with regard to the impact of state ownership. After reviewing the evidence on productivity growth he concludes that: 'There is no evidence of a statistically satisfactory kind to suggest that public enterprises in LDCs have a lower level of technical efficiency than private firms operating at the same scale of operation'. However, Millward's position is not entirely clear, for while he argues that there is no statistically significant evidence of lower technical efficiency amongst state firms, he notes that at: 'a less formal level the tendency seems to be nevertheless pointing in that direction' (p. 157).

Another study that finds a more favourable outcome associated with state ownership is that by Sampson (1995). Sampson studied the impact of privatisation of banking in Jamaica and more especially the performance of the National Commercial Bank Group (NCBG) which was privatised between 1986 and 1992. The study concludes:

Although growth in the financial sector and the economy as a whole was stronger in the post-divestment period, there is no evidence from this specific case that private ownership resulted in higher performance than state capitalism. The pre-divestment rate of real growth in revenues was stronger. Market share increased and peaked under state capitalism. Real growth in assets and deposits was also stronger. The improvement in profit performance in terms of return on equity is not statistically significant. Since competition NCBG's performance has generally been below that of its main competitors in terms of return on equity and assets. However, NCBG has been more innovative under private ownership. The major difference . . . is the higher level of diversification . . . since divestment. . . . [But] NCBG has diversified into riskier investments and areas where it would seem to have no competitive advantage and no special management skills.[3]

(Sampson, 1995, p. 222)

In sum, the international studies do not provide unequivocal support for privatisation programmes. When allowance is made for the fact that generally the industries in which state-sector firms seem to perform as well (or perhaps even better) than private-sector firms tend to be monopolistic and state-regulated, and economic theory suggests that state regulation may lead to inefficiency under private ownership, then the balance of evidence may be interpreted as favouring private ownership but only in competitive markets. Perhaps the existence of taxpayer subsidies and the absence of a take-over threat makes the management of state-owned firms in competitive markets more complacent than their private sector counterparts. Where state regulation will continue, the message from these studies for governments thinking about privatising their monopoly enterprises is a much more cautionary one.

UK STUDIES

It is now time to turn to studies that have looked specifically at the performance of public and private sector firms in the UK. Duch (1991) notes in his study of international telecommunications that national factors, including local attitudes towards public and private enterprise, may be very significant in determining whether state firms operate efficiently. Examples of highly successful state-owned firms, such as China Steel in Taiwan, provide casual support for this claim. If national characteristics can have a significant effect on the way state-owned firms behave, then international findings on relative efficiency may have less significance for the UK privatisation debate than similar studies in the UK.

Table 4.1 above also summarises the main UK studies of public and private sector efficiency undertaken over the last thirty years. What is evident at first glance is once again the diversity of the results. For example, Rowley and Yarrow (1981) using a number of economic indicators, including productivity, for the UK steel industry found a general downturn in performance following nationalisation in 1967 but 'with some ambiguity concerning the highly important productivity variable' (p. 93). By contrast, Lynk (1993, p. 112), looking at the state-owned regional water authorities and the privately-owned statutory water companies before privatisation of the water industry in 1989–90, concludes: 'The average level of inefficiency within the privately owned water industry appears to be substantially higher than that prevailing within the public sector in the period immediately preceding privatisation'. The Pryke studies (Pryke, 1971, 1981, 1982) are also particularly noteworthy not only because they have been widely cited in the past but because of their widely differing conclusions. Initially Pryke praised the productivity record of the nationalised sector for its performance in the late 1950s and early 1960s (Pryke, 1971). A decade later, however, he took a much less favourable view of public ownership, based on his study of the nationalised sector's performance in the 1970s (Pryke, 1981, 1982). Below, more recent research, by Millward (1990, 1991; see also Foreman-Peck and Millward, 1994, ch.9), Hutchinson (1991) and Molyneux and Thompson (1987), is reviewed in greater detail.

Millward (1990, 1991) charted the growth of labour productivity and total factor productivity (TFP) in the UK gas, electricity, water, mining, transport and communications industries between 1951 and 1985. In this period the industries were dominated by publicly-owned suppliers. The results were contrasted with productivity indices for private manufacturing. Millward calculated that on average during this period labour productivity in manufacturing rose by 2.8 per cent and by 3.2 per cent in the state enterprise group. TFP in the state-owned industries rose by a more modest 2.2 per cent, but this still exceeded the growth rate in private manufacturing, which Millward noted averaged a mere 1.6 per cent. He explains these results in terms of job cuts in the public sector, especially in the 1950s and 1960s, and a better performance in terms of capital productivity throughout the period. He concluded, using words very similar to those in Pryke's 1968 survey, that: 'There is therefore no general evidence that productivity growth has been slower in public enterprise than in manufacturing in the post-war period' (Millward, 1990, p. 431).

Like the other studies reviewed, this research has its fair share of problems most notably relating to the sectoral comparisons. The validity of comparing public utilities and service industries with manufacturing industry is questionable because of possible differences in the potential for productivity growth. As a cross-check, Millward went on to compare his group of state enterprises with similar industries in the USA and found that the growth rate of TFP was higher in the UK, though the growth rates of the UK and US manufacturing sectors were identical. The record on labour productivity, he concluded, was more patchy. On the one hand, this comparison is problematic because the US utilities are state-regulated even when they are privately owned and this may explain relatively weak performance. On the other hand, the US utilities are privately-owned so the property rights literature would still lead us to expect a better performance than in state-owned companies.

Hutchinson (1991) categorised seventeen UK firms into five industrial groupings based on the official Standard Industrial Classification (SIC), namely aerospace, electronics and electrical, automobile manufacturing, civil aviation and general freight. He then compared state-owned firms with private sector firms within each category. The measurements used were labour productivity, profitability and what Hutchinson calls 'technology mix', which is a capital/labour ratio. He concluded that: 'The empirical evidence reported is consistent with the literature which suggests that privately-owned firms generally outperform 'comparable' government-owned firms' (p. 95). Again, this result should be treated with care given the use of the SIC as a basis for categorising firms for comparison. SIC classifications are arguably too wide to be useful for direct state versus private sector comparisons. For example, Hutchinson compares Ferranti, normally a private sector firm but briefly in the public sector in the late 1970s because of financial failings, with companies such as Philips and Standard Telephones, whose markets are very different. Similarly, it is doubtful whether much can be usefully learnt from a comparison of British Aerospace with Smiths Industries. The outputs of these two companies are insufficiently similar to make the comparison valid.

Also, Hutchinson's study takes in the 1970s when according to Pryke (1981, p. 257) the performance of the UK nationalised industries was 'third rate, though with some evidence here and there of first class standards'. Hence the question arises, can the results be generalised to other periods? Recent research has recorded a marked turnaround in the fortunes of the nationalised industries since the late 1970s (as reflected in Millward's studies). Molyneux and Thompson (1987), studying the productivity growth of UK nationalised industries between 1978 and 1985, discovered that overall their growth exceeded the performance of the private manufacturing sector over the same period, although the usual caveat about sectoral studies applies (are we comparing like with like?). They put this performance down to three factors: a tighter financial regime for state industries introduced in the late 1970s; the Conservative government's desire that the industries be operated more commercially (the impact of 'Thatcherism' on the public sector); and the threat of privatisation. The good relative performance of state industries appears to have continued, even though some of the most productive have been privatised. According to recent Treasury estimates, between 1979–80 and 1990–1 the average growth rate of output per person in companies remaining in the public sector was 4.2 per cent compared with 3.5 per cent for private sector manufacturing (figures from HM Treasury).

UK PRIVATISATION STUDIES

Until recently, assessing the impact of privatisation in the UK has been restricted by the short period of time since most of the industries were transferred to the private sector. There were a few attempts in the very early days of privatisation to make some preliminary assessment. These studies covered performance in the mid-1980s and therefore capture mainly any static efficiency gains immediately following privatisation. Also, they cover a period which was one of relative economic prosperity in the UK compared with the years immediately before or after. A recent study by Bishop and Green (1995) looks at the period up to 1994, but productivity figures for only three privatised companies are reported and, in terms of the other performance data cited, the coverage is patchy and unsystematic. Also, they make no attempt to adjust their figures for business cycle effects.

Table 4.2 Summary of major studies of performance changes in UK firms following privatisation

Study	Industry(s)	Main performance measure(s) used	Findings
Yarrow (1986, 1989)	7 privatised firms	Various	Only three clear success stories following privatisation (at NFC, ABP, and Cable and Wireless).
Foreman-Peck and Manning (1988)	Telecommunications	Productivity	BT's productivity has risen since privatisation, but some state-owned suppliers in Europe have performed as well or almost as well.
Bishop and Kay (1988, 1989)	12 organisations (not all privatised)	Total factor productivity and financial measures	Performance improved in the 1980s but relationship to privatisation is not immediately apparent.
Vickers and Yarrow (1988)	Various	Various	Varied results
Foreman-Peck (1989)	Telecommunications	Total factor productivity	No substantial improvement in the growth rate for BT since privatisation.
Haskel and Szymanski (1990, 1991, 1992, 1993a, 1993b)	Up to 18 organisations publicly-owned in 1973. Most, however, were not privatised in the period studied	Various	In general, output and profits grew and employment fell in the 1980s, but this applied equally to those organisations which stayed in the public sector and those that were privatised, implying that other factors than privatisation, particularly competition, explained the results.
Hutchinson (1991)	17 UK firms in several industrial groupings	Labour productivity, profitability and technology mix	Privately-owned firms outperformed comparable state-owned firms in the 1970s and 1980s in terms of profitability only. Less certain whether privatisation had improved performance.

Study	Industry(s)	Main performance measure(s) used	Findings
Parker and Hartley (1991a, 1991b) and Hartley et al. (1991)	10 organisations that had changed their ownership status within the public sector or which had crossed between the public and private sectors in the period from 1969 to the mid-1980s	Employment, productivity and financial ratios	Results were sensitive to the performance measure used. But in general, performance improved when organisations were subjected to private-sector or commercial pressures. This result was not, however, guaranteed.
Bishop and Thompson (1992, 1993)	9 enterprises that were either privatised or remained in the state sector	Labour and total factor productivity	Productivity had shown significantly faster growth during the 1980s compared with the 1970s. This applied to firms that remained in the public sector as well as those that were privatised.
Price and Weyman-Jones (1993)	12 production and distribution regions of British Gas, 1977–8 to 1990–1	Productivity	Rate of growth of total factor productivity increased significantly following privatisation.
Burns and Weyman-Jones (1994a, 1994b, 1994c)	12 privatised regional electricity companies	Cost function and productivity	No statistically significant evidence that privatisation had accelerated productivity gains.
Parker (1995a)	10 organisations that were privatised or changed their organisational status within the public sector	Internal restructuring and performance changes	Managerial and organisational restructuring appears to be critical to performance improvement following privatisation or some kind of agency status within government.
Bishop and Green (1995)	A number of organisations privatised or still in the public sector in the 1980s	Profit, turnover, wages and employment data, mainly comparing 1979 and 1990–4. TFP data for 1989 and 1994 but for only three privatised firms	Concludes that competition is very important in explaining the performance results.

The main UK studies are summarised in Table 4.2. As can be seen, the early studies found some evidence that profitability improved immediately after privatisation, though perhaps surprisingly not in all cases (Yarrow, 1986 and 1989; Vickers and Yarrow, 1988; and Bishop and Kay, 1989). Yarrow found that nominal operating profits had doubled at British Aerospace from privatisation in 1981 to 1987. He also recorded impressive profits growth at Cable and Wireless, NFC and Associated British Ports, but more disappointing figures for Britoil, Jaguar and British Airways (Yarrow, 1989, p. 319). Yarrow also considered the possible impact of privatisation on labour and, after studying wages in British Aerospace, NFC, Britoil, ABP and Jaguar, concluded that 'there is little evidence to suggest that, as a result of privatisation, wage rates were significantly reduced relative to those elsewhere in the economy. Indeed, if anything the initial impact of the asset sales on wage rates appears to have been positive' (Yarrow, 1989, p. 323). Improved labour productivity at BA and NFC was associated with employment reductions but he noted that these cuts occurred well before actual privatisation.

Out of the seven firms studied by Yarrow, there were three clear success stories (at NFC, Cable and Wireless, and ABP) but in the other four firms the results were mixed. According to Yarrow a failure to improve competition, the existence of golden shares and dispersed shareholdings, and managerial acquisition binges after privatisation, may all have helped to explain why there appeared to be no clearer link between privatisation and improved efficiency. In summary he wrote: 'the hypothesis that privatization *per se* will quickly lead to substantial improvements in the performances of inefficient state-owned enterprises is not well supported by the data' (Yarrow, 1989, p. 341).

Yarrow's study covered the period up to 1987–8 only and his conclusions were therefore highly provisional. The same applies both to the study by Vickers and Yarrow (1988), which draws on Yarrow's work, and the studies by Bishop and Kay (Bishop and Kay, 1988, 1989). Bishop and Kay attempted a detailed appraisal of the early results of privatisation measuring changes in performance using productivity and financial ratios. They found evidence of performance improvements and their results for TFP are summarised in Table 4.3, but they concluded that generally such improvements were unrelated to privatisation:

> The overall picture to emerge . . . is one of substantial change. Output and profits have grown, margins have increased, employment has declined. But the relationship of these changes to the fact of privatization is not immediately apparent from the data. The privatized industries have tended to be faster growing and more profitable, but it seems that the causation runs from growth and profitability to privatization, rather than the other way round. . . . The significant

Table 4.3 Total factor productivity growth in a selection of mainly former UK nationalised industries

Enterprise	Annual rate of increase in TFP (percentage)			
	1979–88	1979–83	1983–88	Date of privatisation where relevant
BAA	1.4	0.1	2.5	1987
British Coal[1]	2.6	0.6	4.2	1995
British Gas	2.9	(0.2)[3]	5.4	1986
British Rail	1.5	(0.4)	3.4	1995–7
British Steel	7.1	4.6	9.0	1988
British Telecom	1.9	1.6	2.2	1984
Electricity supply	1.3	(1.5)	3.5	1990–1
Post Office	2.9	2.8	2.9	n/a[2]
Average	2.7	1.0	4.1	n/a

Notes: 1 The British Coal results have been adjusted for the effects of the 1984–5 strike.
2 n/a = not applicable. The Post Office is still state owned.
3 Parentheses denote a negative figure.
Source: Bishop and Kay, 1988, p. 5; privatisation dates added.

improvement in the performance of the remaining public sector denies any simple views about the relationship between ownership and performance.

(Bishop and Kay, 1988, pp. 40–1, 45, 53)

A later study by Bishop and Thompson (1992) was able to cover a somewhat longer period (to the late 1980s). In a study of labour productivity and TFP growth at BA, BAA and BT, the coal board, the electricity supply industry, gas, posts, rail and steel between 1970–80 and 1980–90, they concluded that in most cases labour productivity had improved, though the results for TFP growth were more mixed. Results were reported for two sub-periods, the 1970s and the 1980s, and are reproduced in Table 4.4. Productivity growth was usually higher in the 1980s and that: 'in aggregate, both labour productivity and total factor productivity have shown significantly faster growth during the 1980s in comparison with the 1970s' (Bishop and Thompson, 1992, p. 1181). This could be, however, because of national productivity developments as the 1970s was a very poor period for UK productivity growth. Also the dates for their periods do not coincide with the ownership change so it is difficult to relate their figures to the actual act of privatisation as against other possible factors. They went on to argue that changes in the regulatory environment within government rather than privatisation explained the improved performance in the 1980s. In a later paper, Bishop and Thompson (1993, p. 26) observed that performance improvements were more significant when privatised companies operated in competitive markets: 'Performance improvement, although positive, was less impressive in the natural monopolies'. This conclusion is repeated in Bishop and Green (1995) and is broadly consistent with the international studies reviewed earlier.

Table 4.4 UK public enterprises: productivity growth from 1970 to 1990

| Enterprise | Annual average rates of growth[1] | | | |
| | Labour productivity % | | Total factor productivity % | |
	1970/80	1980/90	1970/80	1980/90
British Airways	8.1	6.0	7.9	2.7
BAA	0.6	2.7	4.8	0.3
British Telecom	4.3	7.2	4.6	3.2
British Coal	(2.4)[2]	8.1	(2.2)	2.8
Electricity Supply	3.7	2.5	2.3	1.4
British Gas	4.9	4.9	4.2	1.0
Post Office	(0.1)	3.4	0.0	2.2
British Rail	(2.0)	3.2	(1.7)	1.2
British Steel	(1.7)	13.7	(2.7)	7.0

Notes: 1 Measures are for financial years ending in March of the relevant year.
2 Parentheses denote a negative figure.
Source: Bishop and Thompson, 1992, p. 1187.

Foreman-Peck and Manning (1988) studied the UK telecommunications industry and confirmed an improvement in BT's productivity performance after privatisation, concluding that BT now had the second or third highest productivity in Europe. However, the other systems in Europe were publicly owned, including the most productive, Denmark's, and where some private equity participation existed, as in the Spanish and Italian systems, performance was found to be relatively poor. In the public versus private debate, those on either side can find some satisfaction in the Foreman-Peck and Manning research. The same applies to Hutchinson's study reviewed earlier (Hutchinson, 1991). Although Hutchinson argued that in the industries he studied private sector firms had out-performed their public sector counterparts, he did not find that when privatised relative performance improved. Moreover, recent research into restructuring in the British and West German steel industries in the 1980s, has questioned whether ownership was the critical explanation for British Steel's reported efficiency gains (Bacon *et al.*, 1991, p. 2).

Haskel and Szymanski in a series of papers (1990, 1991, 1992, 1993a, 1993b) gathered data on up to seventeen organisations that were publicly-owned in 1973. They looked at output growth, employment, wages and profits from 1972 to 1988. But only four of their sample actually underwent privatisation in the period studied. The four were the British Airports Authority (BAA), British Telecom (BT), British Airways (BA) and British

Gas. In these four firms output and profits grew. In terms of employment, they found that employment fell with a change towards more commercial objectives in the 1980s, but that wages were only slightly affected being more affected by a loss of market power. The record of the privatised firms was mixed, however. BT and British Gas suffered a loss of employment, while BAA and BA recorded an increase in the numbers employed. Using yardsticks of wages in the production and services sectors, they found the real wage per employee was at a lower level in the privatised industries.

Given the ownership of the firms studied, the Haskel and Szymanski research is better viewed as a comment on the impact of Thatcherism on the public sector than as a study of privatisation. In particular, it remains unclear as to what extent the favourable performance of UK state-owned industries in the 1980s was due to the threat of privatisation, economic and financial reforms in the public sector aimed at tightening the budgetary constraint and reducing waste, or other factors (for example national improvements in economic performance). In further work based on a labour productivity function with dummy variables introduced to capture the impact of unionisation, market share, management, state-regulation and ownership, in only two of their four privatised firms, BAA and BA, was the ownership dummy found to be statistically significant. In other words, there was no evidence of an improvement in labour productivity associated with privatisation in the cases of British Gas and BT. They did find above average productivity growth in the public sector as a whole, which they associated in the main with above average labour shedding and which is consistent with the Molyneux and Thompson (1987) and Treasury figures commented on earlier. But such a finding is not helpful to the privatisation case since it suggests that good performance is quite compatible with state ownership. In terms of winners and losers from UK privatisation, Haskel (1994) observed that shareholders and senior managers were the clear gainers and that privatisation had led to considerable job losses. For those who had retained their jobs, wages had grown in line with the rest of the economy except for top managers 'who have enjoyed very large relative pay rises' (p. 6). But again changes pre-privatisation are not clearly distinguished from trends since and the data used only go up to 1988; it remains unclear what has happened since then.

The studies by Parker and Hartley (1991a, 1991b) and by Hartley *et al.* (1991) concerned ten organisations which had experienced a change of organisational status (nationalisation, privatisation, or a change within government, for instance replacing direct departmental control with a public corporation or a trading fund). The periods studied stretched between the 1960s and the 1980s. Of the organisations, three (National Freight, BA and British Aerospace) experienced privatisation in the 1980s, two were nationalised (Rolls-Royce in 1971 and British Aerospace in 1977), and the others were affected by reorganisation within government (postal services

Table 4.5 Ownership status and performance: whether performance improved or deteriorated as expected[1]

Organisation	Labour productivity	Total factor productivity	Employment function	Financial ratios
British Airways	Yes	Yes	Yes	Yes
London Transport (1984 change in control)	Yes	Yes	Yes	Yes
NFC	Yes	Yes	Yes	Yes?[2]
Royal Mint	Yes	Yes	Yes?	n/a[3]
British Aerospace (privatisation)	Yes	Yes?	Yes?	Yes?
HMSO	Yes	No	Yes	Yes
Post Office	Yes	Unclear	Yes?	Yes?
Telecommunications	Yes	Unclear	No	Yes
Post Office Postal	Yes	Unclear	Yes?	No
British Aerospace (1977 nationalisation)	Yes	Unclear	Yes?	No
Royal Ordnance Factories	No	No?	No	Yes
London Transport (1970 change in control)	No	Yes	No	No
Rolls-Royce	No	No	No	No

Notes: 1 The expectation was for an improvement in performance with a move towards private ownership or a more commercial orientation in the public sector and a deterioration in performance for a move in the opposite direction.
2 A ? denotes some uncertainty in the finding.
3 n/a = not available. For data reasons the Royal Mint was excluded from the financial ratios study.
Source: Hartley *et al.*, 1991; Parker and Hartley, 1991a, 1991b.

and telecommunications in 1969, the Royal Ordnance Factories in 1974, the Royal Mint in 1975, HMSO in 1980 and London Transport in 1970 and 1984). Performance was assessed using a number of measures including an employment function to capture long-run changes in the efficient use of labour, labour productivity and TFP indices, and financial ratios relating to profitability, debtors, stocks and work in progress, wages, fixed assets and value-added.

The results of the research are summarised in Table 4.5. Of the three cases involving actual privatisation, two (BA and NFC) experienced apparent efficiency gains and the evidence for British Aerospace also suggested that privatisation had led to a performance improvement. Again, however, the period studied only extended to the mid-1980s and therefore only covered the first few years of private ownership for British Aerospace and NFC. In the case of BA, the study only considered a period prior to privatisation and it is therefore questionable whether it should be included as a privatisation at all.

The results for those organisations which changed status within government were confused and inconsistent, while the results for the nationalisation cases were perhaps the most surprising. There was some evidence of a worsening of labour productivity at British Aerospace after the state takeover in 1977 (but not necessarily in terms of the other performance measures). In the case of Rolls-Royce, initially state ownership led to an *improvement* in performance, though performance seems to have deteriorated later. Both of these cases may not be typical, however. British Aerospace spent only a very short period under state control and Rolls-Royce was bankrupt when taken over by the government in 1971. More generally, the Parker, Hartley and Martin studies found that corporate performance generally improved when organisations were subjected to commercial objectives or private sector pressures, but that this performance improvement was not guaranteed.

Turning to some very recent studies which have also produced mixed results, Price and Weyman-Jones (1993) looked at the twelve production and distribution regions of British Gas over the periods 1977–8 and 1990–1. They used a production frontier model and confirmed that the rate of growth of total factor productivity increased significantly after privatisation. They claim that privatisation was equivalent to an annual increase in productivity of 2.3 per cent, of which about 0.5 per cent was due to the different regions becoming less dispersed in their efficiency (catching up with the efficiency frontier) and 1.8 per cent was due to the whole frontier shifting. Continuing differences in technical efficiency within British Gas suggest, however, that failure to break up the industry on privatisation has allowed some regions to remain less efficient than they could be.

A similar study, this time of the twelve privatised regional electricity companies (RECs), by Burns and Weyman-Jones (1994a, 1994b, 1994c), used two specifications of the cost function – Cobb-Douglas and translog[4] –

and also measured efficiency by estimating a stochastic cost frontier.[5] They found a wider spread of performance after privatisation amongst the RECs and although they found evidence of productivity growth over the sample period 1971–93, they could find no statistically significant evidence that privatisation had accelerated the productivity gains of the RECs overall (though some RECs had shown significantly higher rates of productivity growth after privatisation). They argued that certain small cost efficiency gains could be put down to accounting changes at the time of privatisation rather to any real privatisation effect. These results may in part be explained by the fact that the UK economy was going into recession at the time of the privatisation of electricity supply and distribution, which occurred in 1990. Another possible explanation, which they favoured, is that the regulatory regime since privatisation has been too lenient allowing the firms to continue with high levels of organisational slack. The RECs are regulated by the Office of Electricity Regulation and both distribution and supply prices are controlled through a RPI–X price cap. This study, therefore, involved features of ownership, regulatory incentives and competition (Button and Weyman-Jones, 1994). Button and Weyman-Jones (1992, 1994) comment that technical efficiency in large utilities varies with the degree of privatisation, but in the light of earlier remarks it remains unclear as to whether such a result is a product of ownership, competition or regulation.

CONCLUSION

There have been a number of public versus private efficiency studies in recent years, including some that have focused on UK privatisation. On balance it seems that neither private nor public sector production is *inherently* or *necessarily* more efficient. In particular, where private sector firms remain state-regulated or protected from competition efficiency may suffer. Also, it appears that some parts of the UK public sector have achieved impressive efficiency gains in the 1980s and, while some economists have chosen to read into such results further support for privatisation (for example, Caves, 1990), an alternative interpretation is that under the right management and the setting of clearer central government objectives, as laid down by Conservative governments in the 1980s, state industries can raise their performance dramatically.

Interpreting the results of all of these studies is complicated by factors impacting on performance other than ownership, notably state regulation and the degree of product market competition. State regulation and limited competition may dull management incentives to operate their firms efficiently irrespective of the legal form of ownership. Also, the studies of actual privatisation are limited in terms of the periods studied and most have not controlled for exogenous factors impacting on performance, notably the stage of the business cycle. Few studies controlled for the effect on performance of either the business cycle or longer-term improvements in the economy, though Haskel and Szymanski comment that cyclical factors may have added over 1 per cent to productivity growth in their study. Also, the studies by Bishop and Kay, Bishop and Thompson, and Haskel and Szymanski compare performance over periods which make it difficult to identify the precise effect of privatisation. For example, Bishop and Thompson's periods are the 1970s compared with the 1980s. How much of the performance improvement they found in the 1980s actually resulted from privatisation remains an open question. The studies by Hartley, Parker and Martin more clearly define the actual dates of organisational change and performance changes are related to these dates, but the studies were mainly concerned with firms that altered their status within government.

In contrast, the research reported in the following chapters involves eleven firms that were privatised in the UK in the 1980s. In each case performance is measured across a number of periods defined to identify clearly both privatisation and restructuring ahead of privatisation. These periods were detailed in chapter 3. In addition, the performance results are assessed in the light of performance changes in the general economy, so as to control for the state of the business cycle.

NOTES

1 A dummy is a binary variable which is introduced into a regression equation to capture a qualitative variable, such as the type of industry or ownership. For example, the variable could take the value of 0 under private ownership and 1 under public ownership. A standard t-test would then be applied to test for the significance of the dummy in the equation. If it proved significant this would suggest that ownership had a statistically significant effect in terms of the overall performance equation.

2 Atkinson and Halvorsen (1986) argue, however, that the US studies showing public utilities to be as efficient as private ones had looked only at productive efficiency and that to get a full picture of performance they should also have considered allocative efficiency. This criticism seems to apply equally, however, to those studies of productive efficiency which have found evidence of higher efficiency in the private sector. One of the relatively few studies concerned with allocative efficiency is that by Lutter (1992), who looked at 23 airlines from 18 countries over the period 1973 to 1983. This study concluded that for private firms output fell as input prices rose, while for state firms the reverse was true, output rose. Lutter concludes that this behaviour is inconsistent with welfare maximising behaviour.

3 Sampson also noted that the NCBG continued to lose market share after privatisation.

4 Cost functions are derived from the underlying production function which relates inputs to outputs. The Cobb-Douglas production function is the most widely known. Its name derives from the work of Professor Paul Douglas and his colleague, C.W. Cobb, who studied the relationship between capital stock, the labour force and output of the US manufacturing sector between 1899 and 1922 (Cobb and Douglas, 1928). The translog production function is more generalised

and less restrictive in form than the Cobb-Douglas function. In particular, it allows the elasticity of scale to change with output and/or factor proportions (Christensen *et al.*, 1973).

5 For an explanation of the stochastic cost frontier, see p.55 above and chapter 6.

5

PRIVATISATION AND PRODUCTIVITY

INTRODUCTION

In this chapter performance is assessed by measuring changes in labour and total factor productivity growth. As we saw in chapter 3, economic performance can be measured in a number of ways; but insofar as privatisation is intended to raise the efficiency with which inputs are converted into outputs (technical efficiency) and factor inputs are more efficiently employed given input prices (price efficiency) this can be captured in a productivity growth series. Testing for the effect on productivity has therefore become a standard approach to assessing the impact of ownership change. In chapter 4, a number of earlier studies were reviewed which have attempted to measure the impact of ownership on productivity growth.

Here *labour productivity* growth is measured by changes in the volume of output in relation to changes in the volume of labour input. Labour input is measured as the average number employed in a given year adjusted, in the absence of firm specific information, by the average hours worked in the relevant industry. Since there is no suitable data, no allowance could be made for changes in the quality (skills) of the labour force, though given the relatively short time scale covered this ought not to be a major problem.

Labour productivity is a partial productivity measure, in the sense that it looks at the relationship between output and one input (labour). If new capital equipment was introduced, which led to higher output, this could be reflected in higher labour productivity figures, though the improved labour productivity results from a larger or technically superior capital stock. Assessing the effect on output of changes in *all* factor inputs requires a total productivity measure or a measure of *total factor productivity* (TFP). TFP takes into account inputs, notably capital, energy and raw materials used as well as labour, and is therefore usually considered to be a superior measure of productivity. It does, in particular, capture the effect of factor substitution when relative factor input prices change. It is, however, subject to the problem of accurately measuring the capital input (Millward and Parker, 1983; Muellbauer, 1986).

96

In this study the capital input was measured on the basis of the firm's recorded depreciation to represent the flow of capital services and a rental charge to reflect the opportunity cost of assets invested in the business. It is recognised that accounting depreciation, especially when based on historic costs, may be a crude indicator of the true resource use. Depreciation charges based on historic costs may bear only a passing resemblance to the true economic amortisation of the capital stock. Depreciation based on current cost accounts may provide a closer approximation, but for the period studied, except for British Gas, reliable current cost accounting statements were not available. The annual rental charge was based upon a real rate of return of 8 per cent (see Spackman, 1991 for a justification of this in terms of the opportunity cost of invested funds). Admittedly, this is a broad brush approximation of the opportunity cost of invested assets when applied over a number of years. Other estimates were tried, however, and they did not affect the overall results materially.

The TFP measure is based upon a weighted index of the growth rates of outputs and inputs based on a Tornqvist index, which, subject to certain assumptions, provides a measure of Hicks neutral technical progress (Diewart, 1976).[1] The underlying production function is assumed to be transcendental logarithmic.[2] TFP growth is measured as:

$$\log(TFP_1/TFP_{t-1}) = \log(Q_t/Q_{t-1}) - \Sigma_{i=1}^{n}[0.5(V_{it} + V_{i,t-1})\log(N_{it}/N_{i,t-1})]$$

where Q is the level of output, t denotes the time period, V_i is the share of input i in total expenditure, and N_i is the amount of input i employed. Wherever possible physical output series are used, but when a figure for the volume of output was not available for one of the enterprises studied, the value of output was deflated using an appropriate price index. For multi-product firms, outputs are weighted by the share of each product in total revenue. Input use is based on expenditure shares for each input. Further details are provided in the appendix.

The use of revenue shares as weights in the output index is appropriate if the firm exhibits constant returns to scale, the prices of outputs are proportional to their marginal costs and there is technical efficiency. The assumptions required for this method to be a reliable measure of TFP are, therefore, quite restrictive. In terms of inputs, the correct weights are the proportional increase in output that a given proportional increase in inputs will provide. Only under strong assumptions will expenditures correspond with these elasticities. Also, when returns to scale are non-constant, the cost elasticities will not be accurately represented by revenue shares since, unlike the revenue shares, the correct weights will not sum to one.

In some of the firms studied, increasing, and with less likelihood decreasing, returns to scale may apply. Where this is so the shares of inputs in total expenditure provide biased measures of the relevant output elasticities.

Also, in so far as public enterprises are wasteful of resources the assumption of technical efficiency will not hold. Moreover, some of the firms sell into markets where prices are not allocatively efficient, while public enterprises may be subject to distortions when raising capital and employing labour. In such cases input shares may not provide reliable measures of output elasticities. Technical progress may also affect productivity growth in certain of the firms studied (notably British Gas, British Telecom and British Airways).

Attempting to decompose productivity growth to identify scale effects, technical progress, technical inefficiencies and distortions caused by inefficient output and input prices in privatisation studies, raises major difficulties. Where an attempt has been made (for example, by Bishop and Thompson, 1992) only qualitative comments were made conditioning their statistical results. It is impossible to make definitive comments about the impact of such factors on productivity growth in the absence of information about the relevant parameter values. Here the results should simply be interpreted with caution. It is also worth noting, however, that year on year results are not used but are averaged over a four-year period and this should reduce bias caused by lags in adjustments of outputs and inputs to price changes. Also, the purpose of this study is to identify changes in efficiency resulting from privatisation. Therefore, there is no need to identify separately efficiency gains resulting from more efficient adjustments to changes in output and input prices from those resulting from higher technical efficiency. The TFP measure will, however, be biased upwards by efficiency improving technical change and this should be borne in mind. In chapter 7 a different approach to efficiency measurement is used and an attempt is made to assess the impact of technical progress directly.

A further problem with productivity growth indices relates to changes in the quality of output which are not reflected in the volume of output figures. Where physical output is approximated by the price-deflated value of output, and insofar as the price series used is biased upwards by improved output quality reflected in a higher price, the resulting output series will be understated. This will result in an underestimate of the true level of productivity growth. Similarly, a reduction in quality as the output volume rises can give a misleading picture of productivity. Unfortunately, there is an absence of data on quality of output changes in the eleven firms studied so no allowance could be made for any such effects. As noted earlier in chapter 3 however, it is not possible for organisations which operate in competitive markets to raise productivity by reducing the quality of service for any length of time since customers will switch to other suppliers. Many of the organisations in our study operate in competitive markets. In other cases, quality of output was regulated by the state before privatisation and since by dedicated regulatory bodies (namely the Civil Aviation Authority, Oftel and Ofgas).

Equally the productivity measures used do not allow for any externalities. As noted in chapter 3, ideally measuring the economic effects of privatisation would look beyond the impact on efficiency in the individual privatised firm to the effect on the wider economy, in terms of, for example, the impact on suppliers and competitors and any environmental effects. In other words, the study would adopt a general equilibrium approach with fully internalised effects, rather than a partial equilibrium framework. In practice, however, the designing of such a model creates insuperable problems. Hence here a much more modest approach is attempted quantifying merely the efficiency effects within the privatised firm. The results, therefore, need to be interpreted recognising the possibility of some input bias and output omissions. Nevertheless, the productivity figures still provide a useful insight into the impact of privatisation on the productive efficiency of the firms.

LABOUR AND TOTAL FACTOR PRODUCTIVITY GROWTH

Changes in labour productivity and TFP are measured across the six distinct periods detailed above in Table 3.2: (a) a nationalisation period; (b) a pre-privatisation period; (c) a period following the first public announcement of the intention to privatise; (d) a post-privatisation period; (e) a period to capture performance during the 1989–92 recession; and (f) a latest period, which captures the productivity growth since 1992 until 1994 or 1995, depending upon the latest data available for each of the variables studied. In general, with the exception of the post-announcement period and the latest period, each period covers four years and the figure reported is therefore a four-year annual average.

Tables 5.1 and 5.2 provide the labour productivity and TFP results. Analysing the results and taking British Airways (BA) first, clearly performance in terms of labour productivity rose in the pre-privatisation and post-announcement periods compared with the nationalisation period. The growth in labour productivity slowed down, however, following privatisation, though it recovered after 1989. This is an impressive performance given the record of many other major international airlines during the recession and 1990–1 Gulf War. However, it should be noted that BA had impressive labour productivity growth in the nationalisation period too.

BA's record on TFP shows particularly strong growth during the run-up to privatisation and more especially after privatisation and during the 1989–92 recession. More recently, however, TFP has stagnated. This alongside the labour productivity figure suggests that recent productivity growth has depended upon improving labour use, while there has been a disappointing performance in the use of other inputs.

In the case of the British Airports Authority (BAA), two output measures were used and the productivity results for both are reported. The first (a) is

Table 5.1 Annual percentage change in labour productivity

Organisation		Nationalisation period[3]	Pre-privatisation period	Post-announcement period	Post-privatisation period	Recession period	Latest period
British Airways		6.6	10.8	8.6	2.9	4.8	6.9
British Airports	(a)	3.0	1.5	0.0	(3.7)[2]	(3.2)	11.8
Authority	(b)	2.8	4.9	3.6	(0.1)	(0.9)	14.5
Britoil		(0.6)	2.7	9.3	6.3	n/a[1]	n/a
British Gas		2.7	8.0	7.1	2.6	1.9	6.0
British Steel		25.4	11.3	13.9	(0.5)	(0.2)	8.5
British Aerospace	(a)	5.8	5.8	9.7	6.8	14.3	3.3
	(b)	0.6	0.6	3.3	6.3	12.4	2.9
Jaguar		34.9	27.0	3.6	3.7	(15.7)	n/a
Rolls-Royce		5.4	6.5	4.0	0.4	2.1	5.3
National Freight		0.7	5.5	10.7	4.0	(0.9)	5.5
Associated British Ports		(1.1)	3.0	9.3	15.4	24.1	10.5
British Telecom		2.8	6.9	8.7	4.3	6.1	15.0

Notes: 1 n/a = not available.
2 Parentheses denote a negative figure.
3 For dates for each of the above periods see chapter 3, Table 3.2.

Table 5.2 Annual percentage change in total factor productivity

Organisation		Nationalisation period[3]	Pre-privatisation period	Post-announcement period	Post-privatisation period	Recession period	Latest Period
British Airways		2.4	4.9	1.4	6.7	5.5	0.4
British Airports	(a)	2.1	(1.0)[2]	(2.6)	(8.3)	(6.3)	3.3
Authority	(b)	1.5	2.2	0.9	(4.9)	(4.3)	5.8
Britoil		15.3	13.4	9.7	9.6	n/a	n/a[1]
British Gas		0.8	4.2	3.5	0.1	(0.1)	(1.3)
British Steel		11.7	4.5	7.5	(4.7)	(5.2)	7.6
British Aerospace	(a)	2.8	2.8	1.9	0.3	(1.3)	(8.3)
	(b)	(2.1)	(2.1)	(4.1)	(0.2)	(2.8)	(8.6)
Jaguar		9.1	6.1	(3.0)	0.7	(14.9)	n/a
Rolls-Royce		(3.7)	5.0	(2.4)	(0.7)	(1.5)	9.6
National Freight		0.2	(1.1)	(0.9)	3.7	(3.8)	0.8
Associated British Ports		(0.1)	6.6	11.0	11.4	2.2	8.7
British Telecom		7.1	4.8	4.8	2.9	2.8	4.7

Notes: 1 n/a = not available.
2 Parentheses denote a negative figure.
3 For dates for each of the above periods, see chapter 3, Table 3.2.

based on the number of air traffic movements, while the second (b) attempts to take into account the volume of all outputs by deflating the total revenue for each year. BAA receives substantial revenues from catering and retail outlets at airports and certain other property ventures; indeed today BAA earns more profit from these activities than from aircraft takeoffs and landings. The two performance measures present a conflicting picture in the run-up to privatisation. In terms of air traffic movements labour productivity growth declined sharply, whereas in terms of all outputs performance improved. On both measures, however, performance seems to have deteriorated badly after privatisation and during the recession period with negative labour productivity growth recorded. More recently, however, it seems that the management has at last acted to stem the decline and labour productivity has rebounded. A similar picture holds for TFP growth, though the recent growth lags behind the rise in labour productivity. In general, it is difficult to avoid the conclusion that since privatisation and until very recently BAA's performance has been disappointing.

Britoil was bought by the oil giant BP plc in 1988 and merged into its operations. Economic performance after 1987 cannot, therefore, be assessed. It seems clear, however, that labour productivity growth accelerated in the pre-privatisation period and remained high immediately afterwards. The slight negative growth in the nationalisation period can be explained by the fact that Britoil began to build up production in the North Sea only in the late 1970s. By contrast, TFP growth, while very healthy throughout the late 1970s and the 1980s, did slow down gradually over the study period.

Turning to British Gas, labour productivity growth seems to have accelerated in the pre-privatisation period, slowed down slightly after privatisation and was affected adversely by the 1989–92 recession. By contrast, TFP growth appears to have been at its highest immediately before privatisation, implying some one-off efficiency gains. TFP seems to have been stagnant immediately after privatisation and then declined.

According to an earlier study, the performance of British Steel was generally poor after nationalisation (Rowley and Yarrow, 1981), but ruthless reductions in staffing and capacity after a major strike in 1980 are reflected in both the labour productivity and TFP figures during the nationalisation period. After privatisation, however, performance seems to have deteriorated until recently, when growth recovered sharply. British Aerospace also seems to have experienced mixed fortunes with labour productivity rising following the announcement of privatisation and continuing to grow impressively after 1989, as the company rationalised in the face of falling defence orders. In this case, however, recently labour productivity growth has slowed. The record on TFP following privatisation and during the recession has been less impressive and no doubt reflects the longer time needed to shed capacity as compared with slimming down the workforce.

For British Aerospace two output measures are used. In both cases physical output was approximated by deflating turnover adjusted for stocks and work-in-progress. In the first case (a) turnover was deflated by a producer price index for manufactures and in the second case (b) by a price series representing input costs in the aerospace industry. They show similar trends, but the level of growth is higher using the first measure. Using the second measure TFP growth is (surprisingly) negative across all of the periods studied. The poorest productivity performance following privatisation occurred at Jaguar. From 1980 the company was increasingly separated from the state-owned car conglomerate, British Leyland (BL), and both labour productivity and TFP responded. The dramatic improvements in performance were, however, short-lived. Productivity growth slowed down sharply in the mid-1980s and collapsed after 1989, following a disastrous loss of markets especially in the USA. This was caused, at least in part, by an adverse sterling–dollar exchange rate movement which caused demand to slump. In 1989 Jaguar was purchased by the international motor conglomerate, Ford, and separate data for Jaguar have not been published by the company since 1992. This has prevented the calculation of later productivity figures.

The performance of Rolls-Royce in the 1980s was not dissimilar to that of Jaguar, though its productivity held up better in the late 1980s. Initial rationalisation in the last years of nationalisation and during the pre-privatisation period led to strong growth in labour productivity and to a lesser extent in TFP, but this performance was not sustained. Immediately following privatisation labour productivity growth slowed down and total productivity growth became negative, in particular during the recession. More recent figures do, however, suggest a sharp recovery in productivity growth, especially in TFP.

The National Freight Corporation (NFC) used to be viewed as one of the most successful of the 1980s privatisations (Veljanovski, 1987, p. 139). According to the labour productivity figures, the management-workforce buy-out certainly was associated with strong growth in performance both immediately before and after privatisation. Although growth was adversely affected by the 1989–92 recession, the previous strong growth has now been re-established. The TFP growth figures suggest, however, that rationalisation of capacity has lagged behind the rationalisation of labour use. There has been a surprisingly poor performance in terms of TFP throughout the periods studied, except immediately following privatisation.

The nationalised British Transport Docks Board which owned many of the largest ports around Britain in the late 1970s was widely regarded as over-staffed and riddled with restrictive working practices. In the 1960s and 1970s what is now called Associated British Ports (ABP) lost market share to other ports. A poor performance under nationalisation is reflected in the productivity figures. Labour productivity declined in the nationalisation period but grew at an accelerating rate in the run-up to privatisation and afterwards. In July 1989 the dock labour scheme, which protected many of the most restrictive labour practices, was swept away by government legislation and this has no doubt helped to sustain the productivity gains. In terms of TFP the record is only slightly less impressive. The abolition of the dock labour scheme and other organisational changes at ABP are discussed in chapter 9.

Lastly, British Telecom (BT) was separated from the Post Office in 1981 and became a private sector company in November 1984. In terms of the labour productivity growth rate there was a noticeable improvement in performance during the 1980s. Since 1989 BT has embarked on a major slimming down of its workforce in the face of tighter regulation and this is leading to even more spectacular growth, most recently averaging 15 per cent a year. TFP has also responded, though interestingly its highest rate of growth occurred, it seems, in the late 1970s. The good performance at this time probably reflects technical progress, as well as a recovery in managerial morale following the demoralisation caused by government interference in pricing in the mid-1970s. Although TFP growth has recently averaged 4.7 per cent a year, this lags well behind the 15 per cent growth in labour productivity. This suggests that there was either exceptional slack in the use of labour inputs at BT or that there is still considerable scope to improve the utilisation of non-labour inputs.

The results in Tables 5.1 and 5.2 reveal that in most cases a performance improvement occurred in the run-up to privatisation, suggesting rationalisation by management in anticipation of having to survive in the private sector. In terms of labour productivity, performance improved after the nationalisation period in eight of the eleven cases: British Airways, the British Airports Authority, Britoil, British Gas, British Aerospace, the NFC, ABP and BT. In the case of two of the three exceptions – British Steel and Jaguar – these were companies that had suffered from poor management and disruptive political intervention in the 1960s and 1970s. Their relatively strong performance in the last years of the nationalisation period is probably a reflection of postponed rationalisation. Similarly, Rolls-Royce had poor productivity growth in the mid to late 1970s (Parker and Hartley, 1991a) which appears to have been followed by a 'catching up' period reflected in the nationalisation period figure.

In terms of TFP the picture is rather mixed. Performance appears to have improved in the run-up to privatisation in the cases of BA, British Gas, the British Airports Authority (on one measure), Rolls-Royce and ABP. The nationalisation period, seems to be associated, however, with the highest TFP growth rates in the cases of Britoil, British Steel, the BAA (until very recently), Jaguar, and BT. These results could reflect rationalisation of capacity use in the late 1970s and early 1980s caused by a 'Thatcher factor'. Mrs Thatcher's governments after the election of 1979 set about introducing more commercial management and financial discipline into public sector activities. Another possibility is that the privatisation anticipation effects extend further back beyond the pre-privatisation periods used in this study. Therefore the productivity figures in the nationalisation period are picking up some performance improvements in advance of privatisation. But there is a further plausible explanation of the variation in the labour productivity and TFP results. They could simply reflect that the main source of efficiency gains both pre-and post-privatisation was rationalisation in the use of labour rather than capital. This would be consistent with the view that nationalisation is associated with large-scale over-staffing. Finally, of course, the rather mixed impact of privatisation on TFP might reflect the fact that ownership *per se* has little consistent impact on performance.

CONTROLLING FOR NATIONAL PRODUCTIVITY TRENDS

The approach adopted involves a study of the annualised growth in labour productivity and TFP over a number of defined periods so as to identify the effect of privatisation on performance. What the results do not take into account is changes in productivity which are independent of privatisation. Notably, productivity growth in the whole economy responds to phases of the business cycle and was generally high in the recovery periods from 1982 and 1992, and poor in the mid to late-1970s and again in the early part of the 1989–92 recession. The performance of a privatised enterprise before and after privatisation may, therefore, simply reflect changes in the opportunity for productivity growth resulting from trends in the economy.

Controlling for the counter-factual is notoriously difficult, however. The counter-factual is what would have happened to labour productivity and TFP in each of the enterprises had privatisation not occurred. The impact of privatisation is measured correctly by the difference between the actual outcome and productivity growth in the absence of a change in ownership. By its very nature this counter-factual is unknown. An attempt can be made, however, to compare changes in the growth in each organisation's labour productivity and TFP with changes in labour productivity and TFP in the whole economy in each of the defined periods of study. Where a privatised organisation is involved in manufacturing activities, a comparison can also be made with changes in productivity in the manufacturing sector as a whole. Admittedly, this adjustment does not fully reflect the counter-factual because other effects on performance unrelated to ownership and national productivity trends are still not revealed, for example the impact of management changes independent of ownership change. Also, the productivity trend for an enterprise may not exactly mirror national trends; indeed,

Table 5.3 Annual percentage change in relative labour productivity

Organisation	Nationalisation period[3]		Pre-privatisation period		Post-announcement period		Post-privatisation period		Recession period		Latest period	
	cf whole economy	cf manufacturing	cf whole economy	cf manufacturing	cf whole economy	cf manufacturing	cf whole economy	cf manufacturing	cf whole economy	cf manufacturing	cf whole economy	cf manufacturing
British Airways	5.1		7.7		5.5		2.3		4.2		4.1	
British Airports Authority (a)	0.2		(1.0)[2]		(2.1)		(4.3)		(3.8)		8.9	
(b)	(0.1)		2.4		1.5		(0.7)		(1.5)		11.7	
Britoil	(3.1)		(0.3)		5.4		3.6		n/a[1]		n/a	
British Gas	(0.2)	(0.6)	5.5	3.5	4.0	3.5	2.0	(1.3)	1.8	(1.0)	2.8	1.8
British Steel	22.3	19.5	9.2	7.8	12.9	9.0	(0.7)	(2.3)	(0.8)	(3.6)	5.6	4.3
British Aerospace (a)	4.5	5.8	4.5	5.8	8.6	10.1	3.6	0.7	13.4	10.9	(0.1)	(0.9)
(b)	(0.6)	0.7	(0.6)	0.7	2.2	3.7	3.1	0.2	11.5	9.0	(0.2)	(1.2)
Jaguar	30.4	28.1	23.9	21.0	4.2	(0.5)	1.5	(0.5)	(16.2)	(18.6)	n/a	n/a
Rolls-Royce	2.8	2.6	3.8	1.8	0.4	0.5	(0.3)	(3.6)	1.3	(1.2)	2.1	1.1
National Freight	(0.9)		3.7		8.5		1.1		(1.7)		2.5	
Associated British Ports	(3.1)		0.4		5.1		12.7		23.2		7.4	
British Telecom	1.3		3.8		6.8		2.3		5.6		12.2	

Notes: 1 n/a = not available.

2 Parentheses denote a negative figure.

3 For dates for each of the above periods, see chapter 3, Table 3.2.

Table 5.4 Annual percentage change in relative total factor productivity

Organisation	Nationalisation period[3]		Pre-privatisation period		Post-announcement period		Post-privatisation period		Recession period		Latest period	
	cf whole economy	cf manu-facturing	cf whole economy	cf manu-facturing	cf whole economy	cf manu-facturing	cf whole economy	cf manu-facturing	cf whole economy	cf manu-facturing	cf whole economy	cf manu-facturing
British Airways	1.9		2.9		(0.9)[2]		6.4		5.8		(1.2)	
British Airports Authority (a)	1.0		(3.1)		(4.4)		(8.5)		(6.0)		1.7	
(b)	0.4		0.1		(0.9)		(5.2)		(4.0)		4.2	
Britoil	15.2		12.5		7.0		7.4		n/a		n/a	
British Gas	(0.3)	(0.1)	2.1	0.3	0.9	0.5	(0.1)	(3.2)	(0.3)	(3.0)	(3.2)	(4.8)
British Steel	9.7	7.2	2.6	0.6	6.3	2.7	(4.5)	(6.7)	(4.9)	(7.7)	6.0	4.2
British Aerospace (a)	2.7	4.8	2.7	4.8	2.3	5.1	(2.2)	(4.2)	(0.9)	(3.3)	(10.2)	(11.8)
(b)	(2.2)	(0.1)	(2.2)	(0.1)	(3.7)	(0.9)	(2.8)	(4.7)	(2.4)	(4.9)	(10.5)	(12.1)
Jaguar	6.3	4.3	3.5	1.5	(2.6)	(6.8)	(1.5)	(3.2)	(14.2)	(16.7)	n/a	n/a
Rolls-Royce	(4.6)	(3.9)	2.8	0.5	(5.3)	(5.0)	(1.2)	(4.3)	(1.1)	(3.6)	7.7	6.1
National Freight	2.0		(1.6)		(0.9)		1.6		(3.4)		(0.9)	
Associated British Ports	(1.2)		5.7		8.8		9.2		2.6		6.7	
British Telecom	6.7		2.8		3.2		1.0		3.1		3.1	

Notes: 1 n/a = not available.
2 Parentheses denote a negative figure.
3 For dates for each of the above periods see chapter 3, Table 3.2.

we would expect some firms to be more affected, say, by an economic recession than other firms, notably those with products that have a relatively high income elasticity. Moreover, economy wide averages will not be as relevant as sector averages. We would expect, for instance, the performance of British Steel to be heavily influenced by changes in the demand for steel in the UK. Sector figures could not be used, however, since in so many of the industries the privatised enterprises dominated their sector. The sector average productivity trend is heavily weighted by the privatised enterprise, making a comparison invalid. But despite these reservations, the approach adopted does help to reflect performance changes which are related to the stage of the business cycle rather than ownership change.

The labour productivity and TFP figures for each of the periods were compared with averages of labour productivity and TFP in the whole economy. The performance of the privatised industries involved in manufacturing activity was also compared with the average for UK manufacturing. The results are given in Tables 5.3 and 5.4. In each case, the change in national productivity in each of the relevant periods is deducted from the productivity growth of the enterprise. Therefore, a positive figure indicates that the performance of the enterprise exceeded that of the whole economy or of the UK manufacturing sector. A negative figure identifies an inferior performance.

Consider Tables 5.3 and 5.4. Relative labour productivity growth appears to have been at its highest for British Airways in the pre-privatisation period and fell back following privatisation. In the case of TFP, the best relative performance seems to have been registered following privatisation. Throughout most of the period, including the nationalisation period, in terms of productivity growth British Airways comfortably exceeded the growth rate for the whole economy. The results are less clear for BAA, however, where the relative labour productivity growth record depends upon which output measure is used. In terms of relative TFP growth, the Authority seems to have under-performed compared to the rest of the economy for a good many of the periods studied. Only recently have both labour productivity and TFP expanded at a rate well ahead of that for the economy as a whole under both measures.

Turning to Britoil and British Gas and in terms of relative labour productivity, performance seems to have been at its worst in the nationalisation period, though British Gas appears to have under-performed compared with UK manufacturing immediately after privatisation and during the 1989–92 recession. The record is more mixed for TFP with Britoil apparently doing well throughout, but British Gas having a patchy performance. In the case of British Steel, a very strong relative growth in labour productivity and to a lesser extent TFP pre-privatisation appears to have fallen away afterwards. After privatisation British Steel's productivity performance was inferior to that of the whole economy and more especially that of UK manufacturing. The demand for steel was adversely affected by the recession which began shortly after privatisation and more recently both labour productivity and TFP have risen sharply. Perhaps, therefore, not too much should be read into the immediate post-privatisation figures. Nevertheless, British Steel's best performance was recorded during our nationalisation period which coincided with a phase of major restructuring.

In the case of British Aerospace in the late 1980s, which was adversely affected by cuts in national defence budgets, labour productivity has performed well except in the most recent period. Relative TFP growth, however, has been lacklustre since privatisation on one output measure and very disappointing in all periods using the other measure (the output measures were detailed earlier).

The record for Jaguar since privatisation is very poor, especially in terms of TFP and especially in relation to other manufacturing industries (although it must be remembered that the figures end in 1991). Labour productivity and TFP growth were both at their greatest in the nationalisation period. The record is slightly better for Rolls-Royce, which seems to have performed relatively poorly in terms of labour productivity compared to other manufacturing immediately after privatisation, but to have performed better since the late 1980s. The TFP record, however, is less good with the enterprise performing relatively poorly from the announcement of privatisation until the latest period. The most recent figures, however, show a marked improvement.

Turning to the NFC, the results confirm that the company's excellent financial record in the 1980s is most strongly linked to improvements in labour use. Since the nationalisation period, NFC has had labour productivity growth rates in excess of those found in the economy in general, but the relative performance in terms of TFP appears to have been less impressive with the best performance occurring under state ownership. By contrast, ABP recorded excellent relative labour productivity and TFP growth rates both immediately before and after privatisation.

Moving finally to BT, as is to be expected in a high technology industry, the relative labour productivity and TFP growth rates are well in excess of those recorded for the whole economy. Relative labour productivity grew much faster after the nationalisation period and is now rising at the heady rate of around 12 per cent a year on average. The relative TFP performance, which was at its greatest in the nationalisation period at 6.7 per cent per annum, has grown less fast since then but has still continued to outstrip national TFP growth rates.

CONCLUSION

This chapter has been concerned with investigating changes in both labour productivity and TFP associated with privatisation in the UK. Average figures were reported for the various periods before and after privatisation. Where possible, four-year periods were used to capture trends in performance and to smooth out the effects of atypical years. Also comparisons were made between each enterprise's productivity growth and that of the whole economy and, where relevant, manufacturing. As explained in detail in chapter 3, no performance measure is perfect. The figures reported should be read bearing in mind the limitations of productivity measures and of the data used. The TFP results need to be interpreted with special care given the restrictive conditions surrounding the measure. In particular, some of the British Aerospace figures are surprising, suggesting a long-run decline in TFP. This may imply that there are some problems with the method that we have used to derive TFP for this organisation. Nevertheless, the results help to shed light on what has been happening to productivity both before and after privatisation. Although we cannot vouchsafe for the precise figures (especially to a decimal place), we have no reasons to believe that the trends shown by the figures are misleading. The mixed results on productivity performance are consistent with the earlier findings from research into UK privatisation reviewed in chapter 4.

Concentrating upon relative labour productivity, and treating the pre-privatisation period as related to privatisation, it appears that ownership change was associated with improved labour productivity in a majority of cases, the exceptions being British Steel, Jaguar, Rolls-Royce, and perhaps BA and the BAA (where the results are sensitive to the output measure used). Note that the word 'associated' has been used. It does not necessarily follow that privatisation caused the improvement. Indeed, it is not possible to be certain that performance would not have been at least as good without privatisation (this is the counter-factual problem again).

Measured by relative TFP, privatisation is associated with clear performance improvements only in the cases of British Airways (until recently) and ABP. In the other enterprises the results are very mixed and it is difficult to find a clear relationship with ownership. Also, ABP's productivity performance was boosted by the abolition of the dock labour scheme in July 1989, which can be interpreted either as a consequence of privatisation or as an independent influence on performance. It is not possible to be certain whether the scheme would have been abolished if the ports had remained state run. Mrs Thatcher's government stripped away existing employment practices in a number of activities which remained state-owned (for example, in the civil service, the universities and the coal mines). It is quite possible, therefore, that the dock labour scheme would have disappeared in a publicly-owned docks.

A better performance in terms of labour productivity than TFP is consistent with the view that state ownership is primarily associated with over-staffing, consequent upon managerial slackness and inefficiency resulting from political intervention.[3] The TFP results do not, however, support the very optimistic assertions sometimes made about the benefits of privatisation in terms of a more efficient use of *all* resources. Indeed, the implication of these results is that although labour productivity generally improves, the productivity of other inputs can deteriorate and that this deterioration can outweigh the positive impact of privatisation on labour productivity.

The relative TFP results are particularly poor and do not support the view that privatisation will necessarily lead to a major change in the use of all inputs leading to higher efficiency. The recession period of 1989–92 was included to see how well the privatised firms have fared in a severe economic downturn. Again the picture is mixed. BA, ABP, BT, and a little less clearly British Gas, appear to have performed relatively well in terms of both labour productivity and TFP, while British Aerospace, and to a lesser extent Rolls-Royce, appear to have performed fairly well in terms of relative labour productivity only. BAA, British Steel, NFC and especially Jaguar performed relatively poorly. Clearly a number of the privatised enterprises have been badly affected by the post-1989 recession. Recent improved productivity figures may simply be a product of the economic recovery, though in the cases of British Gas and BT they no doubt also reflect more permanent regulatory and competition changes, as mentioned earlier and detailed in chapter 9.

This chapter has been concerned with productivity as a measure of performance. In the next chapter two accounting measures – value-added and the rate of profit – are considered.

NOTES

1 Hicks neutral technical change refers to technical change which leaves the ratio in which factor inputs are used unchanged if input prices remain constant. That is such that: $\frac{K}{L} = \Theta_1\left(\frac{Pk}{Pl}\right)$ where Θ_1 is any function. Since, using standard neoclassical equilibrium analysis, $\frac{Pk}{Pl} = \frac{\delta L}{\delta K}$ is the condition for cost minimisation, this means that: $\frac{\delta L}{\delta K} = \Theta_1^{-1}\left(\frac{K}{L}\right)$ This expresses Hicks neutrality in terms of the production function and without reference to prices.

2 Or translog, see note 4, p.94 above. Transcendental means non-algebraic and logarithmic functions are a form of a transcendental function. For more details see Caves *et al.*, 1982; Heathfield and Wibe, 1987, p. 105.

3 It is also consistent with the view that there has been factor substitution, capital for labour.

6

ACCOUNTING RATIOS AND PERFORMANCE MEASUREMENT

INTRODUCTION

There is no single ideal indicator of corporate performance; each has its own strengths and weaknesses (Barrow and Wagstaff, 1989; Davis and Kay, 1990). Accountants have proposed numerous ratios as indicators of corporate performance. In the space available it is not possible to report all such potential performance measures but, that said, we would be unwilling to base an argument on the use of a single accounting ratio, particularly given the difficulties in splitting the periods and in dealing with the accounting policies of different enterprises. In the previous chapter, labour and total factor productivity growth were examined; here, performance is assessed using two standard accounting ratios: first, the rate of return on capital employed; and second, the annual growth in value-added per employee-hour.

The return on capital employed will be of interest to the City and lenders of capital, although a number of economists have disparaged the use of accounting rates of return (for example, Kay and Mayer, 1986; Edwards *et al.*, 1987). Nevertheless, it is a widely used indicator of performance and it provides an interesting comparator for our other accounting ratio, the growth in value-added per employee. In all cases the rate of return is at historic cost except in the case of British Gas which is at current cost. Only British Gas reported current cost figures for the periods studied. The rate of return is normally before interest and tax and on total capital employed (net assets). In the case of Rolls-Royce, however, for reasons of data availability, the rate of return is calculated as profit before tax and after interest payments on capital employed excluding loans.

Value-added is also commonly used to assess business performance. It 'provides the means of recompensing and training new employees for their part and of financing new assets and research and development which are needed for the future of the business and to improve productivity' (Bryant, 1989, p. 34). It is calculated as: ((wages + depreciation + profit before interest and tax)/an appropriate price index))/((average number of employees throughout the year)×(average number of hours worked per week by employees in the industry)).

Value-added is a measure of the company's net output, the difference between its turnover and the value of material and energy inputs. This is deflated by an appropriate price index to obtain a real, rather than nominal, figure for value-added. The total number of employee-hours is calculated as the average number of people employed by the firm throughout the year, multiplied by the number of hours worked by staff in the relevant industry. The division of value-added by the number of employee-hours yields a net measure of labour productivity (gross measures of labour productivity, as reported in the previous chapter, divide turnover by employment). On the basis of this measure, labour intensive industries will, of course, have lower productivity levels than capital intensive industries. To ameliorate this problem, this chapter focuses on the average annual *change* in value-added per employee-hour (over a specified period).

To be a precise measure of net productivity growth, capital and technology inputs need to remain unchanged throughout the sample period (or, for the purposes of this study, to grow at the same rate in each of our study periods). There should also be constant returns to scale. Unfortunately, there are no simple and reliable methods for controlling for capital, scale and technology effects. However, in their study of UK privatisation Bishop and Thompson (1992, p. 1188) argue that scale effects were relatively small in the 1980s 'even in industries where scale effects appear particularly relevant'. They contend that technical progress effects are more difficult to gauge but that 'the limited evidence available suggests that changes in the pace of technical change have not been a material factor' (Bishop and Thompson, 1992, p. 1189). Also, Foreman-Peck and Manning (1988, p. 65) comment that there is no clear evidence of economies or diseconomies of scale in mature telecom networks. Given the length of the period studied, there is no reason to believe that the results are seriously biased by the failure to control for capital, scale and technology, even though technology and capital inputs are unlikely to have grown at precisely the same rate throughout the study period. Nevertheless, the results should be interpreted with this in mind.

With the exception of the data on the average number of hours worked by employees in the industry and the price index used to deflate the figure for value-added, all of the data were extracted from firms' annual reports and accounts. The figure quoted in firms' accounts usually misrepresents true economic depreciation. However, providing that their accounting practices remained relatively constant throughout the sample period, then the focus on the *change* in value-added will reduce the magnitude of this potential error. Where possible, the data were adjusted for any significant changes in accounting practice.[1]

A few former state enterprises were notorious for changing their accounting practices in order to manipulate reported earnings, particularly British Gas (Wright, 1987). These policy changes mainly concerned depreciation policy (for example, changing asset lives) and debt write-offs. In so far as these increased profit and reduced depreciation and interest charges, they did not affect the value-added measure (although such changes will, of course, affect the rate of return on capital employed). First, there is merely a rearrangement of values within the numerator of this measure when lower depreciation leads to higher profit. Second, wherever possible we took profit before interest specifically to avoid distortion caused by variation in interest charges before and after privatisation. Other significant accounting distortions relate to the use of extraordinary charges, often related to restructuring, and were omitted. We recognise that it is always possible for an organisation to massage its accounts but we have taken all possible precautions to remove such artificial distortions.[2]

Wherever possible, an own product/industry price index was used to deflate each firm's value-added. For eight of the eleven firms studied such an index was available (see the appendix for further details). For the three other firms (ABP, BAA and BA), no specific product/industry price index could be found and, in the absence of a more appropriate alternative, value-added was deflated by the non-food retail price index.

Because there is often a considerable lag between the announcement by the government of its intention to privatise a firm and the actual sale of shares to private investors, a simple comparison of corporate performance before and after privatisation was deemed inappropriate and, as in the previous chapter, the sample was divided into six periods: a nationalisation, a pre-privatisation, a post-announcement, a post-privatisation, a recession and a latest period. In a number of cases, there is some overlap between these periods; for further details see chapter 3, Table 3.2.

For each of the eleven organisations studied, the average annual rate of return and growth in value-added were calculated for the six survey periods. Such data are vulnerable to the criticism that they might reflect longer-run, economy-wide adjustments unrelated to changes in the firm's ownership status (for example, an improvement in profitability might be attributable to the business cycle rather than to any change in ownership). Thus alongside each firm's profit rate we also report the corresponding rate for all industrial and commercial companies (ICCs).[3] Clearly, this has its shortcomings as a comparator. For example, it values the capital stock at replacement rather than historic cost whereas, with the exception of British Gas, the data used in this study are based on historic cost accounts. However, the ICC profit series provides an indicator of the direction, if not the precise magnitude, in which one might expect a firm's profits to be moving over a particular period.[4]

For similar reasons, the average annual growth in value-added per employee-hour was calculated for the economy and for manufacturing and, for each time period, this amount was deducted from the corresponding figure for each organisation. This yields a measure of the extent to which the average annual growth in value-added per employee-hour for each of the eleven firms exceeded (or fell short of) that for the economy or, where appropriate, for manufacturing industry, in each of the six survey periods. The method is similar to that used in the previous chapter for labour productivity and TFP comparisons.

Including economy-wide measures of performance provides a benchmark for comparing the performance of our organisations throughout the UK business cycle. As mentioned earlier in the productivity study, this is a rough and ready but the best available counterfactual.

RESULTS

Table 6.1 reports the rate of return on capital employed for the eleven organisations in each of the six survey periods. The corresponding rate of return for all ICCs is also shown. Similarly, Table 6.2 reports each firm's average annual growth in value-added per employee-hour for the six survey periods, having already deducted a comparable figure for the economy or, where appropriate, for manufacturing as a whole. A discussion of each firm's individual performance is followed by some across-industry generalisations.

For British Airways, the announcement of privatisation was associated with a sharp increase in value-added growth which declined slightly as privatisation approached. The intention to privatise was announced in 1980 but the actual sale was delayed until 1987, in part because of a pending law suit arising from the failure of Laker airways. The privatisation of British Airways was, therefore, unusual in that the period between the announcement of the intention to privatise and the actual sale was exceptionally long. Hence the sudden surge in value-added in the first half of the 1980s can be attributed to management attempts to improve performance in advance of privatisation (although there might have been some exogenous benefit from the introduction of wide-bodied aircraft). However, in the immediate post-privatisation period, the growth in value-added actually fell behind that in the rest of the economy, suggesting that the ownership effect prompted a once and for all shake-out rather than a persistently higher level of growth. In the recession period, relative growth improved but it did not differ from that achieved in the nationalisation period. In the latest period, relative growth has declined once more to less than 1 per cent per annum. The profitability results reveal a slightly different picture. Again, there is a sharp improvement in performance in the pre-privatisation and post-announcement periods. However, although profitability subsequently

Table 6.1 Average annual rate of return on capital employed

Organisation	Nationalisation period[3]	Pre-privatisation period	Average annual rate of return on capital employed Post-announcement period	Post-privatisation period	Recession period	Latest period
British Airways	5.9	21.8	22.9	19.9	17.7	9.0
	6.9[4]	*6.2*	*6.9*	*9.0*	*8.7*	*8.5*
BAA	16.3	19.2	19.0	15.2	13.4	13.2
	5.8	*7.5*	*7.8*	*9.0*	*8.7*	*8.5*
Britoil	41.4	47.2	58.9	43.4	n/a[1]	n/a
	4.1	*4.3*	*4.8*	*5.8*		
British Gas	4.0	5.0	4.8	6.3	6.2	1.5
	5.8	*7.5*	*8.3*	*9.0*	*8.5*	*8.8*
British Steel	(7.2)[2]	10.6	15.4	4.3	9.5	4.2
	6.2	*8.8*	*9.2*	*8.2*	*8.7*	*8.5*
British Aerospace	18.8	18.8	17.0	11.0	7.7	8.7
	6.9	*6.9*	*6.4*	*6.0*	*8.3*	*8.8*
Jaguar	7.6	25.2	78.1	41.8	(61.0)	n/a
	5.7	*6.0*	*6.7*	*8.7*	*8.5*	
Rolls-Royce	(10.3)	6.4	25.9	18.5	3.0	5.0
	5.9	*7.4*	*8.5*	*9.0*	*8.3*	*8.8*
NFC	(8.0)	7.6	2.0	25.7	20.9	18.8
	6.3	*6.6*	*5.6*	*6.5*	*8.4*	*8.6*
ABP	15.4	9.5	5.3	9.2	7.4	10.0
	6.7	*5.9*	*5.4*	*7.4*	*8.3*	*8.8*
BT	14.7	19.5	18.3	21.7	22.8	16.5
	6.9	*6.2*	*6.8*	*8.8*	*8.8*	*8.5*

Notes: 1 n/a = not available.
2 Parentheses denote a negative figure.
3 For dates for each of the periods, see chapter 3, Table 3.2.
4 Figures in italics denote the rate of return earned by all industrial and commercial companies.

Table 6.2 Annual percentage change in value-added per employee relative to that elsewhere in the economy

Organisation	Nationalisation period[3]		Pre-privatisation period		Post-announcement period		Post-privatisation period		Recession period		Latest period	
	cf whole economy	cf manufacturing	cf whole economy	cf manufacturing	cf whole economy	cf manufacturing	cf whole economy	cf manufacturing	cf whole economy	cf manufacturing	cf whole economy	cf manufacturing
British Airways	1.5		13.1		10.3		(0.5)[2]		1.7		0.8	
BAA	(0.3)		1.5		1.4		(4.7)		(8.6)		15.0	
Britoil	(5.0)		(2.7)		0.3		(2.3)		n/a[1]		n/a	
British Gas	(6.8)	(7.2)	4.5	2.5	7.7	7.2	5.6	2.2	3.8	1.0	11.1	10.1
British Steel	26.6	23.8	18.1	16.7	18.1	19.0	8.7	10.3	(3.9)	(6.7)	25.8	24.5
British Aerospace	(4.2)	(3.0)	(4.2)	(3.0)	(0.3)	1.2	(1.1)	(4.0)	3.7	1.2	11.1	10.3
Jaguar	406.8	404.8	308.0	306.0	14.9	10.2	(6.3)	(8.3)	(31.9)	(34.3)	n/a	n/a
Rolls-Royce	4.8	6.7	5.4	3.4	1.8	1.9	(4.0)	(7.3)	(8.6)	(11.1)	18.5	12.5
National Freight	(3.0)		2.6		1.7		8.1		(2.0)		1.9	
Associated British Ports	0.0		(6.3)		(6.8)		5.7		(3.9)		75.7	
British Telecom	1.3		0.5		4.5		3.1		5.3		6.4	

Notes: 1 n/a = not available.
2 Parentheses indicates a negative figure.
3 For definitions of each of the above periods see chapter 3, Table 3.2.

declines marginally, it remains significantly greater than that achieved under state ownership in both the recession and latest periods.

The results for the British Airports Authority reveal a similar picture. The announcement of privatisation was associated with a rise in the annual value-added growth rate relative to that in the rest of the economy. However, in the immediate post-privatisation period this rate once again fell behind that for the economy as a whole, and in the recession period this gap widened to over eight percentage points per annum. Similarly, profitability at first increased but then fell back in both the post-privatisation and recession periods to a level below that achieved under state ownership, though this result is affected by asset revaluations. In the latest period value-added growth shows a marked improvement.

The results for Britoil also reveal a rather disappointing performance. Relative value-added growth in the nationalisation period was below that in the economy as a whole. The pre-privatisation period witnessed a slight improvement in the relative rate of growth and this improvement continued in the post-announcement period. However, this growth rate struggled to match that achieved elsewhere in the economy. After privatisation, relative growth fell once more although this result is probably affected by the collapse in oil prices in 1986. If the post-privatisation period is extended by one year (to 1983–7) then Britoil's annual growth rate exceeds that in the economy as a whole by some 18 percentage points. There is evidence for an improvement in profitability in both the pre-privatisation and post-announcement periods as the North Sea oil fields came on stream. However, there is little difference between the nationalised and post-privatisation periods (over the period 1983–7 the average profit rate was 40.2 per cent).

The announcement of the intention to privatise British Gas was associated with a sharp increase in the firm's relative growth in value-added which, in the nationalisation period, had lagged behind that achieved in the rest of the economy. Following privatisation, the rate of growth declined marginally, but was still significantly greater than that under public ownership. This improvement was sustained in the recession and in the latest period. However, in terms of relative, as against absolute profitability, it is difficult to discern any evidence of improved performance following privatisation; indeed in the latest period, profits have declined quite dramatically, probably in response to costs incurred as the company adjusts to increased competition in the industry.[5]

The results for British Steel are mixed. Value-added growth relative to the rest of the economy was at its highest in the nationalisation period when considerable rationalisation of capacity occurred. In the four years before privatisation value-added growth was lower than in the nationalisation period but was still far in excess of that for the economy as a whole. Following the announcement of the intention to privatise, value-added growth remained high but thereafter fell markedly, so that in the post-privatisation and recession periods the rate of growth was considerably lower than in the economy as a whole. Most recently, however, growth has returned to the high levels achieved in the nationalisation period. In the early 1990s British Steel faced increasing international competition but whether this could account for the marked decline in relative value-added growth over this period requires further investigation. With regard to profitability, however, the period of state ownership exhibited the worst performance. In the pre-privatisation period profitability improved markedly but fell back in the post-privatisation period. British Steel's profits seem to have remained fairly resilient to the recession of the early 1990s but more recently profits have fallen.

The overlap of the nationalisation and pre-privatisation periods for British Aerospace makes it difficult to disentangle the results for these two phases. However, relative value-added growth in the privatised (1989–92) recession has clearly exceeded that in all of the previous periods with a further improvement in growth in the latest period. Interestingly, this growth has not fed through into higher relative profitability. Indeed, profitability was at its highest in the nationalisation/pre-privatisation periods and declined markedly after privatisation and then again in the recession period. This may be explained by unwise diversification and the shrinking and increasingly competitive international defence market in the late 1980s and early 1990s.

The lack of relevant data also makes it difficult to examine the performance of Jaguar prior to its privatisation. The unusually high value-added growth rates in the nationalisation and pre-privatisation periods stem from two factors: first, the shortage of data leads to some overlap in the sample periods (the nationalisation period is 1981–3 while the pre-privatisation period is 1981–4); and second, the collapse in sales in the 1980–1 recession and the consequent losses led to a very low value-added per employee figure. When sales and profits recovered, value-added bounced back and the extraordinarily high value-added growth resulted. Even if the nationalisation/pre-privatisation period is shortened to omit 1981–2, however, the qualitative nature of the results remain unchanged; in the two years before its move into private ownership, value-added growth exceeded that in the rest of the economy by almost 50 percentage points per annum. This was a period of rationalisation following the company's separation from British Leyland. In the four years after privatisation, however, the annual growth rate was some six percentage points less than in the economy as a whole, and some eight percentage points less than in manufacturing. In the recession period, Jaguar's performance deteriorated even further and its average annual value-added growth lagged some 33 percentage points behind growth in both the economy and manufacturing. Equally large performance swings are also revealed by Jaguar's relative profitability. Its performance markedly improved in the post-announcement period but declined after its move into the private sector and, as with value-added, was severely affected by the recession. After 1989 Jaguar was in severe financial difficulty but kept in business by the takeover by Ford.

Rolls-Royce presents an unusual picture in the sense that the rate of value-added growth falls following the privatisation announcement. However, the fact that the relative growth rate was lower after privatisation than in the nationalisation period is similar to the result for several of the other organisations studied (such as British Airways, British Airports Authority, British Steel, and Jaguar). In the recession period value-added growth fell even further behind that in the rest of the UK economy, so that it was substantially below the rate in the nationalisation period. In the most recent period, however, value-added growth has soared, presumably making good earlier losses. Again, the use of profitability as the performance indicator reveals a rather different picture. Profits rise in both the pre-privatisation and post-announcement years but then fall back sharply in the recession, but to a level still greater than in the nationalisation period when losses were recorded.

As with the results for Rolls-Royce, the announcement of the intention to privatise the National Freight Corporation was associated with a decline in the amount by which its value-added growth exceeded that of the rest of the economy. These results also differ from those for most other firms in the sense that the post-privatisation period witnessed a marked increase in relative value-added growth. In the recession period, however, the growth in value-added once more fell behind the growth rate of the rest of the economy, although not quite by as much as in the nationalisation period. The rate of profit moved in the same direction as value-added but the magnitude of the movements are typically much larger. Contrary to the results for relative value-added, however, profitability has remained much higher in the recession period than under state ownership.

As was the case for National Freight, the results for Associated British Ports reveal that the announcement of privatisation was not associated with an improvement in its relative performance. Indeed, relative value-added growth in the pre-privatisation period was some six to seven points below that in the nationalisation period. The results for this organisation also follow those for National Freight in the sense that the post-privatisation period was associated with a marked improvement in value-added growth, although in the recession ABP's performance has fallen below that registered in the nationalisation period. In the most recent years, however, growth has soared and more than made good the apparent deterioration registered in the previous period. Again, profits move in the same direction as value-added, but in this instance profitability is much lower in both the recession and the latest periods than under state ownership.

Finally, consider the results for British Telecom which, in many ways, was the flagship of the Conservative government's privatisation programme. In the nationalisation period its average annual value-added growth slightly exceeded that in the rest of the economy. However, in the four years before privatisation this growth rate fell slightly but still marginally exceeded that achieved by the economy as a whole; although taking only the post-announcement period, relative growth is positive and exceeded that in the public ownership period. After privatisation, the relative growth rate fell slightly, but in the recession period it exceeded that achieved in any of the four previous phases. In the most recent period, growth has increased further. The rate of return on capital reveals a similar picture with the exception that in the most recent period profits have fallen below the rate achieved in the recession period. This reflects the increasingly onerous regulatory environment in which BT has to operate and the increasingly competitive market as new firms enter the industry.

In addition to examining the results for individual firms, it is tempting to draw out similarities between those organisations that are in competitive markets and those that are subject to regulatory formulae. A comparison of the nationalisation (earliest *four-year* period) and the recession (most recent *four-year* period) reveals that two of the three organisations where privatisation appears to have had the strongest positive impact on relative value-added growth, British Telecom and British Gas, are both subject to a pricing formulae of the form RPI−X. Independent observers have suggested that the value of X was, in both cases, initially set too low in comparison with cost reductions that had been achieved prior to privatisation (Wright, 1987). If this was the case then the initial relatively good performance of these organisations post-privatisation might follow more from the slackness of the regulatory regime than from the stimulus provided by privatisation. More recent improvements, however, probably reflect tighter regulation and more competition.

The other firm in the sample that has been subject to a RPI−X formula is British Airports Authority. Its post-privatisation productivity results are markedly poorer than those for either British Telecom or British Gas until very recently. This result may in part reflect its less than successful move into the hotel business in 1989–91.

With regard to profitability, there are no obvious differences between the performance of those organisations that are in competitive markets and those whose prices are subject to regulatory formulae, though it could be argued that until recently the regulated firms had a less variable rate of return. Certainly, British Gas and British Telecom appear to perform well (with profitability up by 50 per cent from the nationalisation to the recession period) but BAA's profits are much flatter. Moreover, some of the firms operating in a competitive environment, whose performance, when measured in terms of relative value-added growth, was seemingly lacklustre, appear to have performed well in terms of profitability (for example, British Airways, British Steel and NFC).

It is interesting to compare the performance of each company under state and private ownership. Focusing on only four-year periods and putting to one side the pre-privatisation period (where there is still state ownership but possibly anticipation effects), each firm's performance under state owner- ship can be compared with its performance in either the post-privatisation or recession period. This yields twenty-one comparisons for each of the two performance indicators. Of these, ten reveal an improvement in terms of relative value-added growth, while in fourteen instances profitability improved. The results demonstrate that different indicators can yield dif- ferent results for any given firm and that in the case of the firms studied privatisation was slightly more likely to improve profitability than to improve value-added growth. With profitability improving in two-thirds of the comparisons, there is evidence of a reasonably consistent impact of privatisation on this variable. With regard to relative value-added, how- ever, performance improved in 48 per cent of the comparisons and deterio- rated in the other 52 per cent. Here, the impact of privatisation is more marginal.

It could be argued that the profitability comparisons outlined above do not reveal the whole picture as they ignore the longer-term impact of privatisation. Although there is no way of knowing what the rate of profit will be in, say, five years time, it is possible to use each firm's current share price as an indicator of what the market expects to happen to profitability. Table 6.3 reports the date and price of the first share issue together with, where applicable, comparable figures for the second issue. The price as at 31 January 1996 is also given and, by adjusting the first share issue price for the change in the FT-SE industrial share index, it is possible to examine whether the expected profitability of the privatised companies has improved or deteriorated relative to that of the industrial sector generally. The rele- vant results are in the final column of Table 6.3; a figure of 100.0 indicates that the firm's expected future profits have moved in line with the expected level of profitability for the industrial sector as a whole, while a figure greater (less) than 100.0 indicates that expected profitability has improved (deteriorated) relative to that for all industrial companies. Leaving aside Britoil and Jaguar for which recent stock market data are not available, four companies – ABP, BA, BAA and NFC – have outperformed the market. NFC, in particular, has recorded substantial capital gains with its share price at the end of January 1996 being one hundred times its issue price in February 1982. Over the same period, the FT-SE industrial share index registered a six-fold increase. The other five companies for which data are available (British Aerospace, British Gas, BT, Rolls-Royce and British Steel) have performed worse than the industrial share index. Of course, stock market indices must be used with care since share prices are affected by a number of considerations. Nevertheless, these results suggest that whereas profitability has in two out of three instances increased since

Table 6.3 The share price performance of the privatised companies

Firm	First share issue date	price	Second share issue date	price	Share price lowest[2]	highest	as @ 31.1.96	as @ 31.1.96 relative to the FT-SE industrial share index
ABP	2/83	14p[5]	4/84	270p	14p	319p	289p	465.3
BAA	7/87	123p[5]	n/a[4]	n/a	115p	541p	486p	270.9
British Aerospace	2/81	150p	5/85	375p	124p	899p	892p	94.0
BA	2/87	125p	n/a	n/a	123p	532p	530p	230.0
British Gas	12/86	135p	n/a	n/a	109p	360p	239p	81.5
BT[1]	11/84	130p	12/91	225p	88p	487p	357p	85.4
Britoil	11/82	215p	8/85	185p	n/a	n/a	n/a	n/a
Jaguar	7/84	165p	n/a	n/a	n/a	n/a	n/a	n/a
Rolls-Royce	5/87	170p	n/a	n/a	89p	282p	204p	73.9
BSC	12/88	126p	n/a	n/a	47p	189p	172p	69.8
NFC	2/82	1.7p[5]	n/a	n/a	1.7p	283p	164p	1747.2

Notes: 1 BT had a third share issue in July 1993 at a price of 410p.
2 The lowest and highest share prices are those since the first share issue and up to 31.1.96.
3 The figure in the final column indicates whether the first share issue (as at 31.1.96) had appreciated in value by more or less than the FT-SE industrial share index. A value above (below) 100 indicates a better (worse) performance than the FTSE index.
4 n/a = not applicable.
5 The price of the first share issue for ABP, BAA and NFC has been adjusted for subsequent rights and scrip issues.

privatisation, City investors expect future profitability in four cases to be above and in five cases to be below that in the economy as a whole.

Unfortunately, it is rather difficult to relate this result to privatisation as we do not know how profitable these firms were under state ownership relative to profitability in the economy as a whole.[6] Even if profitability in the state sector was below that overall, then the expected profitability results suggest that an improvement is likely in four of the nine cases. Again, the impact of privatisation is mixed.

CONCLUSION

In this chapter two accounting ratios have been used to examine the impact of privatisation on corporate performance: profitability and value-added per employee relative to value-added in the economy. On the basis of the two performance indicators, and for the eleven firms examined in this study, it is difficult to sustain unequivocally the hypothesis that private ownership is preferable to nationalisation on efficiency grounds. Evidence of an initial shake-out effect, with relative value-added growth improving following the announcement of the intention to privatise, was found in seven of the eleven firms. In addition, in five of the eleven firms relative value-added growth increased in the four years immediately after privatisation, compared with that recorded in the nationalisation period.

However, in the post-privatisation period value-added growth in seven of the eleven firms was less than that in the rest of the economy, while in the recession period the comparable figure was six out of ten firms (there are no data for Britoil for this period). In the nationalisation period five out of the eleven firms seem to have under-performed. Five of the ten firms had higher relative value-added growth rates when nationalised than in the recession period, although eight out of the nine firms (for which data were available) had a higher growth rate in the latest period than in the nationalisation period.

Simply comparing the value-added growth rate for each firm in the nationalisation period with that recorded in the pre-privatisation, post-privatisation, recession and latest periods offers forty comparisons. In twenty-three cases value-added growth increased after the nationalisation period while in the other seventeen instances it declined. The picture with regard to profitability is more favourable towards privatisation with an increase in twenty-eight of the forty comparisons.

Of course, these findings are subject to the usual caveats about the consistency and reliability of data extracted from company accounts, and the assumption about technology and capital inputs referred to earlier. In addition, there is a mix of pre-privatisation periods during which different governments were in power with differing policies towards the management of public enterprises. From 1979 the 'Thatcher factor' led to more emphasis on the efficient management of state-owned industries and less emphasis on other social goals. Moreover, there is the possibility that the nationalisation periods yield a misleading picture of public ownership because management, suspecting future privatisation, might already have taken steps to improve the company's performance. At the same time, to keep going back in history to find a period of state ownership when performance was relatively poor would defeat the object of the study.

In addition, each industry has its own particular history and this will affect the results (for example, both British Airways and British Steel underwent substantial restructuring to facilitate flotation). Ideally, performance results would be reported in relation to a detailed history of each organisation and this is something that is taken up again in chapter 9. We have, however, pointed out particular factors which might have affected performance but which had little to do with privatisation.

Furthermore, comparison with national value-added trends might not correctly reflect a firm's potential for efficiency gains. However, the finding that the effect of privatisation on efficiency has been mixed is confirmed by other studies and the results for value-added growth are similar to those for labour productivity reported in chapter 5. However, the rate of profit figures suggest a general improvement in performance while the TFP results reported in the previous chapter revealed little evidence of any general improvement under private ownership.

Although the labour productivity and value-added results are broadly similar (in terms of the impact of privatisation on performance), a comparison of the growth rates for each firm and for each of the six periods studied reveals that labour productivity growth exceeded value-added growth in two-thirds of all such comparisons. To understand the reasons for this, it is useful to decompose labour productivity into its constituent parts:

labour productivity = gross output/employees

= (wages + depreciation + bought-in supplies + profit

(before interest and tax))/employees

= (value-added/employees) + (bought-in supplies

/employees)

Thus any difference between the labour productivity and value-added figures must be due to the (real) value of bought-in supplies per employee. If, as we have found, labour productivity growth typically exceeds value-added growth, then this implies that the (real) value of bought-in supplies per employee is growing faster than value-added per employee. This might be because more work is being done outside the firm rather than internally (in other words that there is an increase in out-sourcing or contracting-out for supplies). This is an issue which we return to in chapter 8.

It is also interesting to note that the firms in this study have performed better in terms of profitability than productivity. One possible explanation for this is that there has been a re-allocation of business income away from wages to profit. This is another topic examined in chapter 8.

NOTES

1 The accounts of ABP are complicated by a number of asset transfers involving investment and development property (Dyer, 1995). It did not prove possible to adjust the accounts to reflect the transfers and the ABP profit figure might be lower than that reported if computed on a more prudent basis.
2 Value-added can be particularly distorted where profits are not a true representation of actual profitability because of bad debt policy or R&D write-offs against profit. Any change in policy on bad debts and accounting for R&D could affect our figures. We searched for such policy changes and have attempted to adjust for them wherever possible (for example, as in the case of Rolls-Royce).
3 This was calculated as the pre-tax rate of return on capital stock at replacement cost for all industrial and commercial companies in the non-North Sea sector (Sterne, 1993).
4 Both the firm and economy-wide rate of profit are reported as we are less confident about the appropriateness of the national comparator for this performance indicator than for the value-added data, where only a single figure (firm minus the economy or manufacturing) is reported.
5 This is also the case if profits are calculated on the basis of historic rather than current costs.
6 The rate of return data reported in Table 6.1 for the economy as a whole is on a replacement cost basis, whereas only one of the firms in this study (British Gas) reports current cost accounts.

7

ESTIMATING TECHNICAL EFFICIENCY USING DATA ENVELOPMENT ANALYSIS

Aziz Boussofiane, Stephen Martin and David Parker

INTRODUCTION

In this chapter, data envelopment analysis (DEA) is used to assess the level of technical efficiency in ten of our eleven organisations. Britoil is excluded because of inadequate data. As in previous chapters, efficiency is measured for a number of years before and after privatisation. DEA is a nonparametric method that allows efficiency to be measured without having to specify either the form of the production function or the weights for the different inputs and outputs used. It can be viewed as a generalisation of TFP methods in the sense that efficiency is defined as a multi-variate ratio of the weighted sum of outputs to weighted sum of inputs. It is nonparametric because the nature of the functional form between outputs and inputs is not specified in advance. It is therefore highly flexible.

The technique is also capable of handling multiple, incommensurate inputs and outputs. Normally, the DEA model is applied to a single common time period on a cross-section of data and is used to analyse the distribution of efficiency across a number of organisations producing the same or similar output(s). Indeed, DEA has been used to analyse the efficiency of, *inter alia*, air force maintenance units, bank branches, primary, secondary and tertiary education, fast food outlets, hospitals, post offices, refuse collection, and urban transport. However, by pooling time periods, the analysis can be made dynamic and thus can be used to analyse the efficiency effects of a policy initiative such as privatisation (see, for example, Price and Weyman-Jones, 1993). Unfortunately, our data set is not sufficiently extensive to permit a combined cross-section and dynamic analysis. Instead, we focus on the performance of a given company through time and consider whether privatisation has had any impact on the firm's level of technical efficiency.

DATA ENVELOPMENT ANALYSIS

DEA is a linear programming method used for assessing the efficiency of decision making units (DMUs), where the presence of incommensurate

127

inputs and outputs makes the measurement of overall efficiency difficult. It was first introduced by Charnes, Cooper and Rhodes (1978) as a generalisation of the Farrell efficiency frontier within a linear programming framework (Farrell, 1957). The usual aim is to define a frontier of most efficient DMUs and then to measure how far from the frontier are the less efficient units (for surveys of frontier efficiency models see Ganley and Cubbin, 1992; Lovell, 1993; and Färe et al., 1994). Since the initial development of DEA, a plethora of papers have been published exploring both theory and applications of the technique in the public and private sectors (for example, Banker et al., 1984; Banker and Morey, 1986; Banker and Thrall, 1992; Button and Weyman-Jones, 1992; Charnes et al., 1985; Färe et al., 1990; Seiford and Thrall, 1990; Smith, 1990). Recently, the technique has been used to assess the results of the UK electricity privatisation (Burns and Weyman-Jones, 1994a) and to compare the efficiency of electricity transmission and distribution companies, mainly in the US (Pollitt, 1994). These studies were reviewed in chapter 4.

The essential idea in DEA can be explained with the aid of Figure 7.1 which is an extension of the analysis in Figure 3.1 above. This relates the amount of output Y produced along a unit isoquant to levels of two inputs X_1 and X_2. Firms in an industry might produce on or above this best practice isoquant, with firms on the isoquant being technically efficient. For instance, the producers at D, E and F are clearly inefficient as they lie above the best practice isoquant. These firms have technical efficiency indices of less than unity; in the case of F for example this index is OB/OF. Firms A, B and C are deemed technically efficient as they are at points on the isoquant. Of course, neither A, B nor C may be overall efficient as this would also require allocative efficiency which, given the relative prices of the inputs X_1 and X_2, might require them to be at point such as Z. The objective is to construct a production possibility set from the observed output and input levels used by all of the firms in the industry. From this, it is possible to ascertain which firms lie on the frontier and which lie off it. The result is a relative rather than an absolute measure of efficiency and a 'best practice' approximation of the actual production frontier.

Where there is a single input and a single output then often efficiency is simply measured as the ratio of output to input. However, DMUs will more typically have multiple inputs and outputs. Efficiency can then be measured by using a weighted average of the inputs and a weighted average of the outputs. In this case, efficiency is the ratio of the sum of the weighted outputs to the sum of the weighted inputs. When used to compare efficiency between DMUs, the above measure can be most readily applied when a common set of weights for the DMUs is applicable. In practice, however, DMUs might find it difficult to 'agree' on a common set of weights. Certain outputs may be emphasised more by some DMUs than others and the same

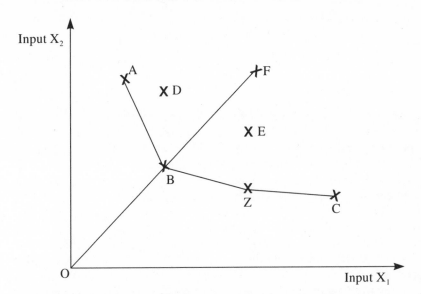

Figure 7.1 Estimated isoquant with two inputs

may be true of the inputs. Thus it may prove very difficult to attach relative values to the outputs and inputs.

DEA circumvents this problem by allowing each individual DMU to choose its *own* set of appropriate weights, so that its own efficiency rating is maximised. This is achieved subject to the constraint that no efficiency rating, obtained using any set of optimum weights, can be larger than an arbitrary constant, usually fixed equal to 100. A linear program is then solved for each individual DMU. By adopting this approach, in contrast to parametric methods of efficiency estimation, no *a priori* assumption as to the analytical form of the production function is required. This is recognised to be a major advantage of DEA over certain other forms of production or cost efficiency measurement (Førsund *et al.*, 1980; Seiford and Thrall, 1990).[1]

If the relative efficiency of DMU_{j_0} is to be assessed, the following linear program is solved:

$$\text{maximise} \quad h_0 = \sum_{r=1}^{s} V_r Y_{rj_0}$$

subject to

$$\sum_{i=1}^{m} u_i x_{ij_0} = 100$$

129

$$\sum_{i=1}^{m} u_i x_{ij} - \sum_{r=1}^{s} V_r Y_{rj} \leq 0 \qquad j = 1, ..., n$$

$$V_r \geq \epsilon \qquad r = 1, ..., s \qquad \text{(M1)}$$

$$u_i \geq \epsilon \qquad i = 1, ..., m$$

where u_i is the weight assigned to input i, V_r is the weight assigned to output r, x_{ij_0} is the level of input i used by unit j_0, Y_{rj_0} is the level of output r produced by unit j_0, and ε a small number (of the order of 10^{-6}) that ensures no input nor output is given a zero weight.

In the above model the variables are the weights u_i and V_r. The unit j_0 will be deemed efficient if its efficiency rating h_0 equals 100.[2] The optimum value of h_0 represents the maximum proportion of current input levels that j_0 should be using to secure its current output levels. If the value of h_0 is 100 then the DMU is efficient, in the sense that no other unit or combination of units can produce more along at least one output dimension without worsening other output levels or utilising higher input levels. Otherwise, the unit is relatively inefficient with a rating below 100. The above model seeks a combination of input and output weights that would maximise the efficiency rating of the DMUs being assessed. The dual of (M1), model (M2), is often solved as it is computationally faster. The dual or side model is as follows:

$$\text{minimise} \quad 100_{Z0} - \epsilon \left(\sum_{i=1}^{m} S_i^- + \sum_{r=1}^{S} S_r^+ \right)$$

subject to

$$X_{ij_0} Z_0 - \sum_{j=1}^{n} \lambda_j X_{ij} - S_i^- = 0 \qquad i = 1, ..., m$$

$$\sum_{j=1}^{n} \lambda_j Y_{rj} - S_r^+ = Y_{rj_0} \qquad r = 1, ..., s \qquad \text{(M2)}$$

where S_i^- is the slack in the ith input and S_r^+ is the slack in the rth output.

M2 seeks a combination of DMUs that will outperform the targeted unit. The combination of DMUs sought uses less resources than unit j_0, while producing at least the same level of output(s). In the side model the variables are the λ s. This particular model carries out an input minimisation where all the inputs are contracted by a proportion Z_0, while the outputs are kept at their current level. The unit j_0 will be efficient if the objective value of Z_0 equals 1 and all slack values are zero. Otherwise, the unit is inefficient. For any inefficient unit a set of peer units is identified. The set of peers consists of units that achieve an efficiency rating of 100 per cent, whilst using the same optimum input and output weights as those derived for the targeted unit.

In M1 the peers are identified by the binding constraints and the λ values are given by the shadow prices of these constraints. By contrast, in M2 the peers are directly identified by the positive values for λ_j. The corresponding set of peer units for any inefficient unit plays an important role in helping the inefficient unit identify sources of its inefficiency. These peer units are used for determining input and output levels that would render the targeted unit efficient. In other words, the percentage of inputs provided by the peer group relative to those of the DMU under consideration is the measure of its technical efficiency.

THE DATA

In this study, rather than comparing several organisations or DMUs at a single point of time, a longitudinal analysis was adopted to assess changes in technical efficiency associated with privatisation *within* each of ten privatised companies. In other words, for each firm we identify the 'best' (most efficient) year(s) and use that to judge the level of efficiency in every other year. Each year's financial results for each of the firms was taken to represent a distinct DMU. Thus, for example, the data for British Steel cover the period from 1978 to 1995 and provide seventeen DMUs: British Steel accounting year ending 1979, British Steel accounting year ending 1980, and so on. The larger the number of outputs and inputs, for a given number of DMUs, the less discriminatory the model becomes. In most situations satisfactory discrimination is obtained if the number of units present in the assessment set is three times the number of inputs multiplied by the number of outputs (Boussofiane *et al.*, 1991).

The first stage of a DEA assessment consists of identifying all of the inputs and outputs pertaining to the function of the organisations being assessed. Ideally, all of the data should be in physical terms, so as not to stray into the area of measuring allocative efficiency when examining technical efficiency. The inputs should represent all the resources being used, and the outputs should include all of the products and services produced or delivered by the organisation. Table 7.1 provides details of the outputs and inputs actually used.

DEA can also allow for the possibility that some of the variables may not be under the control of the managers of the DMU. Depending on how these environmental factors are measured, they may be included in the model either as uncontrollable inputs or uncontrollable outputs. One obvious environmental factor which affects the efficiency of state and privatised firms is demand over the business cycle since this affects the level of capacity working. Demand for outputs is likely to be depressed during the recession phase of the cycle and to expand during the recovery stage, depending upon

Table 7.1 Summary of inputs, outputs and periods studied

Organisation	Years studied[1]	Inputs[2]	Outputs
British Airways	1975–1995	Employee hours Capital Aviation fuel [3] Other inputs[4]	Average tonne kilometres (ATK) flown weighted by length of average sector (AS) flown and passenger load factor (PLF) (output= $ATK \times AS^{-0.2} \times PLF^{0.4}$; Forsyth *et al.*, 1986)
British Airports Authority	1978–1995	Employee hours Capital Other inputs[5]	Turnover deflated by the retail price index for non-food items
British Aerospace	1977–1994	Employee hours Capital Other inputs[4]	Turnover adjusted for stocks and work-in-progress deflated by a total cost index for inputs to the aerospace industry
British Gas	1976–1995	Employee hours Gas mains (mileage)	Volume of gas sold
British Telecom	1974–1995	Employee hours Capital Other inputs[4]	Turnover deflated by a price index for a basket of BT services
Jaguar[6]	1980–1991	Employee hours Capital Other inputs[7]	Number of cars produced
Associated British Ports	1975–1994	Employee hours Capital Other inputs[5]	Tonnes of cargo handled
Rolls-Royce	1979–1994	Employee hours Capital Other inputs[4]	Turnover adjusted for stocks and work-in-progress deflated by an index of total input costs for the aero-engine industry
NFC	1973–1994	Employee hours Capital Other inputs[4]	Turnover deflated by the retail price index for transport
British Steel	1979–1995	Employee hours Capital Raw materials[8] Other inputs[4]	Tonnes of liquid steel produced[9]

Notes: 1 Years studied refers to year in which first accounts studied began to year in which last accounts studied ended. Where a firm's accounts did not coincide with the calendar year all price indices were appropriately adjusted by linear interpolation. 2. With the exception of British Gas, the capital costs for each firm were calculated as depreciation plus a real return of 8 per cent on the net capital stock. The gross domestic fixed capital formation deflator for manufacturing industry was used to calculate capital costs at constant prices. For British Gas, the capital stock was calculated as the length of gas mains in service. 3 Fuel costs deflated by an index of jet fuel prices. 4 Other costs deflated by the input producer price index for manufacturing. 5 Other costs deflated by the retail price index for non-food items. 6 For Jaguar there are no accounts prior to 1980. 7 Other costs deflated by the input producer price index for motor vehicle manufacturing. 8 Raw material costs deflated by the producer price index for inputs to the metal manufacturing industry. 9 Ideally, we should like to be able to distinguish the various types of steel produced but the shortage of observations precluded the use of a more disaggregated data set.

the relevant income elasticities.[3] Later in this chapter, a variable will be included to reflect cyclical effects on output, though the initial results reported exclude this variable. A further environmental factor is technological change. Where improvements in technology lead to higher efficiency this will bias the results in favour of the later (privatised) years. Results reported towards the end of the chapter include a technology variable to control for this effect, though once again the initial results exclude a specific technology input.

RESULTS

The constant returns to scale model

An efficiency assessment for each of the ten organisations was undertaken initially assuming constant returns to scale. Some of the organisations might experience variable returns, a point we return to later. The resulting efficiency ratios are reported in Table 7.2.

Turning to the figures for British Airways first, it seems that efficiency was low in the mid-1970s, rose in the late 1970s (with an efficiency rating of 100 in 1980) but fell back in the recession of the early 1980s. There was a marked recovery between 1983 and 1984 and efficiency then remained relatively high until the recession of the early 1990s. British Airways appears to have adjusted quickly to this recession with good results since 1991. Including the period of the run-up to privatisation in February 1987, it appears that privatisation was associated with relatively high efficiency.

Moving to the British Airports Authority, which was privatised in July 1987, a similar picture emerges with relatively high efficiency recorded in 1979 and between 1984 and 1989. However, efficiency has deteriorated during the recent recession. After 1979 the productivity of other inputs declined although capital productivity increased reaching its zenith in 1984 (hence the 100 per cent efficiency rating). The years 1990, 1991 and 1992 have seen gains in output levels, although these increases have been more than outweighed by the increases in input costs, perhaps reflecting what was, with hindsight, the company's unwise move into the property market in the late 1980s.

The record for British Aerospace reveals a good technical efficiency record under public ownership in the late 1970s. The company was privatised in February 1981. British Aerospace seems to have lost its way in the mid- to late-1980s at a time when management was pursing the takeover of businesses such as the Royal Ordnance factories and Rover cars and also diversifying into property and construction companies. The boom of the late 1980s brought relatively high efficiency levels but more recently the recession and reduction of defence budgets appear to have had an adverse impact on performance.

133

Table 7.2 Efficiency ratings (constant returns to scale model)

Year[2]	British Airways	BAA	British Aerospace	British Gas[4]	BT	Jaguar[3]	ABP	Rolls-Royce	NFC	British Steel
1973									100.0	
1974									100.0	
1975					100.0		59.1		91.5	
1976	77.0			81.5	96.7		68.7		98.8	
1977	76.4		100.0	80.2	93.7		63.1		98.2	
1978	90.5		100.0	86.6	93.3		63.7		100.0	
1979	91.2	100.0	100.0	89.6	100.0		88.1	92.9	97.9	93.3
1980	100.0	90.6	95.8[1]	93.2	100.0	69.0	83.1	98.5	90.2	77.2
1981	94.7	87.7	98.1	90.3	100.0	75.0	96.7	97.0	92.7	75.2
1982	92.8	93.6	94.2	92.3	94.6	100.0	99.6	82.5	91.8	84.3
1983	91.7	94.7	100.0	89.6	94.1	100.0	84.8	82.8	98.2	77.5
1984	100.0	100.0	99.0	93.7	100.0	89.3	92.2	100.0	100.0	100.0
1985	99.8	100.0	94.0	95.5	100.0	100.0	100.0	100.0	100.0	95.7
1986	100.0	98.0	96.2	100.0	96.4	99.5	100.0	98.7	98.8	100.0
1987	100.0	100.0	94.1	100.0	97.8	100.0	100.0	100.0	100.0	98.2
1988	100.0	100.0	96.9	98.3	98.1	95.2	98.6	91.0	100.0	100.0
1989	97.2	100.0	100.0	93.9	100.0	86.6	86.8	98.3	100.0	100.0
1990	95.3	95.0	100.0	95.1	99.2	61.4	75.8	94.7	95.1	99.1
1991	99.5	87.0	93.1	99.4	100.0	n/a[5]	79.0	87.2	92.6	85.7
1992	100.0	86.8	92.6	100.0	99.8	n/a	86.7	96.7	89.6	86.2
1993	100.0	98.7	100.0	98.7	85.6	n/a	92.4	100.0	96.0	85.7
1994	100.0	100.0	87.1	99.5	98.2	n/a	100.0	100.0	95.8	98.7
1995	100.0	100.0	n/a	100.0	100.0		n/a	n/a	n/a	100.0

Notes: 1 Underlining indicates the last year in which the larger part of the accounting period occurred under state ownership. 2 'Year' is defined by accounting year ending in that year, e.g for British Airways where accounts are shown up to 31 March, '1981' is accounting year ending on 31 March 1981; whereas for British Aerospace whose accounts are drawn up to 31 December, '1981' is accounting year ending on 31 December 1981. 3 No figures for Jaguar are available beyond 1991. 4 In 1991 British Gas's financial year end was moved from 31 March to 31 December. The figure for 1991 refers to the 12 month period ending 31 March 1991; figures for 1992 and beyond refer to the 12 month period ending 31 December of the previous year. 5 n/a= not available.

British Gas was privatised in December 1986. The firm's technical efficiency seems to have been relatively low through to 1983. In the pre-privatisation period, the firm's performance improved considerably although in the late 1980s it deteriorated slightly. In the 1990s, its technical efficiency has remained at a very high level.[4]

BT's technical efficiency seems to have fallen in the late 1970s and then recovered in the early 1980s. However, it fell back just before privatisation but recovered in 1984 and 1985. There was a slight decline in productivity in 1986–8 but since then efficiency levels have been close to 100 per cent. The one exception was 1993 when residual (probably redundancy) costs soared. These results accord with the view that from the late 1980s tougher regulation of prices by Oftel and more competition, notably from Mercury, cable and cellular operators, led to rationalisation at BT. It seems that this pursuit of higher efficiency was delayed for a few years after privatisation and, perhaps, was more due to increased competition in the product market than to the change in ownership.

The relationship between privatisation and efficiency is particularly unclear when viewing the ratings for Jaguar cars. Separated from the state-owned giant British Leyland and sold off in July 1984, the company was bought by Ford in 1989. The extent of the company's financial difficulties during the recent recession is reflected in a calamitous collapse in relative efficiency after 1988. Indeed, after 1988 all three output to input ratios are decreasing consistently and hence the poor showing of the company in terms of its technical efficiency record.

Another company which is likely to have been affected by the recession is Associated British Ports. This firm was privatised in February 1983 and its level of technical efficiency has generally remained higher than that under public ownership in the late 1970s. The efficiency of ABP seems poor prior to 1981 with particularly low labour productivity. In 1982, the tonnage of cargo handled per £ of residual cost was at its highest (apart from 1994) and hence the very high efficiency rating. Capital and labour productivity increased by 30 per cent and 24 per cent respectively between 1982 and 1983. Yet 1983, the year of privatisation, is deemed inefficient as its performance is dominated by that of 1985 and 1986. In 1984, the organisation experienced a considerable drop in the productivity per £ of residual cost although this was reversed in 1985. The relatively poor performance between 1989 and 1993 is due to low capital and other input productivity. In 1994, however, other input productivity increased by 25 per cent.

Rolls-Royce was floated on the stock market in May 1987. Here again we seem to have a company where there is no clear difference between the efficiency ratings pre- and post-privatisation, except that the company seems to have come through the latest recession more strongly than that of the early 1980s. The efficiency ratings for NFC suggest a similar result. Efficiency seems to have been consistently high throughout the sample period with the exception of the recessions in the early 1980s and early 1990s.

At British Steel there is evidence of an improvement in performance well ahead of privatisation. The recession of the early 1980s had a major impact on the UK steel industry along with other steel industries in Europe. Particularly low efficiency ratings were registered from 1980 to 1983. After 1983, however, the considerable rationalisation of capacity undertaken from 1980 meant that technical efficiency leaped (the 1985 figure was probably affected by the year-long miners' strike) and through to 1990, the firm's operations were characterised by consistently high efficiency ratings. From 1991 to 1993, however, efficiency fell back considerably due to the low productivity of raw material and other inputs.

The efficiency rating indicates the maximum amount by which *all* inputs could be reduced without affecting the level of output (for example, a rating of 90.0 suggests that all inputs could be cut by 10 per cent). Typically though, it will be possible to reduce some inputs by even more than this and these target input levels can be obtained from an examination of the peer group for each inefficient DMU. Tables 7.3a to 7.3j report the maximum resource savings achievable on each input for each organisation over the sample period. For example, the overall efficiency of the NFC (Table 7.3i) was at a relatively low level in 1975 and 1980. In principle, in those two

Table 7.3a Improvements necessary to achieve 100% efficiency at British Airways

Year	Labour	Capital	Fuel	Other inputs
1976	36.2	45.2	23.0	23.0
1977	38.7	38.3	23.6	23.6
1978	35.6	37.3	9.5	9.5
1979	36.7	24.1	8.8	8.8
1980	0.0	0.0	0.0	0.0
1981	10.7	18.9	5.3	5.3
1982	15.9	7.2	10.6	7.2
1983	19.3	8.3	11.7	8.3
1984	0.0	0.0	0.0	0.0
1985	1.5	0.2	0.2	0.2
1986	0.0	0.0	0.0	0.0
1987	0.0	0.0	0.0	0.0
1988	0.0	0.0	0.0	0.0
1989	2.8	2.8	2.8	2.8
1990	4.7	4.7	9.9	4.7
1991	3.3	0.5	0.5	0.5
1992	0.0	0.0	0.0	0.0
1993	0.0	0.0	0.0	0.0
1994	0.0	0.0	0.0	0.0
1995	0.0	0.0	0.0	0.0

years the Corporation could have achieved the same output but with across the board savings of 8.6 per cent and 9.8 per cent respectively in its resource use. In other words, prior to privatisation poor performance seems to have resulted from inefficiency in the use of *all* inputs, namely labour, capital and other costs. By contrast after privatisation, when efficiency fell in the early 1990s, more of the inefficiency came from the use of capital and other inputs than from the under-utilisation of labour. One interpretation of this would be that the NFC more quickly adjusted its labour input to falling order books in this period than in the recession a decade earlier.

Table 7.3b Improvements necessary to achieve 100% efficiency at British Airports Authority

Year	Labour	Capital	Other inputs
1979	0.0	0.0	0.0
1980	9.4	9.4	9.4
1981	12.4	12.4	12.4
1982	11.9	6.4	6.4
1983	15.4	5.3	5.3
1984	0.0	0.0	0.0
1985	0.0	0.0	0.0
1986	2.0	2.0	2.0
1987	0.0	0.0	0.0
1988	0.0	0.0	0.0
1989	0.0	0.0	0.0
1990	5.0	5.0	5.0
1991	13.0	13.9	13.0
1992	13.2	13.2	13.2
1993	1.3	1.3	1.3
1994	0.0	0.0	0.0
1995	0.0	0.0	0.0

Turning more generally to the results for input target levels, one point that emerges from Tables 7.3a to 7.3j is that there is no single input that is persistently responsible for inefficiency. Rather, the source of potential efficiency gains varies, both through time and across the firms studied. For example, the scope for potential improvements in the use of labour is most notable at ABP from the mid-1970s to the early 1980s, at BSC in the early 1980s, and at British Gas from the mid-1970s to the mid-1980s. These results lend support to the observation in chapter 5 that privatisation has been associated particularly with economies in the use of labour, something discussed at greater length in the next chapter. Scope for improvement in the use of capital can be found at British Aerospace and at Rolls-Royce in the early 1980s. The use of both capital and labour could have been improved at BA and BT in the late 1970s. Finally, all inputs could have

Table 7.3c Improvements necessary to achieve 100% efficiency at British Aerospace

Year	Labour	Capital	Other inputs
1977	0.0	0.0	0.0
1978	0.0	0.0	0.0
1979	0.0	0.0	0.0
1980	4.2	34.4	4.2
1981	1.9	26.7	1.9
1982	5.8	14.2	5.8
1983	0.0	0.0	0.0
1984	1.0	11.7	1.0
1985	6.0	29.1	6.0
1986	3.7	3.7	3.7
1987	5.9	5.9	5.9
1988	3.1	3.1	3.1
1989	0.0	0.0	0.0
1990	0.0	0.0	0.0
1991	7.0	7.0	7.0
1992	7.4	10.2	7.4
1993	0.0	0.0	0.0

Table 7.3d Improvements necessary to achieve 100% efficiency at British Gas

Year	Labour	Capital
1976	39.7	18.5
1977	37.1	19.8
1978	31.7	13.5
1979	30.2	10.4
1980	26.4	6.8
1981	27.7	9.7
1982	24.3	7.7
1983	22.5	10.4
1984	14.0	6.4
1985	8.3	4.5
1986	0.0	0.0
1987	0.0	0.0
1988	1.7	1.7
1989	6.2	6.2
1990	4.9	4.9
1991	0.6	0.6
1992	0.0	0.0
1993	1.3	1.3
1994	0.5	0.5
1995	0.0	0.0

Table 7.3e Improvements necessary to achieve 100%
efficiency at BT

Year	Labour	Capital	Other inputs
1975	0.0	0.0	0.0
1976	3.3	13.5	3.3
1977	6.3	6.3	6.3
1978	6.7	6.7	6.7
1979	0.0	0.0	0.0
1980	0.0	0.0	0.0
1981	0.0	0.0	0.0
1982	5.4	5.4	5.4
1983	7.4	5.9	5.9
1984	0.0	0.0	0.0
1985	0.0	0.0	0.0
1986	3.6	3.6	3.6
1987	17.9	2.2	2.2
1988	5.7	1.9	1.9
1989	0.0	0.0	0.0
1990	0.8	3.1	0.8
1991	0.0	0.0	0.0
1992	0.2	0.2	0.2
1993	14.4	14.4	14.4
1994	1.8	1.8	1.8
1995	0.0	0.0	0.0

Table 7.3f Improvements necessary to achieve 100% efficiency at
Jaguar

Year	Labour	Capital	Other Inputs
1980	43.8	59.1	31.0
1981	38.2	39.6	25.0
1982	0.0	0.0	0.0
1983	0.0	0.0	0.0
1984	0.0	0.0	0.0
1985	10.7	10.7	10.7
1986	0.0	0.0	0.0
1987	0.5	0.5	1.2
1988	0.0	0.0	0.0
1989	4.8	15.8	8.9
1990	13.4	15.0	13.4
1991	38.6	54.0	38.6

been more efficiently utilised at ABP from 1989 to 1992 and at BAA in the early 1990s. Lastly, given that labour is more readily adjustable than capital, it is to be anticipated that in times of recession the importance of capital as a source of inefficiency will increase both relative to its

Table 7.3g Improvements necessary to achieve 100% efficiency at Associated British Ports

Year	Labour	Capital	Other Inputs
1975	85.7	48.0	40.9
1976	84.6	46.6	31.3
1977	85.4	36.9	36.9
1978	74.1	36.3	36.3
1979	73.6	11.9	11.9
1980	86.7	17.4	16.9
1981	85.6	10.4	3.3
1982	68.1	0.4	0.4
1983	29.6	15.2	15.2
1984	25.7	7.8	7.8
1985	0.0	0.0	0.0
1986	0.0	0.0	0.0
1987	0.0	0.0	0.0
1988	1.5	1.5	13.4
1989	13.2	13.2	24.4
1990	26.6	24.2	24.2
1991	21.0	25.9	21.9
1992	13.3	13.3	17.5
1993	7.6	7.6	19.0
1994	0.0	0.0	0.0

Table 7.3h Improvements necessary to achieve 100% efficiency at Rolls-Royce

Year	Labour	Capital	Other Inputs
1979	33.0	27.5	7.1
1980	4.7	17.4	1.5
1981	3.0	16.4	3.0
1982	17.5	27.9	17.5
1983	24.1	17.2	17.2
1984	0.0	0.0	0.0
1985	0.0	0.0	0.0
1986	1.6	1.3	1.3
1987	0.0	0.0	0.0
1988	9.0	9.0	9.0
1989	1.7	1.7	1.7
1990	5.3	5.3	5.3
1991	12.9	12.9	12.9
1992	7.3	7.3	17.7
1993	0.0	0.0	0.0
1994	0.0	0.0	0.0

previous level and relative to other inputs. There is evidence to support this hypothesis for the recession of the early 1980s in the results for BA,

Table 7.3i Improvements necessary to achieve 100% efficiency at
NFC

Year	Labour	Capital	Other Inputs
1973	0.0	0.0	0.0
1974	0.0	0.0	0.0
1975	8.6	8.6	8.6
1976	2.8	1.2	1.2
1977	1.8	1.8	1.8
1978	0.0	0.0	0.0
1979	2.1	2.1	2.1
1980	9.8	9.8	9.8
1981	7.3	7.3	7.3
1982	8.1	8.1	8.1
1983	1.8	1.8	1.8
1984	0.0	0.0	0.0
1985	0.0	0.0	0.0
1986	1.2	17.8	1.2
1987	0.0	0.0	0.0
1988	0.0	0.0	0.0
1989	0.0	0.0	0.0
1990	4.9	4.9	6.5
1991	7.4	12.3	10.5
1992	10.4	16.6	17.7
1993	4.0	16.5	17.8
1994	4.2	25.4	19.5

Table 7.3j Improvements necessary to achieve 100% efficiency at
British Steel

Year	Labour	Capital	Raw Material	Other Costs
1979	67.6	49.7	6.7	6.7
1980	71.0	53.2	22.9	22.9
1981	69.5	43.4	26.8	26.9
1982	54.2	19.4	15.7	15.7
1983	46.1	22.5	24.6	22.5
1984	0.0	0.0	0.0	0.0
1985	4.3	4.3	4.7	15.3
1986	0.0	0.0	0.0	0.0
1987	18.4	1.8	1.8	23.9
1988	0.0	0.0	0.0	0.0
1989	0.0	0.0	0.0	0.0
1990	5.2	20.8	0.9	18.6
1991	14.4	24.7	14.4	33.5
1992	13.8	19.6	13.8	27.3
1993	14.3	14.3	14.3	31.9
1994	1.3	1.3	1.3	19.7
1995	0.0	0.0	0.0	0.0

Table 7.4 Arithmetic means of the cross-efficiency ratings (constant returns to scale)

Year[2]	British Airways	BAA	British Aerospace	British Gas[5]	BT	Jaguar[3]	ABP	Rolls-Royce	NFC	British Steel
1973									77.1	
1974									81.2	
1975					76.1		45.7		75.9	
1976	60.2			76.1	73.7		51.3		80.3	
1977	63.7		89.9	75.6	76.5		49.5		81.9	
1978	71.4		89.8	81.7	80.7		51.3		83.3	
1979	78.0	94.4	84.0	84.4	92.1	51.3	67.5	72.9	81.9	71.4
1980	81.5	86.0	81.6[1]	88.0	89.7	58.1	61.9	88.6	76.3	61.2
1981	77.0	85.2	85.1	85.5	90.0	85.2	70.4	89.1	80.3	61.5
1982	82.0	89.0	85.6	87.8	87.5	94.9	76.1	78.8	79.0	76.3
1983	83.1	88.9	92.9	85.9	86.9	95.6	74.3	78.1	84.3	71.0
1984	93.2	92.9	90.2	90.8	92.9	85.7	70.3	94.4	86.7	94.9
1985	91.4	96.4	83.6	93.2	93.5	97.3	90.3	98.1	87.0	90.0
1986	90.5	95.4	87.3	98.3	91.5	94.5	91.1	94.0	83.3	98.3
1987	79.7	97.4	84.7	98.7	88.2	95.4	77.8	93.7	91.2	89.9
1988	87.3	98.6	87.5	96.9	92.7	87.4	73.3	83.7	94.5	97.9
1989	90.3	97.4	88.4	92.4	95.8	82.6	68.0	90.4	93.9	96.9
1990	87.4	90.1	87.1	93.6	92.5	57.0	71.5	87.3	88.5	88.6
1991	93.0	82.3	81.0	97.8	91.3	n/a[5]	74.1	78.1	84.8	77.8
1992	95.3	83.5	79.9	98.4	90.8	n/a	80.5	78.2	79.7	80.2
1993	94.7	94.5	86.7	95.4	77.7	n/a	82.4	86.7	81.6	80.2
1994	92.7	96.2	69.1	93.1	88.7	n/a	96.4	86.5	79.6	92.7
1995	93.0	95.7	n/a	89.9	90.1		n/a	n/a	n/a	96.9

Notes: as for Table 7.2

British Aerospace, and Rolls-Royce. There is also evidence of a similar result for Jaguar, NFC and BSC in the recession of the early 1990s.

Readers who are more familiar with stochastic methods may be a little disturbed by the absence of anything analogous to a confidence interval for the efficiency ratings reported in Table 7.2 and that, as a consequence, they might feel that it is not really clear what reliance can be put upon the ratings. Responding to this point, Doyle and Green (1994) proposed using the input weights (the u_i in program M1 above) that emerge for each DMU to calculate the efficiency rating for every other DMU (these ratings to be known as cross-efficiencies). In this way a matrix of cross-efficiencies can be constructed to examine the robustness of a DMU's efficiency rating to different sets of weights. Thus for, say, BAA the optimal input weights for 1979 would be used to calculate cross-efficiency ratings for 1980–95. Then the weights for 1980 would be used to calculate cross-efficiency ratings for 1979 and 1981–95, and the weights for 1981 would be used to calculate cross-efficiency ratings for 1979–80 and 1982–95, and so on. For an organisation with n observations (years), there will be $n-1$ cross-efficiencies and for each year the arithmetic mean of these cross-efficiencies is reported in Table 7.4.

With regard to the impact of privatisation on efficiency, the pattern of results revealed by these cross-efficiencies is similar to that suggested by the basic efficiency ratings. On the basis of a comparison of the average efficiency rating pre- and post-privatisation, there is evidence again of an improvement in efficiency at British Airways, British Gas and ABP. In addition, however, there are clear signs of an improvement at BT, British Steel and Jaguar which were not present in the basic efficiency ratings (reported in Table 7.2). But for BAA, British Aerospace, Rolls-Royce and NFC there is again little indication of a change in performance following privatisation.

The variable returns model

The results presented in Tables 7.2 and 7.3 were derived assuming constant returns to scale and the model used should be seen as the 'base model'. In this section, we examine the implications of dropping the constant returns to scale assumption while in the following section technology and business cycle effects are introduced. A constant returns to scale frontier assumes that proportionate input increases (reductions) will be followed by equiproportionate output increases (reductions). A DMU operating under local increasing (decreasing) returns to scale will enjoy input increases that result in more (less) than proportionate increases in outputs.

The model was re-estimated assuming variable returns to scale by introducing the constraint:

$$\sum_{j=1}^{n} \lambda_j = 1$$

to the model M2 (above). This requires that the weights of the comparison group sum to one, ensuring that comparison is by interpolation between DMUs only, and precluding comparison with groups operating at a different scale to the DMU of interest. Figure 7.2 illustrates some of the impacts of assuming variable rather than constant returns to scale in the context of a one input, one output model.

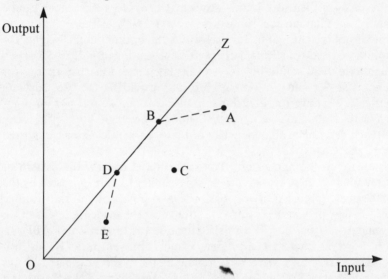

Figure 7.2 Alternative formulations of the production frontier

Assuming constant returns, DEA would fit an efficient frontier given by OZ. Imposition of the scale constraint results in the piecewise linear frontier EDBA. Whereas only D and B are efficient with constant returns, A and E now join them if we allow variable returns. Although A and E are now technically efficient, they are not scale efficient because they do not exhibit the constant returns to scale property demonstrated by D and B. When variable rather than constant returns is assumed, DMUs are no longer penalised for operating at a non-optimal scale. As a consequence, all efficiency ratings are expected to stay the same or to increase. This is confirmed in Table 7.5 which reports the results from re-estimating the initial DEA model but with variable replacing constant returns. For all the units that appear efficient in Table 7.5 but were deemed inefficient in Table 7.2, we conclude that these units are technically efficient, in terms of resource usage, but are operating at a non-optimal scale.

Comparing Tables 7.2 and 7.5, it is evident that the efficiency ratings have increased but that the overall pattern of results – *vis-à-vis* privatisation – is

Table 7.5 Efficiency ratings (variable returns to scale)

Year[2]	British Airways	BAA	British Aerospace	British Gas[4]	BT	Jaguar[3]	ABP	Rolls-Royce	NFC	British Steel
1973										
1974									100.0	
1975					100.0				100.0	
1976	91.0			100.0	100.0		65.2		91.8	
1977	84.6		100.0	100.0	100.0		70.0		100.0	
1978	99.7		100.0	100.0	100.0		68.5		98.6	100.0
1979	92.6	100.0	100.0	99.7	100.0		67.1	97.2	100.0	79.9
1980	100.0	94.1	98.7[1]	100.0	100.0	97.4	88.4	100.0	99.5	87.6
1981	95.1	94.8	100.0	98.5	100.0	100.0	90.2	99.8	94.2	85.7
1982	93.4	96.5	94.7	98.7	100.0	100.0	100.0	82.6	100.0	94.4
1983	93.7	100.0	100.0	97.7	100.0	100.0	100.0	96.4	100.0	100.0
1984	100.0	100.0	99.7	98.9	100.0	100.0	85.5	100.0	100.0	99.2
1985	100.0	100.0	96.7	99.4	98.8	90.7	96.9	100.0	100.0	100.0
1986	100.0	99.3	98.7	100.0	99.0	100.0	100.0	99.7	100.0	100.0
1987	100.0	100.0	95.0	100.0	98.5	100.0	100.0	100.0	100.0	100.0
1988	100.0	100.0	100.0	100.0	100.0	100.0	100.0	100.0	100.0	100.0
1989	97.9	100.0	100.0	99.6	100.0	96.9	90.9	100.0	100.0	99.7
1990	97.4	100.0	100.0	98.5	100.0	90.1	79.5	100.0	100.0	86.5
1991	100.0	93.1	93.2	100.0	92.9	83.5	82.0	88.5	93.3	86.7
1992	100.0	88.8	93.1	100.0	99.0	n/a[5]	90.3	93.9	91.7	89.7
1993	100.0	100.0	100.0	98.8	100.0	n/a	95.6	100.0	96.3	100.0
1994	100.0	100.0	100.0	99.9		n/a	100.0	100.0	100.0	100.0
1995	100.0	100.0	n/a	100.0			n/a	n/a	n/a	100.0

Notes: as for Table 7.2

generally unaffected.[5] For example, looking at the results for BA it is evident that 1985 and 1991 are now years of 100 per cent technical efficiency and that the years 1976 to 1983 still look to be a period of inefficiency, if not by such a large margin as before. The ratings for British Gas are no longer suggestive of an improvement in performance following privatisation and the results for Jaguar indicate a decline rather than no change in efficiency under private ownership (cf. Table 7.2). The result for Jaguar is affected by the sharp decline in the efficiency ratings from 1989.

Incorporating technology and business cycle effects

A number of the organisations studied might be expected to have been affected by important technological change over the period studied and all organisations could reasonably be expected to record productivity improvements through time. These arguments suggest that it may be inappropriate to compare the performance in any given year with subsequent years and that only performance in subsequent years should be able to form the peer group for a given DMU. The results reported so far also suggest that efficiency ratios are affected by the business cycle (witness the decline in the efficiency ratings for many firms in the recessions of the early 1980s and the early 1990s).

Consequently, the variable returns model was re-estimated introducing a technology variable and a business cycle control. Modelling technological change is especially difficult in the absence of information on technology for each of the industries studied. A linear time trend variable was used to capture technological improvements, a method used in numerous previous studies (for example, Hartley and Lynk, 1983; Gao and Reynolds, 1994), though its crudity is self-evident. The business cycle was reflected by changes in real GDP; if an industry's cycle was not commensurate with that of the economy as a whole then again the variable would not capture the intended effects. Unlike labour, capital, and other inputs, these factors were deemed to be largely beyond the control of the individual firm and were therefore entered into the DEA program as uncontrollable inputs; in this case, the DMU is compared with an efficient peer group where the value of the environmental variable is the same as or less than that for the DMU. Given the relatively small number of observations on each firm, the introduction of these additional inputs had a severe effect on the discriminatory power of the DEA program. In particular, very few years were now less than 100 per cent efficient. To minimise the impact of this effect, all controllable inputs were aggregated into a single input, as measured by the firm's total costs. Hence the inputs became 'aggregated inputs' (total costs), technology, and a business cycle variable. Separate runs were also attempted using technology and the business cycle variables separately.

The results were broadly similar to those obtained when both inputs were included.

Space precludes reporting the results in detail but Table 7.6 reports two further sets of efficiency ratings for each organisation assuming variable returns: the figures in column (A) relate to a model with aggregated costs and technology as the inputs, while column (B) adds a business cycle variable as a further input. With regard to the impact of privatisation on efficiency, the results for BT, Rolls-Royce, NFC and British Gas are similar to those reported in Table 7.5; namely, that there is no obvious change in performance. For Jaguar the results in Tables 7.5 and 7.6 are also similar but in both cases there is evidence of a deterioration in performance. The basic variable returns model also suggested no performance change for BAA, British Aerospace and BSC whereas the results in Table 7.6 suggest, if anything, a deterioration in performance for each of these companies. Finally, the initial variable returns results suggested an improvement in performance at ABP and BA whereas in Table 7.6 there is little evidence of any performance change for BA and ABP's results now appear to indicate a (surprising) deterioration in performance! Overall, the impact of the technology and business cycle variable is, as expected, to improve efficiency ratings of the earlier years and/or to reduce the efficiency ratios of the later years.

Of course, the validity of these results depends on the appropriateness of the way in which the cycle and technology effects have been measured, For example, an industry's cycle might not be commensurate with that of the economy (or manufacturing) as a whole and the large fall in productivity recorded by Jaguar in 1992 tends to confirm that for this firm the business cycle indicator is too crude. Similarly, a linear time trend might be a poor measure of technological progress. For example, the idea that ABP was less efficient in the late 1980s than in the late 1970s and early 1980s was not a result that we had anticipated given the labour shake-out during the latter decade. Nevertheless, technology and the business cycle might have important effects and it is therefore appropriate to attempt to incorporate them into the analysis. However, given the preliminary nature of this work we would not want to attach too much weight to these findings and further work on these indicators is required before more definitive conclusions can be reached.

CONCLUSION

This chapter has employed DEA to analyse the technical efficiency of ten of the eleven organisations studied in this book both before and after privatisation. DEA is a linear programming technique used to derive the relative efficiencies of decision-making units, where the presence of multiple inputs and outputs makes it difficult to derive a summary measure of efficiency.

Table 7.6 Efficiency ratings introducing technology and business cycle effects into the variable returns model

Year	British Airways A	B	BAA A	B	British Aerospace A	B	British Gas[2] A	B	BT A	B	Jaguar A	B	ABP A	B	Rolls-Royce A	B	NFC A	B	British Steel A	B
1973																	100	100		
1974																	94.7	94.7		
1975									100	100							91.4	91.4		
1976	100	100			100	100	100	100	90.8	90.8			100	100			97.6	97.6		
1977	96.2	96.2			100	100	100	100	97.4	97.4			100	100			96.2	97.0		
1978	95.0	95.1					100	100	97.7	97.7			98.4	98.4			97.9	98.4		
1979	93.9	93.9	100	100	96.6	98.5	98.1	68.6	100	100	100	100	100	100	100	100	94.7	94.8	100	100
1980	90.1	90.1	92.0	95.1	92.2[4]	100	100	100	97.3	99.2	100	100	90.5	100	100	100	93.4	94.6	97.7	97.7
1981	87.9	100	91.9	100	95.6	100	81.7	100	93.5	100	100	100	91.9	100	100	100	100	100	100	100
1982	93.5	100	97.8	100	93.7	94.5	82.9	98.1	94.8	99.5	100	100	98.5	100	88.0	88.0	100	100	100	100
1983	95.0	96.1	99.8	100	97.7	97.7	79.0	79.0	95.9	96.8	100	100	95.9	95.9	94.3	94.8	99.0	99.7	100	100
1984	100	100	100	100	93.5	93.5	90.8	90.8	97.3	97.3	100	100	90.5	97.7	100	100	100	100	100	100
1985	94.0	94.4	100	100	89.9	89.9	93.7	100	95.9	96.6	87.3	87.3	100	100	100	100	99.8	99.8	91.9	91.9
1986	93.5	93.5	97.8	97.8	92.5	93.2	100	100	94.3	94.3	100	100	96.9	97.7	97.9	97.9	100	100	99.3	100
1987	88.9	88.9	98.7	98.7	91.6	91.6	100	100	92.9	92.9	100	100	88.7	88.7	94.5	94.5	100	100	100	100
1988	91.6	91.6	99.0	99.0			100	100	94.1	94.1	100	100	91.2	91.2	90.7	90.7	100	100	100	100
1989	93.3	93.3	96.2	96.2	95.6	95.6	96.0	97.2	100	100	100	100	79.7	84.7	96.0	96.0	100	100	100	100
1990	90.6	90.6	85.7	86.2	100	100	95.1	100	98.6	100	91.9	94.5	83.9	89.4	100	100	100	100	87.2	90.4
1991	93.8	93.9	78.9	86.0	92.5	100	100	100	94.6	100	89.3	100	100	100	90.9	100	100	100	82.2	89.4
1992	100	100	84.5	100	92.3	94.6	100	100	92.2	95.2	61.6	79.3	91.3	100	90.2	90.3	98.2	98.2	89.0	100
1993	100	100	96.2	100	95.2	95.8	97.4	68.6	99.1	100	n/a	n/a[3]	91.4	96.6	97.6	97.6	96.1	96.1	92.2	98.3
1994	98.5	98.5	100	100	69.5	69.5	97.8	71.3			n/a	n/a	100	100	99.8	99.8	100	100	100	100
1995	100	100	100	100	n/a	n/a	100	100			n/a	n/a	n/a	n/a	n/a	n/a	n/a	n/a	100	100

Notes: 1 Column A figures relate to the model with aggregated (controllable) input and one uncontrollable input (technology) and column B figures relate to the same model but with an additional uncontrollable input (business cycle). 2 For British Gas there was no need to aggregate the controllable inputs (labour and capital) and thus both of these inputs were present separately in the models that generated these results. 3 n/a = not available. 4 Underlining indicates the last year in which the larger part of the accounting year occurred under state ownership.

Essentially three models were estimated: the first took into account the resources used and outputs produced by the organisations assuming constant returns to scale; the second allowed for variable returns; and the third added inputs for technological change and the business cycle to the input/output set. With the exception of two companies, the results were similar irrespective of whether constant or variable returns were assumed. In the cases of British Gas and Jaguar, however, our results depend upon whether the variable returns to scale assumption is invoked. Smith (1993) demonstrates that the inappropriate use of this assumption can lead to wildly inflated efficiency estimates when the sample size is small – which, of course, it is in the present case. For this reason, we would attach the most weight to the results reported in Table 7.2 for these two companies. Thus, our basic DEA model suggests that privatisation has been associated with an improvement in efficiency at BA, ABP and British Gas.[6] There is also some evidence of an improvement at BT and BSC.

There also appears to have been an anticipation effect, in the sense that there is evidence that performance improved at BA, BAA and British Steel in the two or three years prior to actual privatisation. This finding is commensurate with those of earlier studies mentioned in chapter 4 which also attribute substantial gains in efficiency to the period immediately before privatisation. However, for BAA and British Steel this efficiency improvement was not sustained through to the end of the sample period. For British Aerospace, NFC and Rolls-Royce, there is no obvious relationship between ownership and efficiency in these results. Thus, although there is evidence of clear efficiency improvements in some cases, for other organisations there is little discernible difference between pre- and post-privatisation performance. These results are broadly in line with the results of our other efficiency measures discussed in chapters 5 and 6. In other words, there is no systematic evidence that public enterprises are less technically efficient than private firms. We have also found that the source of potential efficiency gains is not confined to a single input; rather, it varies from firm to firm and through time.

These results, however, make no allowance for technical progress and may therefore be biased in favour of the later years, which, of course, will affect the results in favour of private ownership (in all of the firms studied this came after public ownership). But once technology and the impact of the business cycle are incorporated into the model its discriminatory power is considerably reduced and only in the case of the NFC is there any evidence that privatisation was associated with an improvement in efficiency.

The results in this chapter contribute to knowledge about the effects of privatisation on performance, though like the results of all such studies they are not conclusive. DEA makes data demands that have pushed our data set to the limits. Undoubtedly data problems mean that the DEA was not particularly successful when technology and the business cycle were introduced. Clearly more work is needed and hopefully our exploratory study will provide a departure point for further research. In particular, it would be interesting to extend the data set for each company. Not only would this give the DEA model more discriminatory power, but it would enable an extension of the coverage of the input/output set.[7]

Despite the obvious limits of the research reported in this chapter, it is of value. The study has used a technique for measuring performance, DEA, which has been relatively little used in privatisation studies. One important product of this method is that, compared with the methods used in earlier chapters, it has provided further details of where efficiency savings have come from in terms of the inputs used. The ways in which the organisations studied have attempted to improve efficiency in input use is worthy, however, of further discussion. In the following two chapters we turn to consider the impact of privatisation on employment and the distribution of business income, and in terms of business restructuring.

NOTES

1 However, unlike stochastic frontier models (for example, where a cost function is estimated), DEA assumes that there is no 'noise' in the data and that all of the variation in the production possibility set is due to inefficiency.

2 In some studies this is shown as 1.

3 Doble and Weyman-Jones (1991) found that the business cycle was an important determinant of efficiency in the electricity supply industry.

4 This result is in line with the findings of Price and Weyman-Jones (1993). Using Malmquist indices of productivity change, they found that the Farrell efficient frontier is largely composed of the post-privatisation industry.

5 The required improvements in input usage to achieve 100 per cent efficiency (analogous to those reported in Table 7.3) were also calculated but proved similar to those derived from the constant returns model. The main difference was a slight reduction in revealed labour inefficiency in some organisations. For reasons of space these tables are not reported but can be obtained from the authors.

6 This finding is in line with a more detailed study of the technical efficiency of the twelve distribution regions of British Gas over the period 1977–91 (Price and Weyman-Jones, 1993).

7 Moreover, consideration could be given to some issues which are at present out of our reach. For example, currently the assessment of efficiency is based upon the best observed practice across all years without making any distinction between pre- and post-privatisation efficient years. One option would be to assess pre- and post-privatisation years separately, adjust the input values to their minimum and to pool the new data set under one assessment to test for dominance (Price and Weyman-Jones, 1993).

8

THE IMPACT OF PRIVATISATION ON EMPLOYMENT AND THE DISTRIBUTION OF BUSINESS INCOME

INTRODUCTION

The last three chapters assessed the impact of UK privatisation on economic performance using a number of measures (namely labour and total factor productivity, value-added, the rate of profit and DEA). In this chapter the focus is on the impact of privatisation on specific inputs through an analysis of employment, wages, returns to capital and payments to outside suppliers. Economists have been most concerned with the general implications of privatisation for economic efficiency in terms of productivity and costs of production. To date there have been surprisingly few serious studies of the effects of privatisation in the UK on the return to particular inputs and therefore on the firm's income distribution. A few early studies reported higher profitability after privatisation in some though not all cases (Bishop and Kay, 1988; Hyman, 1989; Yarrow, 1989) something we confirmed over a longer period in chapter 6.

The case study research, reported in chapter 9 below, confirms that major reorganisations affecting management, workforce and suppliers have occurred and are still occurring in a number of the privatised firms. These have involved, *inter alia*, a greater consumer focus, more cost control and a greater interest in making profits. This has led to a reduction in the trade unions' scope for collective bargaining, at least in some of the firms (Pendleton and Winterton, 1993). On the impact of privatisation on wage rates, Yarrow argued that the initial effect may actually have been slightly positive (Yarrow, 1989, p. 233), though more recent studies have questioned this view (for example, Bishop and Green, 1995).

It seems that in some cases there was no immediate rush to reduce employment following privatisation. This was true of BT, though since 1989 the company is known to have slashed employment amongst both manual and non-manual staffs in an attempt to cut costs. This led to a national managerial and professional staff strike in 1990. However, part of the change in staffing levels at BT is due to the introduction of new technology, notably micro-electronic exchanges, which probably would have removed large numbers of employees even if BT had remained publicly owned (Ferner and Colling, 1993). Separating out the effects of other factors on resource use from the effects of privatisation remains problematical.

Haskel and Szymanski (1991, 1992, 1993a), looked at between fourteen and seventeen firms that were publicly owned in 1972. Studying employment up to 1988 they reported that employment fell following a change towards more commercial objectives in the 1980s. But they also concluded that wages were only slightly affected by privatisation being more affected by a loss of market power. Their sample includes, however, only four firms that were actually privatised in the period and then only for a very short period after privatisation. Their research, therefore, is best viewed as a study of the impact of Thatcherism on the UK public sector rather than as a study of privatisation *per se*. The research reported in this chapter differs in being concerned only with firms that were privatised and the period of analysis extends to 1994 or 1995.

Here, the impact of privatisation on employment and income distribution is discussed in detail for each of our eleven organisations. It is possible that some firms may have significantly altered their expenditures on bought-in inputs, as suggested towards the end of chapter 6, and this will have implications for suppliers of materials, components and other services. This possibility is investigated. A change in the bought-in supplies term following privatisation could arise due to a number of possible factors: (a) negotiating cheaper inputs (a more aggressive purchasing policy); (b) cheaper purchases resulting from a change in external market pressures leading to lower prices (more competition amongst suppliers); (c) change in the volume of bought-in inputs (more efficient use of inputs per unit of output); and/or (d) through more work being done outside the firm rather than internally (a rise in contracting-out for supplies).

Freed from political constraints, it seems likely that following privatisation firms will test whether continuing to supply components and materials internally is the most efficient way to obtain resources. This would mirror the increased use of competitive tendering for inputs in UK central and local government and the NHS, and the more general reassessment in the 1980s of the make or buy decision by firms which were aiming to reduce costs (Lamming, 1993). Where more work is contracted out, this can often involve redundancies, plant closures and less favourable wages and working conditions for employees transferred. Because of the likely political backlash, such reorganisation may have been unattainable or certainly much more difficult under state ownership. The impact on supplies and the UK supply base is an under-researched area of privatisation.[1]

HYPOTHESES AND METHOD

The approach adopted draws from the public choice and property rights literatures reviewed in chapter 1. These complementary theories suggest that state-owned firms have more complex objectives than private sector firms and that they therefore tend to trade more output for lower profits (Pint, 1991). Hence it is to be expected that privatisation will be associated with a switch from sometimes confused and contradictory objectives towards making profit. In so far as this occurs, it will be reflected in the share of the firm's income going to profits and in the rate of return on capital employed. In chapter 6 rate of return figures for each of the eleven organisations were reported but are repeated here for completeness. It is relevant in a discussion of the distribution of each firm's income to comment again on the rate of return.

Secondly, the public choice and property rights literatures suggest that state-owned firms will be prone to capture by special interest groups and notably public sector trades unions. In turn, rent-seeking behaviour by unions will lead to over-staffing and wages that exceed free market levels. In addition, higher wages and better working conditions leading to higher employment levels may be an objective of government when firms are under state-ownership. As a consequence, it is to be expected that privatisation will be associated with major economies in employment. The impact of privatisation on labour is assessed by considering: changes in employment levels; the percentage of the firm's income paid to labour; and changes in wage relativities. Wage relativities are measured by the wage per employee in each firm relative to wage per capita in the whole economy. In the case of firms involved in manufacturing activities, comparison is made with average wages in UK manufacturing. Labour employment conditions are affected by factors other than wages, such as hours of work, holiday entitlements, stress levels and accidents at work. Other possible changes in labour conditions relate to the substitution of local for national-level collective bargaining, flexible working, de-unionisation and the ending of index linked pensions. A discussion of these changes is postponed to chapter 9.

Thirdly, privatisation provides managements with a new environment freed from the political oversight and political constraints found in the public sector. As a result it might be expected that management will reconsider the boundaries of the firm and will test whether continuing to supply components and materials internally is the most efficient way to obtain resources. We would expect this to be reflected in purchasing policies leading to a more efficient use of materials and a reassessment of the make or buy decision.

Lastly, management have greater freedom to manage and adjust their inputs when state intervention is completely removed. Continued state intervention may reduce the incentives to operate efficiently even though the firm

153

has been transferred to the private sector. Regulation, in particular, may reduce incentives to economise in the use of inputs, as detailed in chapter 1. Hence, we might expect that: where privatised firms remain state regulated there will be a smaller change in profitability, employment and wage levels than in a privatised but unregulated firm. There may also be a less noticeable change in the use of other inputs with a view to reducing costs.

Of our sample of eleven privatised firms, three – BT, British Gas and BAA – were privatised as state-regulated utilities. Insofar as regulation leads to a disincentive to make profits, after privatisation there is less likely to be a rise in both the share of income going to profits and in the rate of return on net assets. There may also be less managerial interest in reducing over-staffing and in removing labour rents. Similarly, there may be less incentive to reorganise the business, out-source and negotiate tougher contracts with suppliers. Some preliminary comment on the relationship between regulation and profitability appeared in chapter 6, but the subject is revisited here.

The above arguments suggest that privatisation will lead to: higher profits; employment economies; a change in purchases of non-labour inputs; and fewer cost-cutting initiatives where firms remain state-regulated following privatisation. These hypotheses were assessed using data on employment and income. Once again the data came mainly from the annual reports and accounts of the firms, supplemented by information supplied by the organisations. Employment data are presented for each year. The other data are reported as averages for each of six distinct time periods, each intended to represent a stage in the privatisation process. These periods have been discussed at length in earlier chapters and are described as: (a) a nationalisation period, to capture performance under state ownership; (b) a pre-privatisation period; (c) a post-announcement period determined by the date of the first public announcement of the intention to privatise; (d) a post-privatisation period; (e) a recession period to capture performance during the 1989–92 recession; and (f) a period covering the years since 1992, termed the latest period. The precise dates for each organisation were given in chapter 3, Table 3.2.

The method adopted mainly involved dividing the turnover of each firm into its main constituent elements. This provided data on the average annual changes in the percentage of income going to manual and non-manual labour combined (unfortunately the wage data are not sufficiently detailed to shed light on wage payments to different types of staff, a point we return to later), capital depreciation, profits and interest, and to other inputs in each of the defined periods. The other inputs category is a residual and is intended to capture mainly the share of income paid out for supplies such as materials, components and energy.

Decomposing business income in this way is equivalent to measuring changes per unit of output in: (a) employment costs; (b) depreciation; (c) profits and interest payments; and (d) the value of raw material, component, energy and other input costs. A change in depreciation per unit of output is especially difficult to interpret and hence not much weight is placed on the resulting figures in this study. If depreciation in accounts accurately reflected capital usage then the figures would provide an insight into the efficient use of capital. However, depreciation as shown in accounts is based on historic costs and arbitrary accounting practices relating to capital usage. It is therefore a crude indicator only of the true economic amortisation of the capital stock, something we have referred to earlier. It should also be borne in mind that the other inputs category can include certain internal costs such as non-labour administrative expenses and certain product support costs (for example, internal sales and marketing expenses). Unfortunately, published accounting data are not sufficiently detailed to identify these items separately on any sort of consistent basis. What figures do exist suggest that these items are usually relatively small in relation to bought-in supplies.

Acquisitions and divestitures can also complicate the use of company data when assessing performance (*cf.* Yarrow, 1989, p. 322), but in the sense that reorganisations were a product of privatisation, we wish to capture such effects. The data still provide, therefore, a useful insight into the way that privatised firms have changed.

The income distribution data were supplemented with figures on the rate of return on capital employed from chapter 6. Also reported are figures for changes in wages per employee compared with national movements in wages. This series was introduced to shed light on whether the relative position of employees in the wage league had changed after privatisation. It should be obvious that the resulting figures are only broad brush because of the aggregated nature of the wage data and because a change in the relative wage level could reflect a number of possible causes. The average wage for each organisation was calculated by dividing the total employment costs by the average number employed each year. National wage data came from *CSO* series (*United Kingdom National Accounts*, various years).

EMPLOYMENT, INCOME DISTRIBUTION AND WAGE RELATIVITIES

Following privatisation productivity and therefore cost efficiency may improve due to better use of capital (improved investment), more efficient use of labour (cost and quantity of labour used) and/or savings in bought-in inputs (out-sourcing economies). At the same time, efficiency gains may be distributed: (a) to labour in terms of higher staffing and/or real wages; (b) to shareholders in terms of bigger dividends and capital growth resulting from greater profits; and (c) to loan creditors in terms of larger interest payments. Profitability results can be affected by a redistribution of income to or from labour without there being a change in the overall value-added. For example, low profitability of public firms could be due to paying higher wages and other labour costs.

Employment

Table 8.1 provides details of the employment levels between 1979 and 1992 for each of the eleven organisations. Looking at each organisation in turn and starting with British Airways (BA), in the early 1980s the airline suffered major financial losses. As discussed in more detail in chapter 9, the survival plan agreed by management in September 1981 required a major reduction in the number of employees. Employment fell from a peak of 58,515 in 1981 to 37,247 in 1984. As the airline's fortunes recovered, employment began to creep up again so that by 1991 it was almost back to its pre-crisis level. This employment growth is exaggerated, however, by the takeover of British Caledonian in April 1988, which added around 7,000 to the labour force. If the effect of this acquisition is left out, the employment recovery is more modest. The airline recession of 1991–2 led to a slight but again temporary slimming of numbers.

In the case of the British Airports Authority (BAA) employment changed little in the run-up to privatisation in July 1987. Following privatisation, however, employment increased, though around 1,400 of this increase was accounted for by hotel acquisitions and increased security staffing at airports following the Lockerbie bombing.[2] Only relatively recently has employment begun to decline. At Britoil, employment was never larger than just over 2,700 and after increasing as the company expanded its operations from the late 1970s, it turned down after the sharp fall in oil prices in 1986. There are no figures after 1987 because the company was absorbed by BP. The record on employment for British Gas contrasts sharply with that of BAA and Britoil. After peaking in 1981 at 106,000, there was a gradual haemorrhaging of employees throughout the remainder of the 1980s. Between 1990 and 1991 employment grew again slightly but, in the face of much tougher regulation and competition since 1992, employment has declined sharply and seems set to decline much further, as explained at greater length in chapter 9. British Steel also saw a major loss of labour, which was especially sharp in the early part of the decade when the corporation was making record losses and closing plants. Since privatisation there has been a further fall in the size of the workforce to just under 40,000 in 1995. This contrasts with over 191,000 employees in 1979.

Assessing the change in employment at British Aerospace is greatly complicated by the spate of acquisitions undertaken by the company from 1987. Employment declined between 1982 and 1986 and increased later in the decade. This increase is entirely accounted for by acquisitions such as

Table 8.1 Privatised companies: average number employed 1979–95

Year[4]	British Airways	British Airports Authority	Britoil	British Gas	British Steel	British Aerospace	Jaguar	Rolls-Royce	National Freight	Associated British Ports	British Telecom
1979	57,741	7,298	1,423	101,600	191,500	73,400	n/a	57,800	35,922	11,571	233,447
1980	56,866	7,640	2,150	103,900	176,200	77,500[1]	9,725	58,300	32,550	11,402	240,056
1981	58,515	7,417	2,238	106,000	144,900	79,180	8,286	57,400	23,943	11,037	243,391
1982	53,148	7,224	2,534	105,800	114,800	80,142	7,832	52,222	24,305	10,221	245,694
1983	45,927	7,191	2,665	103,300	94,800	77,980	8,659	46,344	23,125	9,085	248,812
1984	37,247	7,086	2,721	99,300	76,100	75,998	9,662	41,864	23,158	7,961	244,592
1985	38,240	7,061	2,724	95,600	67,800	75,645	10,440	41,406	25,732	6,876	238,304
1986	39,635	7,196	2,383	91,900	53,720	75,480	11,324	41,875	25,431	6,355	233,711
1987	40,440	7,462	1,689	88,469	54,650	93,100	12,482	42,000	28,366	5,968	236,461
1988	43,969	7,569	n/a[2]	84,587	53,720	131,600	12,835	40,900	30,510	5,478	235,633
1989	50,204	7,936		81,832	55,200	125,600	12,385	55,475	31,763	4,471	242,723
1990	52,054	9,521		80,481	54,000	127,900	12,259	65,900	33,761	3,633	247,900
1991	54,427	10,854		84,540	57,500	123,200	10,389	61,400	33,861	2,759	237,400
1992	50,409	10,338		84,023	51,600	108,500	n/a[3]	55,000	33,850	2,603	219,000
1993	48,960	8,840		79,358	45,600	96,800		49,200	32,955	2,409	183,100
1994	51,530	8,498		69,971	41,300	56,400		43,500	33,989	2,253	165,700
1995	53,060	8,171		n/a	39,800	n/a		n/a	n/a	n/a	148,900

Notes: 1 Underlining indicates before and after privatisation.
2 No figures were available for Britoil after the takeover by BP in 1988.
3 No figures were available for Jaguar after 1991.
4 Years refer to the accounting year ending in that calendar year.

the Royal Ordnance factories, the Dutch company Ballast Nedam and Rover cars. The purchase of Rover added 42,300 to the employment total in 1988. At the same time, the contraction in labour earlier in the decade was only modest. On balance, there is no evidence that privatisation led to a major change in employment. The recession of the early 1990s, along with defence budget cuts, seems to have been far more significant in terms of shaking-out labour. The number employed fell from 123,200 in 1991 to 56,400 in 1994. This decline has been accelerated by recent divestments; in early 1995 British Aerospace sold its car division, Rover, to the German company, BMW.

Turning to Jaguar, employment declined initially but began to rise before privatisation and rose swiftly afterwards. Job cuts came from 1990 under a major rationalisation programme following Ford's takeover of the company, though detailed employment figures have not been published by the company. In July 1993 there were reported in the press to be 6,700 employees (*Sunday Times*, 18 July 1993). Rolls-Royce also appears to have increased its employment levels after privatisation, but in this case it seems that the sharp increase in numbers between 1988 and 1989 was accounted for by the takeover of the engineering firm NEI. Like a number of the other enterprises studied, big job losses were associated with the recession after 1989.

National Freight recorded a decline in employment prior to privatisation in 1981 and, for the first five years in the private sector, the number employed varied only slightly. From 1986–7 until the recession, however, employment rose, though once again there were a number of business acquisitions. At ABP we find the clearest record of continuous economies in the use of labour. The company inherited nineteen ports from the British Transport Docks Board and a history of restrictive working practices (for a fuller discussion see chapter 9). Employment had been declining from the 1960s with the development of containerisation, but the business provides an example of a state-owned firm where there was still considerable scope for employment economies after privatisation. Clearly the opportunity was well and truly grasped. Between 1979 and 1994 employment fell from 11,571 to 2,252 with most of this occurring after the transfer to the private sector in February 1983. Lastly, BT added labour up to 1983. After a small dip in employment immediately following privatisation, the number employed had almost returned to its 1983 level by the end of the decade. Only relatively recently, after a tightening of the regulatory noose and the introduction of increased competition in the telecoms market, has BT mounted a major reorganisation aimed at securing large reductions in its labour force. BT faces growing competition from Mercury Communications, business service suppliers and cable operators (Parker, 1994b). By 1995 employment had fallen to below 150,000 and further job losses have been announced.

Income distribution and rates of return

Table 8.2 gives details of the share of income: (a) going to labour in salaries, wages, pensions and national insurance charges; (b) broadly attributable to owners (government and later shareholders) in terms of profits before interest and tax; (c) the amount accounted for by depreciation charges; and (d) the amount spent on other inputs, including purchases of materials, components and energy. The table also repeats the figures in Table 6.1 above relating to rates of return on net assets. In each case the results are presented as annual averages for the nationalisation, pre-privatisation, post-announcement, post-privatisation, recession and latest periods, as defined earlier in Table 3.2.

Starting again with BA, the figures confirm that the share of wages in income fell during the pre-privatisation period but rose following privatisation and especially during the recession period. This reflects the recovery in employment in the second half of the 1980s referred to earlier. Profit and interest, the return to capital, also rose before privatisation. This is illustrated by the reversal in the poor profit share and rate of return figures during the latter period of nationalisation. It is also evident that a profit share of around 7 per cent has been maintained, despite the rise in labour's share of income in the later 1980s. The figures show how this was achieved. Savings have come from economies in other costs. This has been assisted by lower aviation fuel prices since the mid-1980s.

Turning to BAA, the share of income paid to labour fell during the 1980s, the decline beginning under nationalisation. Indeed, there is almost a continuous decline in labour's share of income from 1979 with only a brief respite in the early 1990s. Some of the sharp increase in the profit share from operations and initially in the rate of return on capital is explained by economies in wages. But another factor has been the sharp fall in income accounted for by depreciation. Again this does not seem to have been obviously related to privatisation. The share of income accounted for by depreciation began declining under state ownership and resulted from extending the expected life of capital assets, especially buildings and runways. The percentage of income accounted for by other inputs appears to have fluctuated over the periods studied. The fall in the rate of return on assets, despite a higher profit share, may be a product of frequent asset revaluations.

Britoil's results show initially a rising and healthy trend in profitability. This was associated with rising output from the investments made in the late 1970s in North Sea oil fields. Profits were, however, hit by the sudden collapse in world oil prices in 1986. Throughout, labour's share of income was extremely low and declined gradually. The major change was an increasing share of income paid out for other inputs and in particular for purchased petroleum. The value of purchased petroleum rose from £51mn in 1982–3 to £332mn in 1984–5.

In the case of British Gas, the rate of return on capital grew modestly after privatisation from around 5 per cent to a peak of 7.6 per cent in 1991 (at current cost). The rise in the share of income going to profits and interest payments was mainly at the expense of income paid out as wages, although since privatisation there also appears to have been some economies in the use of other inputs. Since 1993, profits have slumped in the face of large redundancy costs associated with a major reorganisation of capacity ahead of the liberalisation of the domestic gas market from 1996.

Extremely large losses were recorded by British Steel during the early 1980s and this is reflected in the negative share of income going to interest and profits in the nationalisation period (1 April 1981 to 31 March 1985). As another way of interpreting this, the corporation failed to generate sufficient income from its operations to cover depreciation on its capital stock and to pay for its labour, energy and materials. British Steel's fortunes changed sharply, however, in the mid-1980s as the benefits of rationalisation and restructuring came through. Profitability grew in the run-up to privatisation and initially held up surprisingly well during the severe economic recession from 1989. The share of income going to labour has remained fairly constant since the days of the major employment shake out in the early 1980s. The growth in the share of income going to capital has been partly at the expense of labour and partly achieved by some economies in the purchasing of other inputs. The corporation has made increased use of contractors and joint ventures.

Turning to British Aerospace, the share of income going to labour peaked in 1979 when privatisation was announced and fell almost continuously in subsequent years. In this case, however, the income saved did not go to profit and interest. Profitability also fell, stabilising only very recently. Instead, the additional income went to pay for other inputs. Interpreting the especially large jump in the share of income going to other inputs from the late 1980s is complicated by the purchase (and later sale) of companies, notably Rover cars, which tended to out-source. However, the growth in other input costs pre-dates the company's acquisition binge.

When Jaguar was privatised in July 1984 it initially prospered, but then fell on hard times as the US dollar weakened against sterling. The United States is Jaguar's single largest market and critically affects the company's profitability. Leaving aside the effect of exchange rate movements, the slump in Jaguar's fortunes can also be traced to inherent inefficiencies in the company. Although early rationalisation under nationalisation led to some economies in the use of other inputs, this was not sustained. Equally, there was no rationalisation in labour use to produce a decline in the share of income paid to labour. Indeed, labour's share of income grew and increased especially rapidly after 1989.

Rolls-Royce has a long and varied history. It came under state ownership in 1971 after a financial collapse related to the Lockheed RB211 engine

Table 8.2 Distribution of business income[1]

	British Airways	British Airports Authority	Britoil	British Gas	British Steel	British Aerospace	Jaguar	Rolls-Royce[4]	National Freight	Associated British Ports	BT
Nationalisation period											
Wages[1]	29.4	29.6	4.6	20.0	28.2	45.6	18.3	33.2	40.9	49.6	43.7
Profit and interest	3.0	23.3	48.4	8.3	(5.0)[2]	7.2	(0.6)	6.6	(1.9)	24.1	23.7
Depreciation	4.3	22.2	20.0	16.1	3.0	1.6	1.8	3.3	6.0	6.3	13.0
Other inputs	63.3	25.0	27.0	55.6	73.8	45.6	80.5	56.9	55.0	20.1	19.6
Rate of return[3]	5.9	16.3	41.4	4.0	(7.2)	18.8	7.6	(10.3)	(8.0)	15.4	14.7
Pre-privatisation period											
Wages	24.3	26.1	3.7	16.5	21.1	As above[6]	17.5	33.8	39.2	64.6	39.4
Profit and interest	7.6	30.1	57.2	11.3	8.6		12.2	11.4	1.5	12.0	24.2
Depreciation	4.5	20.5	15.1	10.4	3.7		1.7	4.4	3.9	5.0	12.0
Other inputs	63.6	23.3	24.0	61.8	66.6		68.6	50.4	55.4	18.4	24.4
Rate of return	21.8	19.2	47.2	5.0	10.6		25.2	6.4	7.6	9.5	19.5
Post-announcement period											
Wages	23.3	25.7	3.6	15.6	19.4	46.3	16.8	31.0	38.7	67.8	38.1
Profit and interest	7.3	30.5	52.7	11.2	12.5	7.0	13.7	15.3	0.4	6.5	23.3
Depreciation	4.8	20.5	14.5	10.3	4.0	1.6	1.6	4.4	3.7	5.2	12.7
Other inputs	64.6	23.3	29.2	62.9	64.2	46.6	67.9	49.3	57.2	20.5	25.9
Rate of return	22.9	19.0	58.9	4.8	15.4	17.0	78.1	25.9	2.0	5.3	18.3
Post-privatisation period											
Wages	25.0	24.7	3.9	15.7	20.1	37.6	18.6	30.0	37.3	60.4	34.9
Profit and interest	7.4	37.4	38.4	14.8	3.4	5.7	9.9	15.0	4.7	11.6	25.4
Depreciation	6.1	10.6	15.0	11.2	5.3	2.0	3.8	2.7	8.9	5.0	14.1
Other inputs	61.5	27.3	42.7	58.3	71.2	54.8	67.7	52.3	49.1	23.0	25.6
Rate of return	19.9	15.2	43.4	6.3	4.3	11.0	41.8	18.5	25.7	9.2	21.7

Recession period											
Wages	26.4	25.0	n/a[5]	16.1	19.5	22.3	23.3	30.1	29.8	26.4	33.9
Profit and interest	7.5	37.1		14.0	9.4	2.6	(10.8)	8.7	5.6	20.3	26.0
Depreciation	6.1	8.4		11.5	4.6	2.9	7.5	3.2	2.4	4.7	14.8
Other inputs	60.0	29.5		54.4	66.5	72.2	79.9	58.0	62.2	48.6	25.3
Rate of return	17.7	13.4		6.2	9.5	7.7	(61.0)	3.0	20.9	7.4	22.8
Latest period											
Wages	25.7	20.7	n/a	17.7	20.9	18.6	n/a[7]	30.6	30.8	21.4	29.4
Profit and interest	6.8	38.9		3.6	3.8	2.9		9.9	5.9	43.2	20.3
Depreciation	5.9	8.0		13.5	5.5	3.0		4.4	3.2	4.7	15.7
Other inputs	61.6	32.4		65.2	69.8	75.6		55.1	60.1	30.8	34.6
Rate of return	9.0	13.2		1.5	4.2	8.7		5.0	18.8	10.0	16.5

Notes: 1 With the exception of the return figure, all data are expressed as a percentage of turnover.
2 Brackets denote a negative figure
3 With the exception of Rolls-Royce, the rate of return is calculated as: profit before the deduction of interest and tax / total capital employed.
4 For Rolls-Royce, the rate of return is calculated as: profit after the deduction of interest and non-capitalised R&D expenditure but before deduction of tax / shareholder capital employed. Rate of return figures before R&D expenditure show the same trend but with a less marked decline in profitability after 1989. All figures are based on historic cost accounts, except for British Gas which reported a consistent set of current cost figures over the periods studied.
5 For Britoil post-1987 figures are not available.
6 At British Aerospace the nationalisation and pre-privatisation periods coincide because of the short period of state ownership.
7 For Jaguar post-1991 figures are not available.

contract. During the remainder of the 1970s and in the early 1980s the company's financial fortunes fluctuated (Dunsire *et al.*, 1991). The figures in Table 8.2 suggest a strong continuity in the shares of income going to the differing inputs comparing the first and last of the periods studied. Although the rate of return on capital improved sharply up to privatisation (Rolls-Royce registered a negative return on average in the nationalisation period, 1 January 1980 to 31 December 1983) and remained buoyant until the recession, gains were achieved at only a small cost in terms of the share of income going to labour and in that accounted for by other inputs. What is noteworthy about Rolls-Royce is that, despite fluctuations in the income shares, little seems to have changed between the early 1980s and the early 1990s in terms of the income distribution.

National Freight was bought from the state in a celebrated management and employee buy-out in February 1982. Those managers and workers who took the risk and bought shares in the company reaped large capital gains. Since the company was highly geared, improvements in efficiency passed smoothly through into larger shareholder profits. National Freight suffered a severe financial crisis between 1973 and 1975 associated with OPEC oil price increases at that time and a consequent economic recession. From then performance improved although profits dipped again in the 1979–81 recession. After privatisation in February 1982 profits recovered, as borne out by the figures in Table 8.2, even though margins in road transport and storage were always low because of competition. National Freight remained throughout a volume business. There were savings in terms of the share of income going to labour despite this being a management and employee buy-out. From the mid-1980s the share of income accounted for by other inputs rose. This reflects the management's policy of diversification away from bulk road haulage into higher value-added activities. Perhaps surprisingly for a distribution business, profits held up well in the much more difficult trading conditions after 1989. This is not to imply, however, that National Freight were unaffected by the recession; indeed, in some respects the company seems to have lost its way and this is discussed in the next chapter.

Like National Freight, ABP was affected by the recession at the beginning of the 1980s and again after 1989. The rate of return figures for ABP from the late 1980s are depressed by a large rise in the value of the company's net assets, particularly due to a frequent revaluation of property assets. This helps to explain the large percentage rise in the share of income going to profit, alongside the continued modest rate of return on net assets. Profits have remained buoyant of late because of the large labour savings achieved. The share of income going to wages rose in the late 1970s and early 1980s, but more recently the company has achieved a more than 60 per cent reduction in labour share. This has mainly come about because of the ending of the Dock Labour Scheme in July 1989 which is discussed in the next chapter. Since the Scheme's abolition there has been a re-emergence of the practice of sub-contracting the loading and unloading of ships and other dock work to labour-only contractors and expensive stevedoring has been effectively ended. Also, non-unionism has grown and demarcation lines have been removed.

The company's rate of return on capital peaked in the middle of the nationalisation period and then declined. It did not recover fully until 1987 and similarly the profit share did not reach a new high, of 34.5 per cent, until 1989. The average figure for the subsequent recession period, 21.7 per cent, is depressed by very poor profits in 1992. If this year is left out of the calculation then the period since 1989 shows a much higher profit share (at 28.6 per cent). The poor profit figure for 1992 reflects the company's diversification into property development. The company inherited large amounts of underutilised land and property sales and development paid handsomely in the late 1980s, when there was a property market boom. By 1987, half of the company's profits were generated by property-related transactions. The collapse of the property market after 1989 necessitated large provisions against profits, especially in 1992.

Lastly, BT's figures show that, although employment in the company did not fall significantly until recently, the share of wages in total income declined over the periods studied. This provided scope for the company to improve both profit margins and the return on capital, although recently the effects of stiffer regulation and increased competition have caused a downturn in the rate of return. It is noticeable that the decline in labour's share of income has only been partially accounted for by a growth in the profit share. The remainder is explained by an increase in the purchase of other inputs and higher depreciation charges. The rate of return on capital, however, has increased until late and it might be expected that it is this financial indicator, rather than the profit share, which most influences the regulator when setting the price cap. The rise in the share of income going to depreciation and especially other inputs seems, therefore, more likely to be associated with major restructuring within BT rather than the disincentive effects of state regulation.

Wage relativities

If public ownership is associated with successful rent seeking by public sector unions we might expect the relative position of employees in the wage league to deteriorate after privatisation. This was assessed by comparing the average wage per employee with the average wage per capita in the whole economy, though in the case of manufacturing firms – British Gas, British Steel, British Aerospace, Jaguar and Rolls-Royce – a comparison was made with wages in manufacturing (a comparison with wages in the whole economy was also carried out and showed the same trend so this is not reported).

The way wages are compared here is crude and some allowance should be made for this. It is to be expected that wages will be affected by productivity changes in organisations. Also, an average wage figure calculated by dividing the wages paid by the number employed can be distorted by changes in the hours worked and by changes in the composition of the labour force. For example, more part-time staff and less full-time staff or more unskilled employees and less skilled workers might be employed thus reducing the average wage. At present the necessary data do not exist to adjust the real wage figure to reflect such changes.

The results are reported in Table 8.3. In general, the relative position of BA employees changed little over most of the periods studied and actually improved in the last few years. In the nationalisation period the average wage in the corporation was 82 per cent higher than the national average wage. By the mid-1990s this had risen to around 99 per cent higher. In the case of BAA and more especially British Aerospace there was an opposite gradual trend until recently – in most of the companies relative wages have risen since the recession. In Britoil there was a large increase in relative average earnings as the company benefited from rising oil and gas output in the early 1990s. Turning to British Gas, the run-up to privatisation seems to have been associated with a fall in relative wages, but an especially sharp deterioration in the relative wage position set in after privatisation. This trend has been just as sharply reversed recently, however, and this reflects perhaps a change in the composition of the labour force in favour of higher paid employees during the current capacity rationalisation. A similar trend is evident for British Steel and Rolls-Royce, though the recent recovery in the relative wage at British Steel has been less marked.

Turning to Jaguar, the extent to which management lost control of costs following privatisation is apparent. Relative wages rose by ten percentage points immediately after privatisation. In National Freight wages were always relatively low compared to national wages reflecting the low skill levels of many of its staff. The relative wage improved slightly after privatisation and then fell back before recovering after 1992. In ABP where, as we saw earlier, employment has fallen dramatically, for those who retained their jobs the average relative wage actually seems to have improved up to privatisation and immediately after. More recently, however, there has been a marked deterioration in relative wages. This corresponds with the ending of the Dock Labour Scheme in July 1989. Lastly, the record for BT suggests that on average its employees maintained their relative wage position in the run-up to privatisation and after and, since 1993, have actually improved their rating.

CONCLUSION

In this chapter we have looked at income shares and profitability in our sample of eleven major firms that were privatised in the UK in the 1980s. As

Table 8.3 Wages per employee relative to those in the economy as a whole

Percentage of national per capita wage paid, on average, to employees[1]

Organisation	Nationalisation period	Pre-privatisation period	Post-announcement period	Post-privatisation period	Recession period	Latest period
British Airways	182	183	182	183	187	199
British Airports Authority	154	148	148	147	146	151
Britoil	198	204	215	222	n/a[2]	n/a
British Gas	133	127·	123	108	112	135
British Steel	130	126	118	111	113	115
British Aerospace	134	134	136	124	117	122
Jaguar	118[3]	119	119	129	126	n/a
Rolls-Royce	119	122	118	112	110	123
National Freight	84	84	86	90	88	92
Associated British Ports	121	129	124	133	125	120
British Telecom	141	144	143	141	142	154

Notes: 1 The data are for wages per employee in each organisation relative to wages per capita in the UK economy or manufacturing industry expressed as a percentage (for example, a figure of 154 means that wages were 54 per cent higher in the organisation than in the economy or manufacturing in the period studied). For British Gas, British Steel, British Aerospace, Jaguar and Rolls-Royce wages are expressed in relation to wages in manufacturing. For the other organisations, the comparison is with wages in the whole economy.
2 n/a = not available.
3 For Jaguar, the figure for the nationalisation period is for 1983 only. No reliable wages data are available for earlier years.

explained at the outset, it might be expected that privatisation would be associated with a greater interest on the part of management in making profits and that this would in turn be reflected in a higher rate of return on capital and in the share of income going to profit. Comparing the nationalisation period with subsequent periods, it is evident that profits did rise in the run-up to privatisation, as also discussed in chapter 6. Only in the cases of ABP and British Aerospace does this seem not to have been true (though interpreting the British Aerospace figures is complicated by the pre-privatisation period overlapping with the nationalisation period). Since privatisation the picture is somewhat more mixed with a number of the companies suffering a deterioration in profitability, especially during the recession (at Jaguar profits crashed). More generally, however, privatisation, when interpreted to include the run-up to privatisation, does seem to have been associated with higher profitability.

Another expectation is that privatisation will be to the disadvantage of the workforce; it will lead to a labour shake out and a deterioration in wages for those who retain their jobs. This expectation received partial confirmation. The picture is most mixed in terms of employment. Large job cuts have been posted by British Gas, British Steel, ABP and more recently BT. But in the other organisations there seems to have been a more marginal loss of jobs or even a rise in employment (though the effect of business acquisitions complicates the interpretation of some of the figures). In addition, British Gas and British Steel began cutting their labour forces long before privatisation was mooted.

Turning to relative wages, these declined in the run-up to privatisation at BAA, British Gas and British Steel. They declined immediately after privatisation at BAA, British Gas, British Steel, British Aerospace and Rolls-Royce. Most recent figures do show wage relativities recovering, however, in most of the companies. The exception is ABP, where there is evidence of a sharp fall in wage relativities after 1989. Comparing simply the nationalisation period and the latest period, the wage relativity figure has remained more or less the same at British Gas, improved at BA, Rolls-Royce, National Freight and BT and declined at BAA, British Steel, British Aerospace and ABP. There is a lack of data to make such a comparison in the case of the other two companies, Jaguar and Britoil and it is important in all cases to treat carefully the averages reported. Average wage figures provide no information on the distribution of wages amongst different groups of employees. In particular, a rising average figure may simply reflect the sacking of lower paid workers. Also, it is well known that generally the growth in earnings of top managers has outstripped the growth in pay amongst those lower down the organisation. In terms of the *share* of income going to labour, this has declined in all cases (except for Jaguar up to 1991).

A further argument concerned expenditures on non-labour and capital inputs. The expectation is that privatised companies will search for income gains in terms of more efficient purchasing of supplies. Looking at the shares of income going to other inputs, across the entire periods studied, the shares have fluctuated. They have changed markedly in just under half of the cases – Britoil, British Aerospace, Jaguar, ABP and more recently at National Freight – and more marginally at British Steel, BAA and BT. This development may have reflected a change in policy on out-sourcing in a bid to raise efficiency. Equally it may reflect diversification policies and business acquisitions associated with restructuring the businesses. To be precise about the reasons for these changes requires further research.

Lastly the following observations can be made about privatisation and regulation. Three of the firms studied were privatised as state-regulated concerns: BT, British Gas and BAA. If regulation leads to a smaller incentive to increase efficiency, then we might expect to find fewer changes in terms of profitability, employment practices and purchases of other inputs in these companies compared with the other enterprises studied. At first, following privatisation, no real differences could be found. British Gas posted a small reduction in employment, while employment rose at BAA and changed little at BT. The share of income going to wages fell in all three companies, but this was true of most of the unregulated companies too. The share of income going to profits also rose in all three companies, though only marginally at BT. The rate of return on capital, which regulators seem especially mindful to monitor, declined in the years immediately after privatisation at BAA, while at British Gas and BT it rose. There was no discernible pattern relating to the purchases of other inputs. More recently, however, regulation may have had more effect, especially on British Gas and BT, though growing competition (encouraged by the regulators) has been a further important factor. Both British Gas and BT have seen a sharp fall in the share of income going to interest and profit and in their returns on capital.

To summarise the findings, privatisation does seem to have been associated with higher profitability and labour does seem to have lost out in terms of income share, though to a much lesser degree in terms of employment and wage relativities where the picture is mixed. In a few cases there is evidence of a large change in employment and wage relativities and in the share of income going to other inputs, perhaps implying major changes in purchasing policies including policy on out-sourcing. State regulation seems to have had only a limited impact on British Gas and BT initially, but coupled with growing competition is now leading to major restructuring. This is discussed further in the next chapter.

NOTES

1 The subject of procurement policies in privatised firms is currently being researched by one of the authors of this book, David Parker, along with Professor

Andrew Cox and Lisa Harris in the Centre for Strategic Procurement Management at the University of Birmingham Business School.

2 In December 1988 a PanAm flight from London to New York was destroyed by a terrorist bomb.

9

PRIVATISATION AND BUSINESS RESTRUCTURING

INTRODUCTION

In earlier chapters the performance of eleven privatised companies in the UK has been assessed using a range of measures. What is evident from the results is the degree to which the post-privatisation performance has varied. In a number of the cases studied, productivity and value-added rose around or since the time of privatisation and there is evidence of higher profitability and lower returns to labour. At the same time, however, there are firms where productivity and value-added growth have declined since privatisation. Nor does it seem to be the case that privatisation necessarily leads to higher profitability on the one hand and lower employment and wage levels on the other (see chapter 8).

Privatisation policy has been driven by, *inter alia*, economics. Some economists have argued that private ownership introduces capital market pressures into inefficient state bureaucracies. Private property rights are expected to maximise the incentives for management to achieve a high level of production efficiency, as discussed in detail in chapters 1 and 3. But earlier empirical work, reviewed in chapter 4, and the results of our statistical studies, presented in chapters 5 to 8, suggest that the capital market may not act as an efficient disciplinarian and/or there is a greater complexity to the relationship between ownership and performance than is implied in much of the economics literature on the subject, including public choice theory. If privatisation apparently works in some cases but not in others, this implies that there are other factors that may be crucial in determining the outcome.

In this chapter we argue that in so far as ownership and competition are important, they impact on performance through *an internal adjustment process*. This raises the question: If ownership and competition do provide increased incentives to operate efficiently, how does this translate in terms of managerial decision making and business organisation within the 'black box' of the firm?

Privatisation changes the external environment of the businesses concerned. Instead of being accountable to government, which may pursue goals other than profitability, management become accountable to share-

170

holders who presumably expect high profits so as to maximise shareholder value. In addition, organisations may face more competition after privatisation. Of the eight privatised firms studied in this chapter, this is particularly true of British Telecom (BT) and British Gas, which are seeing former monopoly positions eroded. While always operating in competitive markets, three of the other firms studied (Rolls-Royce, British Steel and British Airways), also saw the degree of international competition intensify during the 1980s.[1] In the cases of the National Freight Corporation (NFC), Associated British Ports (ABP) and the British Airports Authority (BAA), there is less evidence of any material change in rivalry during the decade.

The property rights/public choice literature suggests that the move from state to private ownership will produce an improved performance. Similarly, the move from a monopolistic to a competitive market structure also is thought likely to bring about an improvement. Economists do not dwell, however, on *precisely how* these changes are likely to affect performance, except that both ownership and competition are believed to create incentives for management to search out internal cost savings. Of much less concern has been what impact these changes might have on the firm internally. This largely stems from the dominance of the perfect competition theory of the firm in economics, within which the firm can be regarded as a 'black box' with no discretion over resource allocation issues. The assumptions of the perfectly competitive model allow the innards of the firm to be ignored as each firm is forced to be X-efficient and to produce that level of output where marginal cost equals the market price. Failure to abide by these rules leads the firm to exit the industry. Once the perfectly competitive model is dropped, however, the firm's discretion returns. In these circumstances, delving into the 'black box' becomes rather attractive. It allows us to examine and analyse the internal changes that occur following events such as privatisation and the introduction of a competitive product market.

At one level, privatisation is about *strategic choice* or the direction in which the organisation is to move. Management in privatised companies are clear about the general way that government expects them to change, in particular to be completely self-financing, entrepreneurial and more consumer oriented. More complex is the *strategic implementation*, in the sense of ensuring that the organisation has the structures, processes and internal mind-set necessary to carry through the programme of change. If privatisation is to lead to improved performance, it implies substantial restructuring within firms. Changes must occur to complement those happening in the external environment (Woodward, 1988, 1990; Parker, 1993; Bishop and Thompson, 1994; DeGagné and Goh, 1995; Prokopenko, 1995). Whereas advocates of privatisation, and most noticeably economists, have concentrated almost entirely on the strategic choice question, much less attention has been paid to the importance of strategic implementation.

The public choice and property rights literature suggests that privatisation, via the discipline of the capital market, improves performance but says little about what changes within the black box will bring about this improvement. In this chapter we attempt to make good this omission by examining the way that privatisation impacts upon management and organisational relationships or the *internal environment of the firm*.[2]

THE INTERNAL ENVIRONMENT

Privatisation is popularly associated with a change from a bureaucratic, sluggish and badly managed organisation to one that is dynamic, entrepreneurial and customer focused. What is involved is in essence a culture change within the organisation (United Research, 1990). The change in ownership leads to increased strategic choices which in turn implies new forms of strategic implementation.[3] But so far surprisingly little research has been undertaken into the internal restructuring of privatised organisations (for some initial ideas see, for example, Dunsire et al., 1988; Metcalfe and Richards, 1990, p. 172; Richardson, 1993). In discussing the likely changes in internal characteristics, the management literature provides some, though usually indirect, guidance only (Burton and Obel, 1986; Woodward, 1988; Elcock, 1993). Within the organisational theory, organisational behaviour and strategic management literatures, the idea that there are fundamental differences between public and private sector organisations has tended to be discounted in favour of looking at performance and behaviour in terms of factors such as technology, firm size, competitive positioning, the degree of diversification, organisational structure and management style (Rainey et al., 1976; McKelvey, 1982; Barney and Ouchi, 1986; Grinyer et al., 1988; Rainey, 1989, 1991). These are characteristics that cut across ownership form. Turning to the public administration literature, whereas traditionally differences between operations in the public and private sectors were emphasised, more recently the literature has tended to stress similarities in the challenges facing both sectors and common optimal responses, for example, the use of out-sourcing.

Similarities between the public and private sectors are especially evident in contingency theories of organisational design (Lawrence and Lorsch, 1967; Thompson, 1967). The extent to which a firm achieves goodness of fit between its external environment and its structural characteristics is considered to be the decisive factor in determining performance (Mackenzie, 1986, p. 91; Barrett, 1990). Successful firms are those that achieve a strategic fit with their market environment and support strategy with appropriate structures and management processes (Miles and Snow, 1984, p. 10). In this literature Burns and Stalker's (1961) seminal classification of firms as *mechanistic* with clear hierarchical authority and controls or *organic* with less hierarchy and more lateral communication has been particularly influential. Bureaucratic and hierarchical types are said to be most appropriate to relatively stable external environments; while less stable environments suggest a need for less formal and more decentralised structures. Greater complexity in the external environment implies a need for structures that facilitate quick decision making (Mintzberg, 1979). By contrast, hierarchies are to be preferred in situations of high asset specificity, thin markets, conditions of high complexity, uncertainty and infrequency of transaction, when information impactedness and opportunism are likely to be present and important (Williamson, 1975). In so far as public sector tasks are more clearly defined and static, it may be deduced from this argument that the mechanistic form of organisational structure will be the more appropriate to the public sector, while entrepreneurial private operators will tend to adopt more organic forms of organisation. Nevertheless, in the literature the mechanistic and organic labels were not intended to be applied specifically to public and private sector organisations respectively. It was expected that some private-sector firms would be mechanistic and that public sector firms could be organic.

There can be no doubt that public sector activities have been associated with bureaucracy, but bureaucracy may be more a function of the size of the organisation than legal ownership. A number of empirical studies contrasting the structural characteristics of certain public and private sector organisations have found that characteristics affecting organisational tasks and functions are much more important in determining structures than ownership (for example, Haas *et al.*, 1966; Pugh *et al.*, 1969; also see the discussion of this literature in Rainey, 1991, p. 16 *et seq.*). Wilson (1989) informs us that to ensure a standard product delivery the McDonald's Corporation has a detailed operations manual for its fast-food operation weighing four pounds and extending to some 600 pages. In any event, bureaucracy is not always a bad thing (Goodsell, 1985) and as Hammer and Champy (1993, p. 48) comment: 'If you dislike bureaucracy in your company, try getting by without it'. In the public sector, bureaucracy has been a source of strength in terms of organising and administering large and complex systems and in preventing corruption and misuse of power.

COMPARING THE PUBLIC AND PRIVATE SECTORS

The public and private sectors may include similarities which blur the distinctions between them. At the same time, however, possible differences in environments, constraints, incentives and cultures can be identified. These differences provide a pointer to the ways is which privatisation impacts on performance and, importantly, why sometimes it may fail to do so. The differences relate to the degree of external intervention, an emphasis on rules over discretion and the complexity of strategy formulation and implementation in state organisations.

External intervention

In much of the private sector senior management is ultimately accountable to shareholders and is subject to scrutiny of its policies by the financial institutions which are the major investors and creditors. Annual meetings with shareholders have to be endured and there are frequent meetings with key investors. But by contrast to the state sector, the degree of external intervention in management is usually much smaller and more predictable. This is because state organisations are susceptible to arbitrary political intervention by ministers. Even when the constitutional position of the organisation is supposed to prevent meddling in day-to-day management (as in the public corporations in the UK), experience suggests that political pressures lead to frequent intervention. In terms of the agent–principal argument reviewed in chapter 1, the position of management as agents is more complicated because ownership is more diffused and ambiguous in the public sector than it is in the private sector. Indeed, it may not be entirely clear who is *the* principal for a public sector organisation. The minister, the sponsoring government department and its officials, parliament and the public or taxpayers are all possible contenders.

In turn the more ambiguous agent–principal relationship can lead to more complexity in decision making in the public sector (Hickson *et al.*, 1986; Bozeman and Straussman, 1990). Public sector managers may feel that they too have to satisfy numerous stakeholders (workforce, political masters, local community and consumers), but with the weighting on each changing according to political imperatives. The resulting lack of clarity about purpose can lead to confusion and demoralisation. When state-sector managers appeared before Parliamentary Committees in the 1960s they complained most frequently of inconsistent political direction (*Select Committee on Nationalised Industries*, 1968, paragraphs 89 and 117; Robson, 1969).

The rule book

Under their founding statutes usually public sector organisations are supposed to perform efficiently, while at the same time ensuring public accountability, legality, equity in treatment, standardisation, accuracy and probity in behaviour (Weiss, 1974; Wildavsky, 1979). In sum, the goals are often ill-defined in terms of content and weightings, which makes them vulnerable to the shifting sands of political advantage (this is discussed in more detail in chapter 3). In addition, public-sector managers must ensure that mistakes are avoided that could lead to embarrassment of their political masters. This leads to incoherence in public sector management and managerial cautiousness, low innovation and inflexibility (Stewart and Ranson, 1988).

In this environment, consistency of decision making is sought through a culture developed around professional values and procedural norms and rules (Flynn, 1988, p. 29). Professional values and procedures act to protect the organisation from arbitrary political intervention. In Charles Handy's terminology, state bureaucracies have 'role cultures' conducive to routine and programmed activities (Handy, 1986). With a lack of clarity regarding outputs, the focus of attention in terms of performance measurement tends to lie in inputs (Joubert, 1988; Jackson, 1995). With no bottom line of profit, public sector organisations are inclined to measure their performance in terms of input or process-based measures, for example numbers employed or number of letters answered or cases dealt with. In turn, where outcomes are not easily measurable, the risk of political intervention increases. Political decisions which distort resource use are less easily identified and even when identified, the consequences may be unquantifiable.

Traditionally the public sector has been associated with a strict hierarchy of accountability. This has necessitated clear chains of command and tight central control through detailed rules or the 'rule book'. The fact that the chief executive, chairman or the permanent secretary is accountable through government ministers to Parliament encourages the maintenance of a pyramid structure, reporting up for decision making purposes, and a plethora of highly defined procedures to maintain consistency in working.

In steep pyramid forms of organisation, communications tend to become formal and complex, with information being subject to noise as it flows along the chain of command. Cumbersome reporting relationships mean that bureaucracies can become insular and ritualistic, reactive and inward looking. Potential problems are exacerbated in the public sector by a tendency to under-invest in management information systems. In part this also reflects a lack of clarity about goal – what should be reported and why?

The public sector is commonly equated with the written memo, red-tape and formal committee meetings, though communications may not be more formal than in similarly sized organisations in the private sector. For example, Ammons and Newell (1989) found that mayors and city executives in the USA spent no more time in scheduled meetings than their counterparts in the private sector.

Formalised strategy formulation and implementation

Research suggests that in the public sector policy making is often highly structured with an emphasis on deliberate strategies. This can lead to a formalised and numbers driven style of strategy formulation or planning (Dror, 1971; Allaire and Firsirotu, 1990). The interest in highly formal and visible corporate plans can be part of a PR exercise. Public sector managers may feel that they are *expected* to plan; it gives a semblance of them being in control. Also, a plan may be required by the sponsoring government department (Langley, 1988). Equally, planning can be a means by which management acts to limit political meddling (see, for example, Mintzberg, 1994, p. 354, and his discussion of the role of planning in Air France). By setting out and agreeing precise goals and the means to achieve them, public-sector managers may hope to head-off political interference. Al-Bazzaz and Grinyer (1981, p. 163) found more written planning in the four nationalised companies in their sample than in the other firms they studied.

Such formalised planning often becomes ritualistic, summed up in the term 'the annual planning round'. Equally, planning can act, intentionally or unintentionally, to reinforce the status quo. Plans can prevent strategy emerging incrementally according to changes in the external environment, such as changes in demand conditions. Despite the existence of highly formalised planning in the public sector, consequently there can often be a sense of strategic drift. Public-sector organisations may find it difficult to evolve and change. Ring and Perry (1985) found public-sector managers were less likely than their private-sector counterparts to make large shifts in terms of decision making and were more likely to pursue limited objectives. At least in part, strategic drift occurs because there is far less freedom for top management in the public sector to make strategy (Sorensen, 1993, pp. 230–40). Managers are more likely to be administering strategies designed elsewhere in the political system.

What this amounts to is a dominance in the public sector of what Argyris and Schon (1978) labelled 'single-loop learning'. Under single-loop learning new skills are added to what has already been mastered. This translates into an emphasis upon fine-tuning existing ways of working, or what Hofstede (1981) called 'dynamic conservatism', when what may be required is 'double-loop learning', where old methods are jettisoned and new approaches are adopted. There is certainly evidence that top managers in the public sector have to concern themselves much more with petty day-to-day management matters than their counterparts in the private sector (Mellon, 1993, p. 29) and this may divert their energies from strategic appraisal.

Strategy formulation and implementation is also affected by motivation. In the public sector pay tends to be linked to longevity within the post (salary gradings) rather than with performance, as in much (though by no means all) of the private sector. Also, secure employment has traditionally been a hallmark of the public sector with few redundancies and with dismissal usually occurring only for clear breaches of regulations. Such an environment favours a cautious and incremental style of management.

Moreover, the terms of employment may lead to a particular type of person being attracted to working in the public sector. Research in this area is patchy and on the whole not conclusive. Nevertheless, there is some evidence that public-sector employees may be more concerned with job security than pay (Rainey, 1991, p. 131 *et seq.*) and that they differ from private-sector employees, not in being lazy and bureaucratic, but in terms of 'work-related values, reward preferences, needs, and personality types' (Kettl, 1988, pp. 12–13; Wittmer, 1991, p. 369). When working they may achieve lower levels of job satisfaction and commitment, especially at managerial grades. Research also suggests that public-sector workers may place a higher value on public service and a lower value on financial rewards; perceive a weaker relationship between pay, promotion and job security; and that public-sector management may be less enthusiastic about the possibility and desirability of change (Dopson and Stewart, 1990, p. 38).

It has also been suggested that authority limits are a key ingredient in defining publicness (Nutt and Backoff, 1992, p. 46). Where government sets charges, borrowing and capital expenditures for state organisations and is inclined to intervene in other matters, there is precious little scope for managerial discretion in terms of strategy formulation and implementation. Not surprisingly, therefore, there is empirical evidence that public managers see their environment as *predictable but complex*; whereas private managers see the environment as *simple but in a state of flux* (Pugh and Hickson, 1976). In the public sector competitors are known (or non-existent), technology changes slowly, and prices and financing are determined along agreed lines. What uncertainty there is results from the political interface, where there is a kind of 'fishbowl management' (Blumenthal, 1983). Open to more public scrutiny through the political machinery and perhaps in terms of media attention, the public sector manager may seek to become a defender, set on protecting the organisation from outside attack. It is hardly surprising if the management style is consequently risk averse (Miles, 1982).

PRIVATISATION AND THE MANAGEMENT OF CHANGE

The above discussion suggests that, though there are similarities between the public and private sectors, there are certain possible differences in operations and focus. It is presumably in respect of these differences that privatisation must impact if it is to lead to significant performance improvement. Table 9.1 provides a list of stereotypical distinctions between the public and private sectors. The distinctions are stereotypes, since, as we have seen, such sharp differences between public- and private-sector organisations may not always exist. Such a listing does provide, however, a useful benchmark for analysing the possible impact of any privatisation.

The distinctions are summarised under six headings and in our view it is in terms of changes within these characteristics that privatisation or quasi-privatisation can be expected to impact on performance. The six characteristics are: goals; management; labour; communications and reporting systems; organisational structure; and nature and location of the business.

The following discussion sets out the expected direction of change for five of these characteristics when privatisation occurs. Unfortunately, we were unable to obtain sufficient information on internal communications and

Table 9.1 Stereotypical distinctions between the public and private sectors

Public sector	Private sector
Management	
Agent–principal relationship: blurred	Clear
Orientation: inward/production/professional interests	Consumer/marketing focus
Style: reactive	Proactive
Politically constrained	Stakeholder interests but less constrained
Goals	
Multiple and sometimes vague and conflicting (public interest)	Uni-dimensional(profit)
Equity and probity	Entrepreneurial
Closed system leading to continuity/consistency	Open/adaptable
Focus on inputs	Focus on outputs/outcomes
Non-market prices/state subsidies	Market prices/subsidy free
Organisational structure	
Hierarchical pyramid/centralised	Decentralised/diversified
Functional	Business based/profit centres
Labour	
High unionisation/centralised bargaining	Lower unionisation/decentralised bargaining
Salary gradings	Employment based on performance
High security of employment	Less security of employment
Communications and reporting systems	
Bureaucratic and formal/external environment more static	Non-bureaucratic/informal/external environment more turbulent
Internal communication via written memoranda	More face-to-face
Formal committee structures	*Ad hoc* team working
Rule book procedures	Financial targets; outcomes
Accounting and management information systems under-developed	Strong accounting and MIS systems
Nature and location of the business	
Politically and geographically constrained	Commercially determined
Business development limited	Diversification, investment and divestment/mergers/overseas ventures
Location: mainly national	International/global orientation

reporting systems in the organisations studied to comment usefully on this characteristic.[4] Also, the discussion is limited to eight of the eleven firms whose performance was studied in earlier chapters. Two of the three omitted organisations, Britoil and Jaguar, were taken over by large transnational companies a few years after their privatisation. This prevents a useful discussion of internal changes within these organisations. The third, British Aerospace, has undergone a particularly complex number of changes and therefore for reasons of space discussion could not be included here. Those readers particularly interested in British Aerospace should see Dunsire *et al.*, 1991, for an overview.

Goals

Perhaps the most obvious way in which we might expect a privatised organisation to change is in terms of its goals or objectives. Freed from political intervention, the expectation would be that emphasis will switch towards commercial goals. In the UK state-owned firms were expected to perform efficiently and at various times had economic, financial and service level performance targets to meet: from the 1960s rate of return targets and test discount rates and, after 1978, required rates of return and service-quality measures (Winward, 1994). At the same time, however, and as already discussed in chapter 3, state-owned firms were expected to pursue goals that were generally incompatible with these targets, including macro-economic goals concerned with employment and inflation, and concern for equity, probity and accountability in service delivery. By contrast, private-sector firms exist primarily to make profits for their owners. The expectation, therefore, is that privatisation will be associated with more emphasis on making profits and this is borne out by the profit figures reported in the previous chapters. During the 1980s profitability, as measured by the rate of return on net assets, grew in nearly all of the eight organisations, although much of the profit growth occurred in the run-up to privatisation, that is to say while the firms were still state-owned. ABP is the main exception, where most of the profit improvement came later when staff cuts intensified and working practices were radically altered. The recession from 1989 did lead to a fall in profits in a number of the privatised firms, in common with a fall in profitability across the economy.

Commercial success and profits can only come in a competitive market environment from winning and retaining customers. Therefore, one important indicator of a determination to be more profitable will be a new interest in marketing and customer service. Any earlier 'production orientation', in which engineering and production staff dominate decision making, should give way to a 'marketing focus'. The degree to which there was such a change in the character of the organisation may be expected to depend upon the degree to which it operated in a competitive market both before and after privatisation. Those privatised organisations which have traditionally had to compete for customers are likely to have inherited a stronger customer focus than those that operated in monopolistic markets. Also, organisations that face limited competition after privatisation face less external pressure to change. In the eight organisations studied the importance of competition is borne out. The most obvious change in focus occurred in BT and more recently, as competition has been introduced into gas supply, in British Gas. There has also been an important change in BA, though this arose for a different reason.

As part of the Post Office, the forerunner of BT was essentially a production-focused business, dominated by an 'excellence in engineering' culture (Carter Committee, 1978, p. 42). Prior to the 1980s marketing was almost unknown within BT and supply was very much a case of selling what the network had to offer (Duch, 1991, p. 244). Since privatisation, the company has become noticeably more market oriented (BT, 1987; Brunnen, 1989). The company has been grouped into service divisions, the marketing function has been developed and the power of the engineering function in the organisation has diminished (Morley, 1986; Smith *et al.*, 1986, 1988; Brunnen, 1989; Pitt, 1990). Launched in April 1991, 'Project Sovereign' has been the most ambitious effort yet by BT to change its approach to the consumer and has involved training courses, a new corporate image and further organisational restructuring. This change in focus has been forced on the company by growing competition in both telecommunications services and equipment supplies and by new regulatory pressures coming from the industry's regulator, the Office of Telecommunications (Oftel).

A similar movement away from a production-based focus to more emphasis upon marketing is evident at British Gas, where the old certainties of a monopoly market are also fast disappearing. The industry's regulator, the Office of Gas Supply (Ofgas), announced the gradual deregulation of gas supplies in 1991 and a series of Monopolies and Mergers Commission Reports in August and September 1993 led to a speeding up of the process (MMC, 1993). From 1998 it is intended that all of British Gas's UK markets will be open to competition.

BA's objectives in the 1970s were the usual set of meritorious commitments typically laid down by governments for state industries. The corporation was to meet target rates of return set from time to time, compete in world markets, generate sufficient cash, be a responsible employer, promote technical and commercial innovation, and adopt a practical attitude to environmental problems (BA, 1977, p. 1). In the late 1970s BA's corporate plan had looked to solving productivity problems without redundancies by doubling output (Ashworth and Forsyth, 1984; Green and Vogelsang, 1994, p. 90). This had led to an emphasis upon volume through price competition. But with increased competition margins declined, while poor labour relations and organisation led to a deterioration in service reliability (Pryke, 1981, p. 138). In 1978, for example, 40 per cent of long-haul services were delayed (Graham, 1983, p. 31). In 1981–2 the airline reported losses of £545mn.

Central to changing the orientation of BA in the 1980s was a management-driven programme aimed at instilling a commercial and competitive culture. A 'Putting the Customer First' training programme for all levels of staff in the organisation was introduced, along with new staff uniforms, aircraft livery, logo and a consumer-oriented mission statement (Labich, 1988; Hampden-Turner, 1990). New management at BA realised that air travel had become an increasingly homogeneous product with customers deciding which airline to use largely on price. If higher margins were to be earned then the product would have to be differentiated. In addition, it was clear that BA's standing with customers had been severely damaged by the fall in the quality of service in the second half of the 1970s. If BA was to prosper over the longer term there had to be large investment in marketing and in improving service quality (King, 1987).

From 1982–3 a new marketing group was created within BA drawn from younger managers and with a brief to plan and co-ordinate world-wide marketing. New marketing talent was brought into BA from fast-moving consumer goods industries with the objective of branding BA's services and differentiating the market. New products, such as World Traveller and the later launch of a new look Club World and First Class Service, were specifically aimed at differentiating the company's services from those of other airlines (Batt, 1990). This strategy was supported by a skilful advertising campaign that, prematurely, portrayed BA as 'the world's favourite airline' (Campbell-Smith 1986, p. 88).

The strategy worked. The new chairman of the corporation, appointed in February 1981, Sir John (later Lord) King, was mandated by the government 'to take all necessary steps to restore the' Group to profitability and prepare it for privatisation' (BA, 1987, p. 9). By the late 1980s BA was one of the world's most profitable airlines.

Compared with the markets served by BT and British Gas, at privatisation ABP's main business, port services, faced a competitive market. The forerunner of ABP, the British Transport Docks Board, had been losing business for many years to other ports. After privatisation ABP adopted a strategy of competing on price coupled with speed of cargo handling. Increased profitability was achieved by disposing of surplus assets and driving down costs, of which the major item was labour costs.

Turning to the other companies studied there is less evidence of a change in orientation immediately before or after privatisation. In the cases of NFC, British Steel and Rolls-Royce the markets had always been competitive and this had necessitated a commercial culture even when in the state sector. All three demonstrate a strong sense of continuity in business orientation. The same is true of BAA. The regulation after privatisation was more visible than under state ownership, but it was still largely administered through the Civil Aviation Authority (Roth, 1987; Heath, 1988).

The competitive and regulatory pressures to change, apparent in the cases of BT and British Gas, were largely absent at BAA.

Management

Research has found that good leadership is an important factor in the successful adaptation of a business to changes in the external environment (Mintzberg, 1979; Torbert, 1989; Alderson and Kakabadse, 1992). It is top management that must aim to provide the new strategic direction by example and by implementing organisational and other changes which signal the new culture (Greenwood and Hinings, 1988). In moving from the public to the private sector a form of discontinuous change is needed, involving Argyris and Schon's (1978) 'double-loop learning'. Existing practices, indeed existing thinking, needs to be challenged and this can be difficult for management steeped in a public-sector culture and ill-prepared by experience for dynamic change with its inherent tensions and risks. Certainly existing management can disrupt and thus slow down internal changes if they are mindful to do so.

Existing management may be reluctant to impose the radical changes that a new external environment requires. They may either not understand the need for change or they may have so much personal capital tied up in the status quo that they oppose change. Studies of corporate turn-arounds have therefore confirmed the importance of hiring new chairpersons and chief executives to achieve the necessary strategic shift (Bibeault, 1982; Slatter, 1984; Kotter and Hesketh, 1992).[5] Importing management with experience can also be important in bringing in the skills needed to undertake new business developments or to make good major deficiencies in accounting and marketing talent (Helm *et al.*, 1992, p. 7).

Looking at the eight organisations, there appears to be an even split between those that brought in new management from outside and those that demonstrate continuity in management. There were important senior management changes at BA, NFC, BT and BAA, though in the cases of BA and the NFC the new management were imported well before privatisation and in the case of the NFC well before the possibility of privatisation was seriously discussed. At both BA and the NFC the changes of management were triggered by financial crisis rather than the prospect of a change in ownership.

At BA new management headed by Lord King as chairman and Sir Colin Marshall as chief executive reshaped the business. Both came from outside the air transport industry; King had been chairman of the engineering group, Babcock International, while Marshall's background was in Hertz, Avis and Sears Holdings. On taking control in 1981 King began an immediate shake up of the existing management, which he considered to be wedded to the past and blackened by failure. In particular, he instituted a major board restructuring in which nine of the existing fourteen members were removed.

Management was also changed at other levels in the organisation and in their place high-fliers were promoted, many of them aged in their mid-30s. The new marketing effort was later placed under the direction of a Director of Marketing, Jim Harris, and a Head of Products and Brands, Mike Batt, who joined BA from Mars confectionery in 1987. Other noteworthy appointments included Gordon Dunlop from the Inchcape Shipping Group as Finance Director in June 1982. By 1985–6 performance appraisal schemes had been brought in for middle and senior management grades (Marshall, 1988; Campbell et al., 1990, ch. 5). Most recently, the appointment of Robert Ayling as chief executive, a former lawyer and civil servant who joined the company in 1985, has been followed by management changes to provide a flatter management structure. Ayling is on record as criticising what he perceives to be continuing vestiges of public sector culture within BA, including bureaucracy, an unwillingness to accept responsibility and inadequate staff communications (Skapinker, 1995).

At NFC, senior management changes occurred after a major financial crisis in the mid-1970s, triggered by oil price increases and a trade recession. In 1975 the corporation chalked up a deficit of £30.9mn and had to resort to borrowing to meet its interest charges. The result was a government-financed recovery package and a wholesale replacement of senior management. By 1978 there was no one left at the top of the NFC's operational management who had been there when the large losses were incurred (Thompson, 1991, p. 59). Management changes affected the entire top management team with new personnel brought in, many from BRS, one of more successful parts of the NFC's operations.[6] A majority of the new team also had earlier outside industrial or financial experience. It was this new management, headed by Sir Peter Thompson (formerly with Unilever and then BRS), that brought about the new market-focused organisation that became such a success story for privatisation in the 1980s. For the first few years following the company's transfer to the private sector the executive management remained very stable with few board changes. More recently, however, the effect of recession and a clear faltering in the NFC's performance has led to a series of board changes in an environment of crisis. First, Peter Sherlock was brought in from the brewery and leisure giant Bass in 1993 as chief executive with an agenda to shake up the company. Also a new chairman was appointed, Sir Christopher Bland, previously chairman of LWT (Holdings) plc. Sherlock was the first outsider for a number of years to be brought into the company at senior management level, but he left suddenly after only eighteen months following a bitter board-room row over future strategy. In 1994–5 five new board members were introduced, including further talent from outside the company in what was the biggest set of board changes since privatisation. Sherlock's replacement, Gerry Murphy, was appointed in June 1995.

Another organisation which imported senior management was BT. BT was established in 1981 when telecommunications was separated from the Royal Mail and other postal services. The company's first chairman, Sir George Jefferson, was appointed in October 1981 from outside the Post Office (PO). The Deputy Chairman, D. Vander Weyer, came to BT from the Barclays banking group. Of the ten members of the executive board who managed BT's transfer to the private sector, six came from outside PO telecommunications. This importing of new management continued after privatisation. Although Jefferson's successor, Sir Iain Vallance, who became chairman in October 1987, was a career BT man, of the seven executive directors on the board in 1990 four had joined since 1984, three from outside.

BAA was guided into the private sector in July 1987 under the chairmanship of Norman Payne. Payne had joined BAA in 1965 and had become its chief executive in 1972 and chairman in 1977. He remained chairman until his retirement in July 1991. Though the chairmanship of the BAA was unaffected by privatisation, there were major changes elsewhere on the board. For example, of six executive directors in 1989, five had been appointed since 1986. Moreover, in September 1990 further new blood was imported in the shape of Sir John Egan as chief executive and Dr N. Brian Smith as non-executive chairman on Payne's retirement.

In the other four organisations studied there was a much stronger sense of continuity at board level at the time of privatisation and immediately after. The changes were generally no more than should be expected as directors reach the age of retirement. British Steel underwent a large-scale restructuring involving a major slimming down of capacity in the early 1980s under a new chairman, Sir Ian MacGregor. Once again, the driving force for change was financial: in 1980–1 the corporation made a total loss of £1bn on a turnover of just under £3bn. MacGregor was appointed with a mandate from the government to place British Steel on a sound financial footing even if this meant plant closures and redundancies. It was the MacGregor restructuring programme that restored the business to profit and hence enabled privatisation to take place in December 1988 (Aylen, 1988; MMC, 1988). Although there were management changes during the restructuring, during the run-up to privatisation and immediately afterwards senior management turnover was low. The chairman at the time of privatisation, Sir Robert Scholey, had taken over from MacGregor in 1986 and had been chief executive of British Steel since 1973. When he retired in July 1992, his replacement, Sir Alastair Fame, suffered ill-health and was replaced within a year. The new chairman, Brian Moffat, had joined the company in 1968 and had been appointed to the board in 1978. Looking at other board appointments, as directors retired their replacements came almost entirely from within British Steel. Of the six executive directors in 1993, five had been with the company since 1972 or earlier.

British Gas entered the private sector with its senior management essentially intact. A sentiment of continuity was articulated by the chairman's statement on the day of the flotation: 'The company will be run in the same way in the private sector as it was as a nationalised industry' (Sir Denis Rooke quoted in Chapman, 1990, p. 28). Rooke was part of that continuity having been appointed chairman in 1976. When he retired in 1989 his successor, Robert Evans, was a career British Gas manager having joined the corporation in 1950.

Only recently, as the regulatory and competitive pressures on British Gas have built up, has the Rooke attitude become untenable. By 1993 the whole of the company's executive membership had changed and the first executive director from outside the company had been appointed. When Robert Evans retired in December 1993 he was replaced by the American, Richard Giordano, as chairman and Cedric Brown, as chief executive. Giordano was brought in from outside British Gas having most recently been chairman and chief executive of the BOC group. Giordano did not make immediate changes, but in October 1995 the company announced the departure of three of its seven executive directors in what was the biggest senior management shake-up since privatisation. This left Cedric Brown as the only executive director left on the British Gas board who had worked for the company before privatisation. In early 1996 British Gas launched the second phase of its board changes with the appointment of two new executive directors from outside, including a new finance director, and a realignment of responsibilities among top managers. In February, in the face of mounting City concern about the performance of British Gas, Cedric Brown announced his retirement.

Rolls-Royce was taken into the private sector in May 1987 under the chairmanship of Sir Francis (later Lord) Tombs, who had been elected to the board in 1982 and at a time when there were a number of other board changes. Of the eight executive directors at board level in 1990 two had careers within the company dating back to the 1950s and one since the 1970s. Only two directors had been appointed after 1984. Sir Ralph Robins became chief executive in January 1991 having joined the board in 1982, after a long career as a manager in Rolls-Royce. He succeeded Lord Tombs as chairman in October 1992. The new chief executive appointed at this time, Dr Terence Harrison, was relatively new to the board having joined in 1989. There was also a new finance director, Michael Townsend, who had joined the company in 1990. Nevertheless, the changes of board membership both before and after privatisation were gradual and privatisation does not appear to have prompted changes. Traditionally, Rolls-Royce recruited most of its senior management internally and this continued.

Turning lastly to ABP, the story is similar. Sir Keith Stuart became chairman of ABP in May 1982 and remains chairman. Before taking the chair he had been managing director of the corporation's forerunner, the British Transport Docks Board, for a number of years. Also, all of the executive directors at privatisation had been on the board since at least 1980. In general, since privatisation new board appointments have occurred only as existing directors have retired. In early 1995, of the five executive directors at board level three had long careers with ABP or its forerunner.

Employment and labour relations

Traditionally the public sector in the UK aimed to be a model employer providing secure employment and good working conditions and pay. Trade unions were recognised and usually collective bargaining was highly centralised. The trade unions have argued that privatisation leads to a deterioration in employment conditions and widespread redundancies (TUC, 1986) and this fear has been reinforced by economists who have argued that public sector organisations are over-staffed (for example, Pint, 1991; Haskel and Szymanski, 1993a). Part of the leaked Ridley Report on privatisation in 1978, when the Conservative Party was in opposition, centred on the role of privatisation in reducing the power of trade unions. A succession of Conservative Secretaries of State have justified privatisation since in similar terms (Beaumont, 1991).

It is to be expected, therefore, that privatisation will lead to important changes in employment practices, including a much reduced role for trade unions (Pendleton and Winterton, 1993). Figures on employment and wage levels were provided in the previous chapter. In terms of employment, the record varies considerably between British Steel and ABP, which recorded extensive job losses, and the other firms, where employment reductions were more modest or did not really begin until some years after privatisation. Notably in the cases of BT and British Gas, restructuring and resulting redundancies have been a product of the introduction of competition in the product market rather than of privatisation *per se*. Looking at wage levels, it seems that in most of the organisations studied those who retained their jobs may have maintained their relative wage position comparing the years immediately before privatisation with the most recent data. As stressed in the previous chapter, however, the figures computed are averages which may mask important changes in wage relativities between particular groups of employees; for example, higher pay for management and lower pay for unskilled and semi-skilled workers. Privatisation has led to some well-publicised increases in the pay and benefits of top managers.

Concentrating on specific changes in employment and employment conditions, of the eight companies studied the one that has undergone the most extensive changes is ABP. There has been a long-run trend of reduced employment in the ports as a result of new cargo-moving technology, notably containerisation. Nevertheless, on privatisation in February 1983 the management of ABP believed that the company was still seriously hampered in competition for cargo handling work by excessive staffing. Many of the working practices that led to over-staffing arose out of the National Dock Labour Scheme, which legally defined dock work and limited it to registered dock workers. Also, under the Scheme the trade union was given joint control over a number of aspects of recruitment, dismissal and disciplining, and employment was guaranteed irrespective of the actual amount of work on hand. The result was a pool of labour which had to be paid even when it was not required.

Although the management of ABP were keen for the Scheme to be axed, the government feared the economic and political consequences of a major strike in the docks and hesitated. It was not until July 1989 that the Scheme was abolished. Since then the slimming down of the workforce has been dramatic. New forms of shift working have been introduced, historic demarcation lines have been removed and a flexible labour force has been established within the company; any grade of worker can now be required to work cargoes and expensive stevedoring has been effectively ended. Also, the company has moved away from direct employment of labour, including former registered dockers. Of 1,720 registered dock workers employed in July 1989 less than fifty remained in the company's employment by the end of 1990. In the place of directly employed labour there has been a re-emergence of the practice of sub-contracting the loading and unloading of ships and other dock work to labour-only contractors. This reverses a policy in the docks from the 1960s, which had moved work in-house. The result is the restoration of a form of casualised labour (Turnbull, 1993; Turnbull and Weston, 1993). It was the abolition of the Scheme rather than the ownership change that led to these large-scale changes in employment conditions but, once privatised, government could distance itself from the employment implications of terminating the Scheme.

In addition to the ending of the National Dock Labour Scheme, there have been other important changes in employment conditions within ABP, again aimed at increasing labour flexibility. In April 1980 pay bargaining for manual grades was devolved to local ports and a job evaluation scheme dating back to 1969 was abandoned. Personal contracts were extended from senior to middle managers early in 1989, replacing nationally negotiated salaries and employment terms, and personal contracts were gradually extended to supervisory and other grades a little later. A major strike in 1989 ended in defeat for the main union in the industry, the TGWU, and since then it has been largely side-lined by management (Turnbull, 1991 and 1993, p. 186).

Another organisation where there have been substantial changes in employment and negotiating rights is British Steel, though in this case the changes were well underway before privatisation occurred. The collapse of a three-month strike over pay early in 1980 was followed by a large shake-out of labour. Between 1979 and 1984 the numbers employed fell by over 110,000. This was matched by plant closures and an increased use of subcontractors, some of whom re-hired redundant steel workers under inferior conditions of employment and pay rates (Fevre, 1986). Important changes in working practices were pushed through by management, which ended many of the traditional demarcation lines in steel plants. In particular, the boundary between production and craft areas of work and shop-floor and staff gradings was substantially modified. Also, local productivity-based bonus schemes, first introduced in 1980, became more widespread so that by the end of the 1980s quarterly productivity bonuses accounted for almost 20 per cent of workers' earnings. Today a quarter of white-collar and 35 per cent of blue-collar labour costs are variable thanks to bonus schemes. This has helped British Steel to reduce the impact of demand changes on profits in what is a highly cyclical industry (Heller, 1995). Paralleling the changes in pay, more negotiations with the union have moved to the local level; national pay bargaining ceased in December 1989, shortly after privatisation (Blyton, 1993, p. 178). Since this time pay decisions have become the responsibility of the individual businesses within British Steel. Earlier in the same year the company ended the formal negotiating role of the TUC Steel Committee.

The record on employment and labour relations is clearly one of substantial change at ABP and British Steel. But in a number of the other organisations studied the degree of change has been more limited. At BAA performance related pay was introduced for senior management in 1987 and for other management and employees in 1990 and there have also been changes along similar lines at Rolls-Royce. Turning to BA, during the run-up to the privatisation of BA employment fell, from over 58,000 in 1981 to around 40,000 by 1987, but most of this reduction relates to the financial rescue strategy introduced in September 1981. Certain restrictive working practices, for example relating to baggage handling, were removed following a show-down with industrial staff at Heathrow in April 1982 and pay was linked more closely to individual performance. But with the recovery of the airline's fortunes in the mid-1980s, the emphasis switched from cost cutting to winning the commitment of staff through improved communication and training schemes.

During the 1970s employment at British Gas remained broadly constant. But from 1980–1 the numbers employed were reduced from around 106,000 to 90,000 immediately before privatisation in late 1986. This gradual reduction in the number of workers continued after privatisation so that by 1991–2 the figure stood at 84,000. Also, more flexible patterns of working were introduced to provide a quicker response to customer service requests. Union negotiating rights and national wage bargaining, however, were largely unaffected by privatisation and experiments with performance related pay for managers have been dogged by problems. A scheme introduced in May 1993 was quickly abandoned when it threatened to become too expensive. By the end of 1993 individual contracts and pay levels existed only for senior management grades, while lower down the organisation gradings and pay continued much as they had done under state ownership. The new competitive threat, however, is now leading to major changes with sharply reduced employment and the introduction of new employment conditions.

— Like British Gas, BT faced little competition when privatised, though the pace of change intensified from the late 1980s. Initially, management proceeded cautiously in reforming working practices so as to avoid a rift with the unions. Even so industrial relations did not proceed entirely smoothly. In 1986–7 there was a serious dispute over an attempt by management to link pay increases to efficiency gains and over the introduction of changes in working practices, and in 1990 the first ever national managerial and professional staffs strike occurred. Since 1990 the regulatory and competitive pressures on BT have increased and as a result there has been a noticeably more aggressive management style. Major job losses have been announced – 30 per cent between March 1990 and March 1993 – affecting both managerial and non-managerial grades. By the early 1990s performance related pay had been introduced throughout the management structure and pay linked to performance has since been extended to other grades. Also, although the company has continued to consult and negotiate with recognised trade unions, the scope for bargaining and consultation has been gradually restricted from senior management levels downwards (Pitt, 1990; Ferner and Colling, 1993). To date there have been only minor changes in the formal positioning of the trade union within BT proper, but in some of the new subsidiary businesses set up after privatisation union negotiating rights have not been recognised. —

At the NFC in the 1970s there had been a cost-cutting mentality which had led to a fall in the workforce from 66,000 in 1969 to 24,000 by 1981. By contrast, because of business expansion following privatisation, employment gradually increased reaching around 34,000 by 1994. The most prominent feature of employment relations in the privatised NFC has been the share-ownership scheme. The NFC is different to the other organisations studied in having been privatised through a management and workforce buy-out. The percentage of employees with shares in the company rose from 37.5 per cent in 1982 to around 80 per cent by 1989. The company has also made a conscious effort to relate pay and promotion to performance through profit-sharing and an employee appraisal scheme. But at the same time trade union negotiating rights seem to have continued much as before; the main change, the decentralisation of wage negotiations in 1981, had the active support of the unions. Joint consultation has been encouraged at branch, depot and company levels and management made a major effort from the early 1980s to communicate with the workforce regarding current performance and future business strategy.

In all of the privatised companies management have stated their desire to cultivate a consensus around the need for commercial operation and to move away from a 'them and us' mentality. This has been promoted through training and communication programmes and by encouraging staff to own shares in the company and partake in other profit-sharing schemes. This is particularly true of the NFC, though studies of attitudes within the company by Bradley and Nejad (1989) and of the privatised water industry by Nichols and O'Connell Davidson (1992; also O'Connell Davidson, 1993) discount much of the hype about the resulting worker commitment and motivation. A recent survey of almost 300 middle-managers in thirty-eight privatised companies found confusion resulting from inadequate communication by top management and a fear of redundancy (Gemini Consulting, 1995).

Organisational structure

As indicated earlier a hierarchical pyramid is an obvious structure for state activities given the political need to hold a small group of senior management accountable for all of the organisation's actions. To maintain top down control, line management is instructed through the 'rule book'. The rules set out authority boundaries for grades of staff and actions to be taken under different contingencies. Little is left to chance or individual discretion.

In the light of these remarks, we would expect privatisation to lead to significant changes in organisational structure. At its most general, this would involve a movement away from a bureaucratic or mechanistic and functional structure towards a more organic and decentralised form or away from a unitary or 'u-form' structure to one that is more multi-form or 'm-form' in nature (Dunsire et al., 1988; Dunsire, 1991).[7] Functional structures tend to be associated with single and dominant business strategies; while diversity/complexity require a more varied structure (Rumelt, 1974). This may involve flattening the pyramid to encourage local decision making and accountability and the introduction of profit centres managed by their own senior management. In m-form firms the responsibility for management is devolved to individual product lines or units serving particular market segments. A related aim would be to end a culture of referring up and to judge local management by its ability to achieve performance targets. There may also be an increased use of out-sourcing for supplies previously provided in-house, as management search for means to reduce costs. In some cases separate operating companies might be established.

Certainly there is evidence of substantial restructuring along these lines at BT. The company inherited a hierarchical organisation from the Post

Office, which until 1969 had been a government department (Newman, 1986, pp. 23–4; Beesley and Laidlaw, 1989, p. 21). The structure was based around functions, some centralised at HQ level and with financial control clearly separated from line management (Pitt, 1990, p. 64; Parker, 1994b). Local managers were essentially administrators of the rules and head office directives. There was little delegation of authority (Corby, 1979, p. 84; King, 1986, p. 79; Wheatley, 1986, p. 122). The HQ lorded over ten regions and the regions lorded over 61 areas in a classic example of a pyramid of control (Harper, 1989, p. 21).

Privatisation was associated with the sweeping away of the regions in favour of geographic and later product-based divisions. The sixty-one areas were amalgamated into thirty-one districts responsible to the divisions and operating as profit centres with local management accountability for services. This was only the beginning, however, of what was to be an even more substantial restructuring. Indeed, since privatisation there seems to have been a relentless search within BT for the optimal organisational form. Accelerating changes in competition and regulation have meant a series of restructuring exercises, a new one beginning as soon as the last one has been completed. As to be expected, this has brought about a degree of organisational confusion and anxiety amongst staff.

As the organisation has changed decision-making has been pushed downwards. This has brought decision-making closer to the consumer but has not produced unqualified gain. In particular, in the period immediately after privatisation more discretion for district managers led to some loss of consistency in service quality, in what customers still perceive to be a national service. Also, the centre became worried about local management decisions that conflicted with nationally negotiated labour agreements (Ferner and Colling, 1991; Colling and Ferner, 1992). The result was some recentralisation of decisions in the late 1980s. This has not stopped, however, the sweeping away of the districts along with the regional tier of management. Many of the remaining middle-management grades at HQ have also disappeared or are about to go in a further and extensive bout of delayering (Bartram, 1994, p. 63).

Major restructuring also occurred at British Airways. Early changes resulted from the survival plan agreed with the government in September 1981, when there were large cuts in capacity and asset sales. In May 1982 the corporation was reorganised into three main divisions as profit centres, but this led to co-ordination problems. Hence, a further restructuring took place in July 1983. This imposed eight market-centred divisions alongside three business centres (cargo, charters and tours). Each market division was based on a geographical region (for example, Africa, Far East, Northern Europe). An operations division sold aircraft, pilots, cabin crew, engineering, catering and ground operations to the market centres. Headquarters consisted of an expanded number of functions, namely finance, air safety, human resources, planning, information management, legal and secretarial, market place performance, medical, public affairs, security and training. Essentially it was with this structure that BA underwent the financial recovery that permitted privatisation in 1987.

At British Gas change occurred only gradually. Pre-privatisation there was no significant restructuring. The business comprised of an HQ, responsible for co-ordination and centralised operations, for example gas purchasing and bulk transmission, and twelve regions each with its own management. This structure dated back to the formation of the corporation in 1973, the twelve regions being the legacy of an even earlier structure.

For the first two years of private ownership there was little change. In 1989, however, three business areas each under the direction of its own senior management team – gas business, exploration and production, and global gas – were created and a new local management structure began to be introduced. In 1990 the regional organisation was reviewed and streamlined and by 1991 reorganisation within the gas regions was completed with the appointment of general managers to take control of each of the ninety-one new districts. These districts were intended to cover the whole of Britain in a bid to make the company flatter and less hierarchical. This structure was soon affected, however, by the government's decision, following the Monopolies and Mergers Commission investigation in 1993, that the company should separate its trading and production activities. The aim of this restructuring was to prevent unfair competition between British Gas and new entrants into gas supply that would need to use the company's pipeline and storage system.

In response, in December 1993 British Gas announced the dismantling of its regional structure and the creation of new businesses involved in the domestic market, namely public gas supply, business gas, service, and retail. Each of the new businesses was designed to be geared to serving particular market segments with its own staffing and management. Transco was the pipeline and storage organisation to be at the heart of the new British Gas; while another part of the company was to be concerned with the selling of gas to domestic and business users, the markets facing a rapid increase in competition. As part of the reorganisation British Gas aimed to reduce bureaucracy and service delays. But in the face of growing financial pressures, compounded by unfavourable gas supply contracts entered into before privatisation and immediately after, in February 1996 the company announced plans for a further restructuring into two separate companies. The two companies are British Gas Energy, which will take over the UK supply business and Morecambe Bay gas fields, and a company to be called TransCo International, which will include all other exploration and production, gas transport and storage, power generation and businesses outside the UK.

Leaving aside the substantial closure of capacity at British Steel in the early 1980s and more recourse to out-sourcing in that industry, the extent of restructuring in the other organisations studied has been more modest than at BT, BA and recently at British Gas. Under state ownership both the NFC and ABP had highly devolved structures and these have been retained. The NFC has a holding-company structure with day-to-day management undertaken in the subsidiary companies. Privatisation saw some restructuring of business units into product-based divisions to support the development of higher value-added services and in 1988 the company was reorganised into four principal divisions concerned with distribution, transport, home services and travel and property interests (the latter proved unsuccessful and was closed in 1991). Also, since privatisation more power at the local level has been accompanied by tighter central control of strategy and development plans, though this change was underway well before privatisation (Thompson, 1991). Most recently the NFC has begun to reorganise its domestic activities after posting poor financial results.

Traditionally the British Transport Docks Board had treated each port as a profit centre and this has continued and been reinforced since the privatisation of its successor, ABP. After the acquisition of Grosvenor Square Properties Group plc in 1987 the company operated through three, largely autonomous, operating companies – ABP (the largest subsidiary and responsible for the core port operations), Grosvenor Square Properties (property development) and the Red Funnel Group (ferry operations).

At BAA recommendations of an internal study group in 1982–3 into the Authority's organisation led to some increased delegation to airport management. Most of these changes had come into effect by April 1986, however, since which time restructuring has been limited. Turning to Rolls-Royce, between 1981 and 1983 the company changed from a product-based divisional structure to one more matrix in form. Later in the decade organisational change was dominated by the acquisition of the engineering company NEI in 1988. This led in January 1991 to the formation of two separate business groupings: aerospace (responsible for aero engine design and production) and the industrial power group (responsible for power generation projects and the industrial and marine gas turbine and nuclear businesses).

British Steel introduced an m-form structure in place of a unitary form as part of its major surgery of the early 1980s. Product-based divisions became largely autonomous businesses each with its own management and HQ took on more of a supporting than a directing role. Since then this structure has been reinforced by performance targets. What other change there has been has resulted mainly from ups and downs in the demand for steel products. For example, early in 1986 the company's engineering steel business (specialist grade steels for forging), that was in difficulty, merged with the engineering steel interests of GKN, a major UK engineering firm, to form United Engineering Steels (UES). This left British Steel better positioned to concentrate upon the revitalisation of its core bulk steel operations. As part of further restructuring, in April 1989 a new Distribution Division was created and the former Tubes Division was disbanded. In 1992 British Steel's stainless operation was merged with Avesta of Sweden. In February 1995 British Steel purchased GKN's share in UES, thus taking full control of what is now Europe's largest engineering-steels producer.

Nature and location of the business

Usually public sector organisations do not have the freedom that exists in the private sector to move into new areas of activity. Activities are normally tightly controlled and legally defined. The nature of the trade of UK nationalised industries was set out in their founding statutes. Since any major extension of activities would be likely to bring the industries into competition with private sector producers, business development was highly constrained. A move to compete with the private sector quickly led to claims of unfair competition because of the possibility of taxpayer funding or cross-subsidisation from monopoly markets. Also, changing the location of state activities and closing plants aroused political friction and moving production off-shore was generally out of the question, even if it made good commercial sense. Political opposition to exporting jobs, a lack of access to capital markets and restrictions imposed by founding legislation combined to limit the functional and geographic diversification of state organisations.

A dynamic world economy and the consequent need for continuous organisational reconfiguration have sat uneasily alongside the concept of state-ownership, involving as it does highly defined firms operating in politically protected markets. In the past relatively few state-owned firms have ventured heavily into international investments, including mergers and acquisitions (a notable exception are French public enterprises). As a rule, state corporations have accounted for less than 5 per cent of a country's cross-border acquisitions activity. This record led Stevens (1992, p. 17) to conclude that 'the dilemma facing state-owned enterprises is that the pressure to internationalise their activities is growing rapidly, but that the corporate strategies needed to respond adequately are ultimately best pursued in a privatised context'.

Privatisation is an opportunity for companies to diversify and restructure with a view to repositioning both in terms of product range and geographical location. Privatisation gives management much greater freedom to develop new lines of business and close down old ones. A privatised company may use the new freedom to restructure its businesses, diversify, merge and divest activities, and perhaps relocate operations.

All of the privatised firms studied have taken advantage of the opportunity to reassess the nature and location of their business. In 1987 BA bought out its main domestic rival British Caledonian and since then has made marketing agreements with the US carriers Delta and United Airlines.[8] In

1992 it took over another domestic airline mainly concerned with charter flights and near to bankruptcy, Dan Air. BA has also taken shareholdings in US Air (25 per cent of the shares), the Australian airline Qantas (a 25 per cent shareholding), TAT the largest independent French airline (49.9 per cent of the shares), and a regional German airline Deutsche BA (a 49.9 per cent holding), though only Qantas has traded profitably.

Since privatisation NFC has concentrated upon moving away from bulk general haulage and storage services to more specialised distribution activities giving higher value-added. The first major step in developing an overseas presence was the acquisition of a large removals firm in Australia, renamed Downard-Pickfords, in December 1981. By 1985 the company had gone from owning no foreign firms to owning businesses in five overseas countries. Since then NFC has continued to pursue international acquisitions as part of a mission to be a global transport and logistics group, though disappointing German acquisitions have contributed to the firm's recent lacklustre profits. In the state sector the company was not allowed to develop property. Since privatisation NFC's income has been usefully supplemented by developing and disposing of surplus land and buildings (Foster, 1992, p. 45).

Shortly after privatisation in 1988 Rolls-Royce purchased NEI, a company primarily involved in engineering and project management and with an emphasis upon supplying power generation equipment. It is difficult to believe that this purchase, like BA's acquisition of BCal, would have gone ahead if the company had remained state-owned. Through the acquisition management aimed to reduce Rolls-Royce's exposure to cyclical demand for aero-engines, while taking control of another engineering-focused business. Another development has been a rationalisation of production involving site closures as well as foreign joint ventures and acquisitions, such as the £336mn purchase of the Allison Engine Company, a US military engine supplier in 1994. Also, although Rolls-Royce has always been active in marketing its products overseas, privatisation has given a fillip to its foreign activities.

A similar story holds for British Steel. In the early 1980s, joint ventures under the Phoenix programme and plant closures were driven by overcapacity in the European steel industry and the need to rationalise production. Since privatisation the company has strengthened its international position by overseas investments and co-operative alliances. For example, recently the company agreed a major investment in steel making capacity in the USA, in association with LTV Steel of the US and Japan's Sumitomo corporation. The company has also closed loss-making steel works kept open in Britain under state ownership for political and social reasons, most notably the Ravenscraig plant in Scotland in February 1990. Today British Steel's bulk steel making in Britain is on only four principal sites, managed in effect as two: Scunthorpe/Teeside and Llanwern/Port Talbot.

The mission of British Gas since privatisation has been to become 'a leading international exploration and production business over the next decade . . . ' (British Gas, 1991, p. 3). Since privatisation the company has aimed to increase the proportion of its profits from non-regulated activities through investments, joint ventures and the marketing of consultancy services. In 1988 a stake in Bow Valley Industries, a Canadian oil and gas company, was acquired and this was followed in March 1990 by the purchase of Canada's largest gas distributor, Consumers' Gas, though in 1994 both were re-sold. Gas distribution in Canada is highly regulated and it seems that British Gas has decided to concentrate upon investing where there are fewer trading restrictions. Today British Gas is active in over forty-five countries both directly and through joint ventures. The company has also moved back into oil and gas exploration, an activity it was made to divest prior to privatisation. The company now generates a quarter of its profits from exploration and from its global gas business.

Prior to privatisation, ABP and its forerunner the British Transport Docks Board had been heavily restricted from diversifying out of port-related activities. Parliamentary approval was required even for port development projects (Turnbull, 1993, p. 197). Since privatisation ABP has capitalised on its under-utilised dockland property for commercial and residential developments. The company has also entered into joint ventures with port users and operators, including purchasing a 40 per cent stake in Tilbury Container Services Ltd in 1992. In addition, new research and consultancy and property development subsidiaries were established in the mid-1980s.

BT has invested heavily overseas since privatisation in an effort to become a global telecommunications supplier, though, as in the case of a number of the companies, not all of the acquisitions have proved profitable. BT's post-privatisation mission statement articulates management's objective as being 'to provide world-class telecommunications and information products and services, and to develop and exploit our networks at home and overseas . . . ' (BT, *Annual Report and Accounts* 1988, n.p.). Noteworthy acquisitions immediately after privatisation included the Canadian equipment supplier Mitel (later re-sold at a loss) and ITT Dialcom, a world leader in message handling. Later acquisitions included the data communications group Tymnet, from the McDonnell Douglas Corporation in 1989, and a 20 per cent stake in MCI, the second largest US long-distance telephone company, announced in May 1993. Through alliances and joint ventures the company is now active in a number of foreign countries and is marketing managed network services internationally. Potentially of major importance is Concert, a joint venture with MCI, to provide one-shop telecommunications services for transnational corporations. During 1995 BT also formed a series of alliances and joint ventures in continental Europe, in anticipation of the further liberalisation of the EU telecommunications market from 1998.

Lastly, BAA has transformed itself from an airport operator to a retail property investor; by 1993 revenue from airport shopping exceeded income from aircraft landing fees and airport charges. BAA's stated strategy from the late 1980s was one of staying close to its airport businesses: 'our strategy is to concentrate on our core business' (BAA, 1993, p. 2). This followed some disappointing diversification immediately after privatisation. In particular, in July 1988 Lynton, a property investment and development company, was acquired, mainly to develop land around BAA's airports, though it had non-airport business. The property recession from 1989 sent Lynton into losses. A move into the building and running of airport hotels was particularly unprofitable and was reversed (Helm *et al.*, 1992). By 1992 BAA had sold its non-airport hotels and granted leases on new hotels at airports to the Forte and Hilton groups. BAA has not, however, ignored the potential for business expansion. The company won a contract to manage Pittsburgh airport's retail operations and more recently bid successfully for a ten year contract to operate the airport system for Indianapolis. The company now hopes for further US airport business and is eyeing the Australian airports, which are to be privatised in 1996. Also, BAA's consultancy work for airports overseas has continued to expand and in the last two years the company has opened two factory-outlet centres, one in Britain and one in France, to provide retail space for manufacturers to sell directly to the public. Other factory outlet shopping malls are being built and as sites are away from airports this suggests that the earlier commitment to stick to the core business has weakened.

CONCLUSION

To date privatisation has been advocated with surprisingly little exploration of the internal changes within the privatised companies that may be necessary if performance is to improve. The literature is thin when it comes to exploring the type of strategy that we might expect to see. This seems to be a product of a dialectical difference between economists on the one hand and management theorists on the other. Whereas many economists have emphasised the differences between public and private ownership and the impact on performance, the management literature has tended to be more concerned with common issues affecting organisations in the public and private sectors. In this literature ownership is but one of a large number of contingencies that might affect management behaviour and hence performance.

This chapter has been concerned with investigating internal changes when privatisation occurs. The main theme has been that the proximate source of performance improvement lies within the 'black box' of the organisation (although, of course, these changes may well be driven by pressure from the capital and/or product market). In other words, the outcome of privatisation might be dependent upon changes in the internal environment, as summarised in Figure 9.1. Table 9.2 provides a summary of the main changes in each of the eight privatised firms studied.

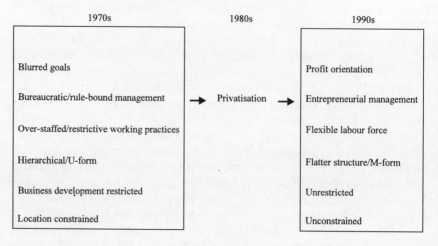

Figure 9.1 A stereotypical view of the change process from nationalised industry to private sector producer

On the one hand, what is apparent from Table 9.2 is the difference in the scale and form of restructuring across the privatised companies. In general terms, change has occurred more noticeably at BT and now at British Gas – two organisations previously largely protected from competition. By contrast, British Steel, Rolls-Royce and the NFC, in particular, have traditionally operated in a competitive market place and were therefore commercially orientated when in the state sector. Change in these three organisations since privatisation has mainly built upon structures and systems already in place. There has not been the kind of discontinuity in development evident at BT and now at British Gas. Turning to BAA and ABP, they have also continued to build on structures that pre-date privatisation, though large changes in employment and employment practices have occurred within ABP, especially since the abolition of the National Dock Labour Scheme in 1989.

On the other hand, there are certain similarities between the experiences of the eight organisations. In particular, while trade unions may have retained some negotiating rights their role has generally diminished (although this occurred throughout the entire UK economy in the 1980s). In addition, some form of performance related pay seems to have become universal, at least among management grades, and local-based pay bargaining has developed. Where privatisation may also have made a difference is in respect of the nature and location of the business. All of the organisations studied have taken advantage of the new freedom that comes from being in the private sector to invest, make acquisitions and to enter into joint ventures, both at home and overseas. BT, BA, British Gas and the

Table 9.2 Whether there have been changes in the internal environment since privatisation

	Goals	Management	Labour	Organisational structure	Nature and location of the business
British Airways (BA)	Yes: clear shift towards a consumer focus, supported by new products and marketing.	Yes: senior management and board changes after 1981. New marketing expertise.	Yes: new staff training, performance related pay. New working practices. Mainly pre-privatisation.	Yes: new profit based centres. Ending of remaining divisions between the old BEA and BOAC operations. Mainly pre-privatisation.	Yes: initial divestment of peripheral activities. Later, a move towards takeovers, e.g. BCal, shareholdings in foreign airlines, e.g. Qantas and US Air, and joint ventures, e.g. computer booking system. Mission to be a global airline.
British Gas	Limited: a more consumer oriented operation has developed only gradually.	Not immediately: came later as competition intensified.	Limited at first: increasing pace recently as competition intensifies, especially more flexible working practices and de-staffing.	Limited at first: now major restructuring of regional structure, movement towards product based divisions.	Yes: still heavy dependence on UK, though some high focus investments overseas, including joint ventures. Desire to become a global gas supplier has developed. Investments in exploration.
British Telecom (BT)	Yes: consumer orientation, under pressure from regulator and as competition has increased. Reduction of production/ engineering focus.	Yes: new chairman (outsider) from 1981. Some board changes. Some importing of staff with marketing and financial expertise.	Limited at first: recent downsizing again associated with competition. New more flexible working practices. Less favourable attitude to collective bargaining in subsidiary companies.	Yes: restless search for optimal structure. Decentralisation (followed by some recentralisation). Abolition of districts. Product based divisions.	Yes: mission to be a global telecommunications operator; joint ventures; some unhappy acquisitions e.g. Mitel.
NFC	Yes: to be more global.	Yes: but pre-dates the decision to privatise.	Yes: worker/management buy-out. More flexible working.	Limited: always devolved and product based.	Yes: takeovers and other investments overseas to support global ambitions.

Associated British Ports	Yes: new commercial orientation.	No: strong continuity.	Yes: considerable de-staffing; 1989 abolition of Dock Labour Scheme.	Limited: more use of contractors, but always had a devolved structure.	Limited: e.g. acquisition of property development company.
Rolls-Royce	No.	No: continuity and elevation from within.	Limited.	Limited: mainly resulted from acquisition of NEI.	Limited: takeover of NEI was intended to diversify the company.
British Airports Authority	Limited: profit now more important but continued emphasis upon safety and security.	No: continuity.	Limited.	Limited.	Limited and relatively unsuccessful at first. Then largely content to concentrate upon core business apart from overseas management and consulting services. Now signs of renewed expansionary ambitions.
British Steel	Yes: to reverse the staggering losses of the early 1980s and become self-financing.	Limited: new high-profile chairman imported from outside in 1980 with mandate to rationalise the industry. Other changes limited after early 1980s shake out.	Yes: decentralised negotiations, sweeping de-staffing, ending of many traditional working practices and demarcation lines.	Limited: major retrenchment and a return to more autonomous businesses operating as profit centres pre-dates decision to privatise. Demand driven reorganisation since then.	Yes: though already had overseas operations and joint ventures.

NFC have been particularly vigorous in diversifying into new business areas. With the benefit of hindsight, however, some of these diversifications have proved unwise. BT lost money on some of its early acquisitions and BA has had to make provisions against the losses notched up by US Air, in which it has a minority holding. BAA's diversification into property related ventures proved a mixed blessing when the property market slumped after 1988.

Earlier in this chapter a stereotypical view of the public and private sectors was presented (Table 9.1). What is evident from a study of the privatised firms is the diversity of change, but alongside some common themes that accord with the stereotypes. The history of each of the organisations since privatisation has reflected industry specific factors, as well as ownership change, but the following seem to be common themes:

(a) commercial goals – a clearer emphasis upon profitability to be achieved by focusing on consumer needs;
(b) employment relations – a reduced role for trade unions, the introduction of new methods of working, including the removal of traditional demarcation lines; new remuneration methods; devolved bargaining; and in some cases large job losses;
(c) organisation – a flattening of the organisational pyramid; devolved management; m-form in place of u-form structures, including the introduction of profit centres;[9]
(d) nature and location of the business – disposal of surplus assets; expansion of the business into new areas of work and new geographical regions; acquisitions and joint ventures to support a new mission to become a global operator. The repositioning of companies to combat growing international competition and to take advantage of new business opportunities overseas (sometimes associated with privatisations in other parts of the world).

It is important to stress once again, however, that the degree to which the firms have changed in these respects has varied. From the UK experience there is no simple template of internal change resulting from privatisation. Also, the degree of management change is less easy to summarise, for in this case the experience has been noticeably different across the eight firms. For example, ahead of privatisation at BA there were important changes in senior management, including the importing of a new chairman and chief executive from outside the corporation. The NFC underwent similar wide-sweeping changes in senior management at board level, but in this case in the mid-1970s and well before privatisation was planned. More contemporaneous with privatisation were the board level changes at BAA and BT. In the other organisations management change was less obvious. In these organisations there seems to have been relatively little change in the senior management over the privatisation period and for some time after. In particular, significant management changes have occurred at British Gas only recently as it has become necessary to face up to a new competitive environment.

It is interesting to consider the extent to which performance improvement is associated with internal change. Clearly there are some organisations, such as British Airways, that have registered a clear performance improvement as well as undergoing considerable changes in their internal environment since privatisation. But there are other organisations, such as ABP and British Gas, where performance has improved with a much more modest degree of internal change.

The changes that the privatised companies recorded are paralleled by those in certain other organisations that remained in the public sector, such as the coal industry, British Rail and the Post Office. Also, some of the reorganisation, notably at BT and British Gas, resulted from technological change rather than ownership. For example, micro-electronic exchanges in telecommunications, which probably would have removed large numbers of employees even if BT had remained state owned (Ferner and Colling, 1993).[10] Also, changes directly resulting from privatisation are not easy to distinguish from the effects of recession and from organisational changes affecting all parts of the economy. In the 1980s there was a general movement towards the flattening of organisational structures, more flexible labour markets, joint ventures and global trading (Ohmae, 1989).

We acknowledge, therefore, that the changes experienced within the privatised firms are part of a wider set of changes affecting the management and organisation of firms in the UK economy, and it is impossible to separate out the results of privatisation from these broader changes. Nevertheless, it is difficult to believe that the change in ownership was irrelevant. At the very least it freed management to undertake the reforms, which would have proved more difficult to introduce had the firms remained in the state sector. This is consistent with one of the government's privatisation objectives, freeing management to manage (Moore, 1983).

NOTES

1 BA has, however, consolidated its dominant position in the UK domestic market through acquisitions detailed later and has retained its leading position at Heathrow airport. This despite a recommendation by the CAA prior to privatisation that the company should surrender some landing slots to facilitate competition.

2 The chapter builds on earlier published papers, notably by Dunsire *et al.* (1988, 1991) and by Parker (1993, 1995a, 1995b).

3 As Paul Bate (1994, p. 26) reminds us: 'structure, strategy and "organization" are all important in the culture concept; when we change culture, we are, in effect, changing strategy, structure and organization'.

4 In terms of research into internal change, the subject of communications and reporting systems could be one of the most fruitful, but it is also one of the most problematic. Ideally, interviews, observations on site and access to internal memoranda are needed to track changes in the systems used and the type of

information that flows through the systems. By its very nature, however, such research is highly labour intensive and requires considerable levels of co-operation from the organisations concerned.

5 Only one of the privatisation studies discussed in chapter 4 looks in a systematic fashion at the possible connection between management change and post-privatisation performance. Megginson *et al.* (1994) discuss the turnover amongst boards of directors and top managers in fifty of the companies they study. They find that board membership and board size changed in a significant number of cases. They also find some evidence, though it is not statistically significant, of larger performance improvements in those firms that experienced the most board turnover. They conclude (p. 445): 'Changes in the firm's ownership and control structure, rather than more government divestiture or cash infusions into the firm from share issues, clearly seems to be the driving force in explaining all of the results we document in this study.'

6 BRS is British Road Services, a long-standing business within the NFC mainly concerned with domestic road-freight haulage.

7 Such organisational restructuring during the privatisation process has been observed in other countries (see, for example, Vacha, 1995, pp. 74–5).

8 The charter operations, in the shape of Caledonian Airways, were re-sold early in 1995. At the time of writing BA was negotiating an alliance with American Airlines which awaits regulatory clearance.

9 This is consistent with the findings of Bishop and Thompson (1994).

10 Since privatisation BT has invested heavily in network modernisation. For example, in 1989 digital exchanges accounted for under a quarter of all BT's exchanges yet by 1994 three-quarters of the exchanges were digital.

10

SUMMARY AND CONCLUSIONS

INTRODUCTION

Privatisation is now a major part of industrial policy in many developed and developing countries. One of the main objectives of privatisation is to improve efficiency, defined usually in terms of achieving higher productivity, lower-cost production and higher profitability. This book has been concerned with exploring the nature of the privatisation argument, considering public choice and property rights theories, the nature of efficiency and empirical studies of public versus private ownership. In particular, the performance of eleven organisations that were privatised in the UK in the 1980s has been studied using a range of performance indicators.

The empirical work presented in chapters 5–8 is based on various performance measures and has painted a mixed picture of the impact of privatisation. Here we attempt to summarise the findings. This is not an easy task. First, there is a large amount of empirical material. The performance of the privatised firms has been studied using data envelopment analysis as well as four other performance indicators – labour and total factor productivity, value-added per employee and the rate of return on capital – and data on the distribution of business income. Second, we have looked at the performance of these firms before and after privatisation but such an apparently straightforward comparison is not without its difficulties. Indeed, six different periods have been identified: in the public ownership phase there are the nationalisation, pre-privatisation and post-announcement periods; under private ownership, a post-privatisation, a recession and a latest period have been identified. If we wish to summarise the performance of these firms under public and private ownership, it is not obvious which periods should be compared. Clearly, with three periods of public ownership and three periods of private ownership, there are several possibilities. However, for nine of the eleven firms, the post-announcement period is relatively short (one or two years) and usually overlaps with another period (the pre-privatisation period). A similar objection could be raised against the use of the latest period but in this phase no firm's results are based on fewer than two years' figures and four firms' figures are based on three years' worth of data. Another complication is that although the pre-privatisation period occurs under public ownership it could be argued that this period's results reflect the effect of the anticipation of private ownership.

In the following summary of the results, we concentrate on making four comparisons: in each case we take the results for the nationalisation period to reflect the performance under public ownership and compare these with the performance under four periods of (actual or anticipated) private ownership. It is to be expected that a once-and-for-all shake-out effect might show up in a comparison of the nationalisation and pre-privatisation periods, although these are both periods of public ownership. Also, a persistent differential between the performance of public and private companies would be expected to lead to a difference between the results for the nationalisation period and all three periods under private ownership.

Within this framework, the approach adopted is to take each company in turn and to present a summary table with details of the firm's performance in the various periods but with the post-announcement period omitted for the sake of clarity. Four performance indicators are reported: labour productivity (LP) growth, total factor productivity (TFP) growth; the growth in value-added per employee; and the rate of profit. With the exception of the latter indicator, each firm's performance is relative to that for the economy as a whole or, where applicable, to that for manufacturing (for further details see chapters 5 and 6). The results of the data envelopment analysis are also discussed together with relevant material from the discussion on the distribution of business income in an attempt to construct a coherent picture of the impact of privatisation on each firm's performance. Finally, the results for all firms are brought together to see if, overall, privatisation has had any consistent impact on performance.

COMPANY RESULTS

British Airways (BA)

One consistent picture to emerge from the results in Table 10.1 is that BA's performance improved in the pre-privatisation period. The labour force had already been cut by 20 per cent between 1979 and 1983 and this contributed to considerable labour productivity growth. In the immediate pre-privatisation period, it was reduced by a further 10 per cent. Hence the further increase in the rate of labour productivity growth and the reduction in the share of income going to wages (see chapter 8). Value-added per employee soared in the pre-privatisation period, driven by employment reductions and considerably increased profitability. Thereafter, however, the results become more mixed. Labour productivity and value-added growth have been below their levels in the nationalisation period, yet TFP growth and profitability have continued to outperform the results in this period. In the latest period, however, BA's performance has deteriorated with three of the four performance indicators registering a poorer performance than in the nationalisation period. With regard to the DEA results reported in chapter 7, the basic model suggests that private ownership is associated with an improved performance but once technology and business cycle variables are included (the augmented model), this differential disappears. Since privatisation, employment has increased by one-third and the average wage paid by BA has increased considerably relative to that paid to all employees in the economy (chapter 8).

Table 10.1 Summary of performance indicators: British Airways

Performance indicator (% per annum)	Period				
	Nationalisation	*Pre-privatisation*	*Post-privatisation*	*Recession*	*Latest*
LP growth	5.1	7.7	2.3	4.2	4.1
TFP growth	1.9	2.9	6.4	5.8	−1.2
VA growth	1.5	13.1	−0.5	1.7	0.8
Rate of profit	5.9	21.8	19.9	17.7	9.0

British Airports Authority (BAA)

The results in Table 10.2 reveal a fairly consistent picture but not in the direction suggested by the public choice and property rights literatures. A comparison of the nationalisation and post-privatisation periods reveals a deterioration in all four performance indicators as does a comparison of the nationalisation and recession periods. There is no obvious difference in performance between the nationalisation and pre-privatisation periods. This latter result is confirmed by the basic DEA model, with the augmented model revealing a deterioration under private ownership (see chapter 7). In the latest period, however, substantial improvements in productivity growth have been recorded. Since privatisation in 1987, employment has increased by about 10 per cent yet the share of income paid in the form of wages has declined. There is some evidence that relative wages have fallen. The share of income going to profit has increased (by 50 per cent) while depreciation charges have been cut by a similar amount (see chapter 8).

Britoil

With the exception of TFP growth, the three other performance indicators improved in the pre-privatisation period and are also above their nationalisation levels in the post-privatisation period (see Table 10.3). The shortage of data for Britoil precluded the use of DEA in this case. Employment fell by one-third between privatisation in 1982 and the last date for which data are available (1987) although for those who remained employed the relative wage rate increased on average by one-quarter (see chapter 8).

Table 10.2 Summary of performance indicators: British Airways Authority

Performance indicator (% per annum)		Nationalisation	Pre-privatisation	Period Post-privatisation	Recession	Latest
LP growth	(1)	0.2	−1.0	−4.3	−3.8	8.9
	(2)	−0.1	2.4	−0.7	−1.5	11.7
TFP growth	(1)	1.0	−3.1	−8.5	−6.0	1.7
	(2)	0.4	0.1	−5.2	−4.0	4.2
VA growth	(2)	−0.3	1.5	−4.7	−8.6	15.0
Rate of profit		16.3	19.2	15.2	13.4	13.2

Notes: 1 Output calculated as number of air traffic movements.
2 Output calculated as turnover deflated by the retail price index for all non-food items.

Table 10.3 Summary of performance indicators: Britoil

Performance indicator (% per annum)	Nationalisation	Pre-privatisation	Period Post-privatisation	Recession	Latest
LP growth	− 3.1	−0.3	3.6	n/a[1]	n/a
TFP growth	15.2	12.5	7.4	n/a	n/a
VA growth	− 5.0	−2.7	2.3	n/a	n/a
Rate of profit	41.4	47.2	43.4	n/a	n/a

Note: 1 n/a = not available.

British Gas

The picture revealed by British Gas (in Table 10.4) is a reasonably consistent one. For all four performance indicators their pre-privatisation values are greater than the comparable nationalisation figures, and three of the four indicators are also greater in the post-privatisation period than in the first period. There is also evidence of an improvement in performance in the pre- and post-privatisation periods from the DEA results. For the recession and latest periods, however, the results are more mixed. Although the constant returns DEA model indicates an improvement in performance, labour productivity and TFP growth are lower in the recession than in the nationalisation period. In the latest period profitability and TFP growth have declined below their nationalisation values, the former probably as a result of Ofgas's determination to increase competition in the industry and the associated costs of restructuring. It should be noted, however, that if the labour productivity, TFP, and value-added results were relative to those for the economy as a whole rather than manufacturing, they would present a more favourable picture of the impact of privatisation. In the pre-privatisation period, employment fell by 15 per cent but it was only in 1993 and 1994 that further substantial job cuts were made. Until recently, relative wages

207

had decreased sharply, while the share of income going to profit and interest had increased by over two-thirds. In the latest period, however, relative wages bounced back to their nationalisation level while employment was cut by another 15 per cent.

Table 10.4 Summary of performance indicators: British Gas

Performance indicator (% per annum)	Nationalisation	Pre-privatisation	Period Post-privatisation	Recession	Latest
LP growth	−0.6	3.5	1.3	−1.0	1.8
TFP growth	−0.1	0.3	−3.2	−3.0	−4.8
VA growth	−7.2	2.5	2.2	1.0	10.1
Rate of profit	4.0	5.0	6.3	6.2	1.5

British Steel

The results for British Steel (see Table 10.5) are pleasingly consistent but not in the hypothesised direction. With the exception of the rate of profit, the value for each of the other three performance indicators is lower in the pre-privatisation, post-privatisation and recession periods than it is in the nationalisation period. Again the basic DEA model, reported in chapter 7, suggests that privatisation was associated with an improvement in performance whereas the augmented model, including technology and business cycle effects, is more consistent with the other performance results in finding no evidence of improved performance. The nationalisation period used in this study covers the period of considerable restructuring in the industry, however, and this explains the large performance gains in these years. Between 1981 and 1985, employment fell by over 50 per cent and, by 1995, had fallen by a further 20 percentage points. Relative wages have fallen too (by about 15 percentage points) and, as the share of income going to labour has declined, the share attributable to profit has increased (see chapter 8). The history of British Steel in the 1980s confirms that major restructuring can occur under both state and private ownership.

British Aerospace

Here comparisons are difficult because of the relatively short period of state ownership. While there is some evidence of an improvement in labour productivity and value-added growth, both TFP growth and the rate of profit were lower in the post-privatisation and recession periods than they were under state ownership (see Table 10.6). Similarly, neither the basic nor the augmented DEA models, reported in chapter 7, are suggestive of a performance improvement under private ownership. In the latest period,

Table 10.5 Summary of performance indicators: British Steel

Performance indicator (% per annum)	Nationalisation	Pre-privatisation	Period Post-privatisation	Recession	Latest
LP growth	19.5	7.8	−2.3	−3.6	4.3
TFP growth	7.2	0.6	−6.7	−7.7	4.2
VA growth	23.8	16.7	−10.3	−6.7	24.5
Rate of profit	−7.2	10.6	4.3	9.5	4.2

TFP growth is particularly poor yet value-added growth is unusually high. The decline in TFP is attributable to the result for 1994 when a number of companies, including Rover cars, were sold. Output fell by one-half but total expenditure on inputs fell one-third. The value-added result stems from the significant loss recorded in 1992 following restructuring in the company's regional aircraft division (15,000 jobs were axed). With the considerable number of acquisitions and sales, as well as the more recent cuts in defence budgets, it is difficult to discuss the change in employment that can be associated with privatisation. Nevertheless, since 1981, employment at British Aerospace has fallen by about one-third and relative wages appear to have fallen by about twelve percentage points (see chapter 8).

Table 10.6 Summary of performance indicators: British Aerospace

Performance indicator (% per annum)	Nationalisation	Pre-privatisation	Period Post-privatisation	Recession	Latest
LP growth	0.7	0.7	0.2	9.0	−1.2
TFP growth	−0.1	−0.1	−4.7	−4.9	−12.1
VA growth	−3.0	−3.0	−4.0	1.2	10.3
Rate of profit	18.8	18.8	11.0	7.7	8.7

Jaguar

The performance of Jaguar has been particularly poor under private ownership (see Table 10.7) up until 1991, the last year for which data are available. Apart from an improvement in the rate of profit in the pre-privatisation and post-privatisation periods, the figures for all the other performance indicators deteriorated in each of the three periods after natio-nalisation. The very high value-added growth rates in the nationalisation and pre-privatisation periods stem from two factors: first, the shortage of data leads to some overlap in the sample periods; and second, the collapse in sales in the 1980–1 recession and the consequent losses led to a very low value-added per employee figure. When sales and profits recovered, value-added bounced back and the results reflect this growth. The DEA results, reported in chapter 7, also offered little evidence of an improvement in performance under private ownership. There is some evidence that under private ownership in the late 1980s both relative wage rates and employment levels improved (see chapter 8).

Table 10.7 Summary of performance indicators: Jaguar

Performance indicator (% per annum)	Nationalisation	Pre-privatisation	Period Post-privatisation	Recession	Latest
LP growth	28.1	21.0	−0.5	−18.6	n/a[1]
TFP growth	4.3	1.5	−3.2	−16.7	n/a
VA growth	404.8	306.0	−8.3	−34.3	n/a
Rate of profit	7.6	25.2	41.8	−61.0	n/a

Note: 1 n/a = not available.

Rolls-Royce

Labour productivity and value-added growth both fell after the nationalisation period (see Table 10.8). At the same time, however, TFP growth and the rate of profit increased, although in the post-privatisation and recession periods, TFP growth remained considerably below that in UK manufacturing industry as a whole. The DEA results were also rather mixed. More recently, however, TFP growth has increased sharply at Rolls-Royce with a rate of growth far in excess of that achieved by the rest of UK manufacturing. The decline in employment, which commenced in 1980, ceased in the year before privatisation (1985) with a total loss of about one-third of all employees. Thereafter, a number of corporate acquisitions increased employment by almost two-thirds but the recent recession has seen employment fall back to just over its pre-privatisation level. Overall, there appears to have been little change in the average wage paid by the company relative to that received by all employees in the economy (see chapter 8).

Table 10.8 Summary of performance indicators: Rolls-Royce

Performance indicator (% per annum)	Nationalisation	Pre-privatisation	Period Post-privatisation	Recession	Latest
LP growth	2.6	1.8	−3.6	−1.2	1.1
TFP growth	−3.9	0.5	−4.3	−3.6	6.1
VA growth	6.7	3.4	−7.3	−11.1	12.5
Rate of profit	−10.3	6.4	18.5	3.0	5.0

National Freight Corporation (NFC)

With the exception of TFP growth, the three other performance indicators all improved in the pre-privatisation period (see Table 10.9). A similar picture of improvement emerges by comparing the post-privatisation and nationalisation periods and, although labour productivity and TFP growth were lower in the recession years than in the nationalisation period, profitability is some 30 percentage points higher. The basic DEA model, presented in chapter 7, revealed no change in performance under private ownership while the augmented model suggested a slight improvement. The augmented model is the more consistent with the other performance results summarised in Table 10.9. Employment fell by one-half at NFC from the beginning of the nationalisation period (1973) to the end of the pre-privatisation period (1981). Since privatisation, however, employment levels have slowly increased so that by 1994 NFC employed about 40 per cent more people than at privatisation. There is also some evidence that relative wage rates at NFC have increased (see chapter 8).

Table 10.9 Summary of performance indicators: NFC

Performance indicator (% per annum)	Period				
	Nationalisation	*Pre-privatisation*	*Post-privatisation*	*Recession*	*Latest*
LP growth	−0.9	3.7	1.1	−1.7	2.5
TFP growth	2.0	−1.6	1.6	−3.4	−0.9
VA growth	−3.0	2.6	8.1	−2.0	1.9
Rate of profit	−8.0	7.6	25.7	20.9	18.8

Associated British Ports (ABP)

At ABP labour productivity and TFP growth were at their lowest in the nationalisation period and were below the rate achieved in the economy as a whole (see Table 10.10). Profitability, however, was at its highest in this period. Labour productivity growth was particularly strong in the post-privatisation and recession periods and this growth has continued in the latest period. This growth has contributed to considerable TFP growth. The basic DEA model, outlined in chapter 7, suggested that private ownership was associated with an improvement in performance, although the results from the augmented model revealed a less favourable picture. Employment was at its peak in the nationalisation period and, since then, has declined almost continuously. By 1994, only 20 per cent of the jobs that existed at privatisation remained although there was little evidence of any change in the relative wage paid by ABP relative to that paid in the rest of the economy (chapter 8).

British Telecom (BT)

At BT, TFP growth was at its zenith in the nationalisation period (see Table 10.11). However, labour productivity growth, value-added growth and profitability all improved with privatisation and the DEA results, on balance, were also indicative of an improvement in performance under

Table 10.10 Summary of performance indicators: ABP

Performance indicator (% per annum)	Nationalisation	Pre-privatisation	Period Post-privatisation	Recession	Latest
LP growth	−3.1	0.4	12.7	23.2	7.4
TFP growth	−1.2	5.7	9.2	2.6	6.7
VA growth	0.0	−6.3	5.7	−3.9	75.7
Rate of profit	15.4	9.5	9.2	7.4	10.0

private ownership. In the latest period, the breaking up of the BT–Mercury duopoly in 1991, with the resulting increase in competition, has contributed to the pressure on BT to improve its performance. With regard to employment levels, there is little discernible difference in the pattern of employment until 1990. Thereafter, increasing competitive pressures forced BT to embark on a severe cost-cutting programme with the loss of 100,000 jobs. However, the evidence suggests that, if anything, the average wage paid by BT has increased relative to that in the rest of the economy. Nevertheless, the share of income paid to labour has fallen and this has been matched by an increase to other inputs. Together, these changes suggest that BT has been substituting bought-in supplies for in-house production (chapter 8), though this needs further investigation.

Table 10.11 Summary of performance indicators: BT

Performance indicator (% per annum)	Nationalisation	Pre-privatisation	Period Post-privatisation	Recession	Latest
LP growth	1.3	3.8	2.3	5.6	12.2
TFP growth	6.7	2.8	1.0	3.1	3.1
VA growth	1.3	0.5	3.1	5.3	6.4
Rate of profit	14.7	19.5	21.7	22.8	16.5

OVERALL VIEW

Taking an overall view of the eleven organisations and each of the performance measures, the picture with regard to the impact of ownership on performance is mixed. This is clearly demonstrated in Table 10.12 where the results of comparing the nationalisation period with the pre-privatisation period, with the post-privatisation period, with the recession period, and then with the latest period are summarised.

With regard to the first comparison, there is clear evidence of an improvement in labour productivity growth and profitability in the pre-privatisation period. However, in spite of such an improvement, TFP growth declined in six of the ten companies for which figures were available.

Table 10.12 Comparative performance indicators for all firms

| | Performance Comparison | | | | | | | | | | | | | | | |
| Firm | Nationalisation v pre-privatisation | | | | Nationalisation v post-privatisation | | | | Nationalisation v recession | | | | Nationalisation v latest period | | | |
	LP growth	TFP growth	VA growth	Rate of profit	LP growth	TFP growth	VA growth	Rate of profit	LP growth	TFP growth	VA growth	Rate of profit	LP growth	TFP growth	VA growth	Rate of profit
British Airways	up	up	up	up	down	up	down	up	down	up	up	up	down	down	down	up
BAA	?	down	up	up	down	down	down	down	down	down	down	down	up	up	up	down
Britoil	up	down	up	up	up	down	up	up	n/a	n/a	n/a	n/a	n/a	n/a	n/a	n/a
British Gas	up	up	up	up	up	down	up	up	down	down	down	up	up	down	up	down
British Steel	down	down	down	up	down	down	down	up	down	down	down	up	down	down	up	up
British Aerospace	n/a	n/a	n/a	n/a	down	down	down	down	up	down	up	down	down	down	up	down
Jaguar	down	down	down	up	down	down	down	up	down	down	down	down	n/a	n/a	n/a	n/a
Rolls-Royce	down	up	down	up	down	down	down	up	down	up	down	up	down	up	up	up
NFC	up	down	up	up	up	down	up	up	down	down	down	up	up	down	up	up
ABP	up	up	down	down	up	up	up	down	up	up	up	down	up	up	up	down
BT	up	down	down	up	up	down	up	up	up	down	up	up	up	down	up	up
Total: up	6	4	5	9	5	2	5	8	3	3	5	6	5	3	8	5
down	3	6	5	1	6	9	6	3	7	7	5	4	4	6	1	4

Note: 'Up' denotes an increase in the performance indicator in the latter of the two periods being compared; 'down' denotes the reverse; and a '?' denotes no appreciable change.

A comparison of the results for the nationalisation and post-privatisation periods reveals that labour productivity growth was greater under private ownership in six out of the eleven cases studied. However, TFP growth was only greater under private ownership in two of the eleven cases and value-added growth improved in five cases. Only the rate of profit showed any clear evidence of an improvement with eight firms recording greater profitability under private rather than public ownership.

One purpose of this study was to assess the performance of privatised companies across the business cycle including the recession years from 1989. Comparing the nationalisation and recession periods reveals a less favourable picture towards private ownership than that revealed in more favourable economic times even after adjusting for national trends (for details of this adjustment see chapters 5 and 6). Both labour productivity and TFP growth were greater in the nationalisation period than in the recession for seven of the ten firms studied (this comparison could not be made for Britoil). Profitability, however, held up well and despite the recession remained higher than in the nationalisation period in six cases (although the maintenance of a relatively high rate of profit in the recession was achieved throughout the economy as a whole (Sterne, 1993)).

Finally, the nationalisation and latest periods can be compared. In this case there is strong evidence of an improvement in value-added growth with eight of the nine firms recording a better performance under private rather than public ownership (this comparison could not be made for Britoil and Jaguar). Labour productivity growth was also better in six firms but the results for TFP growth are in the opposite direction with six firms recording a better performance under public ownership. With regard to the rate of profit, five firms have recorded an improvement and four firms have shown a deterioration under private ownership.

The 159 comparisons reported in Table 10.12 can be aggregated by performance indicator thus obtaining the results reported in the upper half of Table 10.13 (part 'a'). These suggest that overall privatisation has had no impact on labour productivity growth but that value-added per employee has increased with just over four improvements for every three deteriorations. Profitability has increased in twenty-eight of the forty comparisons made. Although labour productivity growth shows no overall change, total factor productivity growth has declined in twenty-eight of the forty comparisons made. This suggests that the growth in the efficiency with which capital and other inputs are used has declined with privatisation. This is a rather controversial result. Calculating TFP growth is difficult because of the problems in measuring capital inputs. Although the method we used was a standard approach and we have no reason to believe that it would only depress the post-privatisation figures rather than all of the TFP results, such a possibility cannot be ruled out. Consequently, the TFP results may be less reliable than the other results reported here.

Table 10.13 Summary of all comparisons with the results
for the nationalisation period

Comparing the results for the nationalisation period with all others	Up	down
(a) By performance indicator		
(i) LP growth	19	20
(ii) TFP growth	12	28
(iii) VA growth	23	17
(iv) rate of profit	28	12
(b) By comparative period		
(i) pre-privatisation	24	15
(ii) post-privatisation	20	24
(iii) recession	17	23
(iv) latest period	21	15
(c) Total	82	77

The results summarised in the lower half of Table 10.13, parts 'b' and 'c',
suggest that overall, if anything, corporate performance (as we have measured it) was better in the nationalisation period than either the post-privatisation or recession periods. However, there is slightly more evidence that
performance was better in both the pre-privatisation and latest periods than
in the nationalisation period, with three improvements for every two deteriorations. Overall, moving from public to private ownership yielded a total
of 82 instances where performance improved (51.6 per cent) and 77 cases
where it deteriorated (48.4 per cent). We realise the limitations of such a bald
comparison. For example, we could have calculated separate indicators for
capital productivity and other input productivity. These would have been
particularly unfavourable to privatisation. The TFP results are a weighted
average of the results for labour, capital and other input productivity and, as
we know, while the TFP results are rather poor, the labour productivity
results show no change. Thus if the overall (TFP) result is poor, and one of
the constituents (labour productivity) reveals no change, the other constituents of the overall result (capital and other inputs) must offer a particularly
poor result. Nevertheless, this omission of the explicit consideration of
capital and other input productivity would not alter our overall result: that
we cannot reject the null hypothesis that there is no difference between the
performance of publicly and privately owned companies.[1]

Of course, this result must be subject to a number of caveats. In particular, no account has been taken of any improvements in the quality of
service offered by the companies in this study. Moreover, we have been able
to identify companies whose performance has improved following their

move into the private sector, notably British Gas. Similarly, there is evidence, for some of the comparison periods, and for some of the performance indicators, that private ownership is associated with an improved performance. But at the same time there is almost an equal amount of evidence in the opposite direction. Consequently, taking all eleven companies together, the overall picture reveals little evidence of any systematic improvement in performance. And, notwithstanding the difficulties in measuring performance (discussed in chapter 3), we have arrived at this conclusion using a range of measures.

It is interesting to consider why privatisation leads to higher efficiency in some cases but not in others. As was outlined in chapter 1, there is a body of theoretical and empirical literature which suggests that the capital market is unlikely to be an efficient disciplinarian of poorly performing firms. In addition, some economists have searched for an explanation in terms of the degree of competition and regulation in the product market pre- and post-privatisation. As a recent World Bank report comments:

> Two main factors affect the strategy for privatization and the outcomes in terms of economic productivity and consumer welfare: (a) country conditions, a composite factor that takes into account the extent to which the microeconomic framework is or is not market-friendly and the effectiveness of regulatory and supervisory institutions, and (b) the nature of the market into which the enterprise is directed – competitive or potentially competitive, or noncompetitive.
> (Kikeri, Nellis and Shirley, 1992, p. 39)

Where a privatised firm retains monopoly power then the incentives to raise efficiency are reduced (Bös, 1991). Where a firm is state-regulated after privatisation (for example, as in the UK telecommunications, gas, electricity and water industries) regulation may lead to smaller improvements in efficiency than would occur without regulation, although the natural monopoly element of these industries precludes total deregulation.

Interestingly, however, although a number of the studies reviewed in chapter 3 found a relationship between ownership, competition, regulation and performance, in this study of the eleven privatised organisations there was no clear evidence that regulated firms were performing worse after privatisation than their unregulated counterparts. This is not to say, necessarily, that competition and regulation are unimportant. Rather the findings suggest that the relationship between ownership, competition, regulation and performance seems to be much more complex than many have imagined.

In chapter 9 we examined whether and to what extent the proximate causes of performance improvement could be traced to changes *within* the privatised organisations. Ownership, competition and regulation involve incentive structures which must impact on performance through *internal*

216

organisational responses. This approach to performance complements the agent–principal literature in economics and the roles of contracts, incentives and information reviewed in chapter 1. It looks to management and organisational relationships, or the internal environment of the firm, for an understanding of the nature of performance change after privatisation. Simplistic views of privatisation, leading automatically to improved efficiency (Hanke, 1987; Pirie, 1987) ignore internal adaptation. We would argue that it is the way in which the organisation's management responds to changes in the external environment in the form of ownership, competition and regulation that is the critical explanation of the success or failure of any privatisation.

Where privatisation does not involve deregulation and competition remains muted, the expectation would be that the previous public sector culture will continue because the pressure for change is reduced. Where organisations remain state-regulated much will depend on the extent to which the regulator can force the pace of *internal* change within the organisations. Certainly reorganisation and redundancies within two of the regulated organisations studied, BT and British Gas, have resulted from recent initiatives by their regulator and government to increase competition and intensify regulation. But what the histories of these and the other organisations studied suggests is that we need a far better understanding of organisational adaptation to changes in the external environment including ownership and competition. Traditionally economists have steered clear of the study of internal processes within organisations. This has led to a voluminous literature on privatisation, competition and incentives but little on the *process* of change. Currently we have no coherent model let alone a well-developed theory of organisational adaptation following privatisation. The contents of chapter 9 were designed as a point of departure for future studies.

The empirical material presented in chapters 5–8 provides little evidence that privatisation has caused a significant improvement in performance. Generally the great expectations for privatisation evident in ministerial speeches have not been borne out. Certainly, privatisation has been associated with improvements in some of the eleven firms studied, especially in terms of profitability and value-added per employee, although what performance improvement there was often pre-dated privatisation. This raises the intriguing question of whether privatisation was necessary or would the performance improvement have occurred without the sell-off?

What our studies could not do was answer this question and determine whether the performance results and the internal restructuring would have occurred in any case, even if privatisation had not happened. The 1980s was a period of considerable change in UK industry brought on by growing international competition and by the government's programme of market liberalisation and trade union reform. In the public sector 'Thatcherism'

217

with its efficiency audits, hardened budget constraints and a new managerialism had important effects on the remaining public sector (Metcalfe and Richards, 1990; Farnham and Horton, 1993). Organisations that were not privatised, for example the Post Office, underwent wide-scale organisational changes and performance improvements that appear to match those taking place in privatised industry (Parker, 1995a). The extent to which the privatised industries acted as a role model for the remaining public sector or whether privatisation was irrelevant or largely so must remain controversial. The suspicion might remain that industries would not have been able to develop as they did had they remained in the state sector because of the controls on external financing and the threat of constant political intervention. Nevertheless, the Post Office managed to reinvent itself despite these obstacles.

In the UK generally, the policy priority has been privatisation with the introduction of competition being a secondary (or later) concern. There must remain the issue of whether resources would have been more effectively used had policy focused on the introduction of competition in the product market rather than the transfer of ownership. For while the impact on efficiency of ownership remains uncertain, few would doubt the beneficial effects of competition. Indeed, while British Gas was privatised in 1986, the introduction of competition in the supply of gas to domestic consumers did not come about for another decade. When competition arrived, however, it brought discounts of as much as 25 per cent on British Gas prices in the trial area of south-west England (Corzine, 1996). Consumers might justifiably wonder why they had to wait ten years for this development.

NOTE

1 The nonparametric sign test, for example, can be used to test formally whether there is the same number of 'ups' and 'downs' after the nationalisation period (Siegel, 1956, 68–75). The calculated test statistic is 0.1 and, with a critical χ^2 value of 2.71, we cannot reject the null hypothesis that the proportion of 'ups' is the same as the proportion of 'downs' at the 10 per cent significance level.

APPENDIX

To calculate labour and total factor productivity (chapter 5), value-added (chapter 6), and to undertake the data envelopment analysis (chapter 7), data are required which reflect how, for each firm, the volume of output adjusts to changes in the volume of inputs. Unfortunately, such volume indicators for outputs were sometimes not available and it was necessary to deflate a value series (turnover) to obtain an indicator of the volume of output. Input use is based on expenditure shares. Unless stated otherwise in the relevant chapter, this appendix reports how the volume series for each organisation's inputs and output were constructed.

For all firms, the volume of labour input was taken to be the organisation's average number of employees throughout the year multiplied by the average number of hours worked by each employee in the industry. Unit labour input costs were calculated as total labour costs divided by the number of employee-hours worked in that industry. The gross domestic fixed capital formation deflator for manufacturing industry was used as an index of capital input costs. The capital costs for each firm were calculated as depreciation plus a real return of 8 per cent on capital employed (Bishop and Thompson, 1992). This imputes a flow of services on the basis of the depreciation policies followed by each enterprise, and a rental charge reflecting the opportunity cost of holding the assets in the business.

Where a firm's annual accounts referred to a year ending 31 March or 30 September, all price indices were appropriately adjusted by linear interpolation having been extracted from various issues of *Annual Abstract of Statistics*, *British Business*, *Digest of United Kingdom Energy Statistics*, *Economic Trends*, *Monthly Digest of Statistics*, *New Earnings Survey*, *Transport Statistics Great Britain* and *UK National Income Accounts*.

ASSOCIATED BRITISH PORTS (ABP)

Output index: tonnes of cargo handled. Input price index to deflate total expenditure: unit labour costs, capital costs, and the retail price index for all items excluding food (for other costs), weighted by the annual share of each input in total expenditure.

BRITISH AEROSPACE

Output index: turnover plus the change in the value of stocks and work in progress deflated by a total cost index for inputs to the aerospace industry (on the grounds that much of the firm's public sector work will be on a cost-plus basis). Input price index to deflate total expenditure: unit labour costs, capital costs, and the input producer price index for manufacturing (for other costs), weighted by the annual share of each input in total expenditure.

BRITISH AIRPORTS AUTHORITY (BAA)

Output indices: (i) number of air traffic movements; and (ii) turnover deflated by the retail price index for all items excluding food. Input price index to deflate total expenditure: unit labour costs, capital costs, and the retail price index for all items excluding food (for other costs), weighted by the annual share of each input in total expenditure.

BRITISH AIRWAYS (BA)

Output index: $ATK^aAS^bPLF^c$ where ATK is the available tonne kilometres, AS is the length of the average sector flown and PLF is the passenger load factor. The parameters a, b and c take the values of $1.0, -0.2$ and 0.4 respectively (see Forsyth et al. (1986) for a justification of this approach to the measurement of airline output). Input price index to deflate total expenditure: unit labour costs, capital costs, an aviation jet fuel index (for fuel costs), and the input producer price index for manufacturing (for other costs), weighted by the annual share of each input in total expenditure.

BRITISH GAS

Output index: volume of gas sold to domestic, commercial and industrial customers. In 1991 the company ceased publishing this figure. However, British Gas continued to disclose the number of customers that it had and, by assuming that the amount of gas sold to each type of customer in 1992, 1993 and 1994 was the same as that sold on average, over the previous five years, we were able to obtain estimates of the total amount of gas sold over the period 1992–4. The retail price index for gas was used to deflate the value-added series reported in chapter 6. Input index: weighted average of the number of employee hours worked and the length of the transmission mains, with weights reflecting the relative importance of labour and capital costs (capital costs were calculated as current cost depreciation plus an amount reflecting a real return of 8 per cent on the organisation's capital employed).

BRITISH STEEL CORPORATION (BSC)

Output index: tonnes of liquid steel production. The output producer price index for steel was used to deflate the value-added series reported in chapter 6. Input price index to deflate total expenditure: unit labour costs, capital costs, the input producer price index for metal manufacturing (for material costs), and the input producer price index for manufacturing (for other costs), weighted by the annual share of each input in total expenditure.

BRITISH TELECOM (BT)

Output index: turnover deflated by the retail price index for telecommunication services. Input price index to deflate total expenditure: unit labour costs, capital costs, and the retail price index for all items excluding food (for other costs), weighted by the annual share of each input in total expenditure.

BRITOIL

Output index: weighted index of the volume of gas and oil sold with weights reflecting the share that each activity contributes to total turnover. The oil price index was used to deflate the value-added series reported in chapter 6. Input price index to deflate total expenditure: unit labour costs, capital costs, and the retail price index for all items excluding food (for other costs), weighted by the annual share of each input in total expenditure. In the case of Britoil there was no reliable hours of work figure and therefore the labour input is number employed only.

JAGUAR

Output index: number of cars produced. The output producer price index for motor vehicles was used to deflate the value-added series reported in chapter 6. Input price index to deflate total expenditure: unit labour costs, capital costs, and the input producer price index for motor vehicles (for other costs), weighted by the annual share of each input in total expenditure.

NATIONAL FREIGHT CORPORATION (NFC)

Output index: turnover deflated by the retail price index for transport. Input price index to deflate total expenditure: unit labour costs, capital costs, and the input producer price index for manufacturing (for other costs), weighted by the annual share of each input in total expenditure.

ROLLS-ROYCE

Output index: turnover plus the change in the value of stocks and work in progress deflated by an index of total input costs for the aero-engine industry. Input price index to deflate total expenditure: Unit labour costs, capital costs, and the input producer price index for mechanical engineering (for other costs), weighted by the annual share of each input in total expenditure.

ECONOMY/MANUFACTURING

Output index: as found in official statistics. Input index: an index of labour input, calculated as the number employed multiplied by average hours worked per week, and an index of capital input, calculated as the value of the gross capital stock, weighted by the annual share of income attributable to labour and capital respectively.

REFERENCES

Adhikari, R. and Kirkpatrick, C. (1990) 'Surveys of Practice and Principles', in J. Heath (ed.) *Public Enterprise at the Crossroads*, London: Routledge.

Aharoni, Y. (1982) 'State-Owned Enterprise: an Agent without a Principal', in L.P. Jones (ed.) *Public Enterprise in Less-Developed Countries*, Cambridge: Cambridge University Press.

Aharoni, Y. (1986) *The Evolution and Management of State Owned Enterprises*, Cambridge, Mass.: Ballinger.

Al-Bazzaz, S. J. and Grinyer, P. H. (1981) 'Corporate Planning in the UK: the State of the Art in the 70s', *Strategic Management Journal* 2: 155–168.

Alchian, A. A. (1965) 'Some Economics of Property Rights', *Il Politico* 30: 816–829.

Alchian, A. A. (1977) *Economic Forces at Work*, Indianapolis: Liberty Press.

Alchian, A. A. and Demsetz, H. (1972) 'Production, Information Costs and Economic Organization', *American Economic Review* 62: 777–795.

Alderson, S. and Kakabadse, A. (1992) 'Strategic Change and the Role of the Top Team', in D. Faulkner and G. Johnson (eds) *The Challenge of Strategic Management*, London: Kogan Page.

Allaire, Y. and Firsirotu, M. (1990) 'Strategic Plans as Contracts', *Long Range Planning* 23 (1): 102–115.

Ammons, D.N. and Newell, C. (1989) *City Executives: Leadership Roles, Work Characteristics, and Time Management*, Albany, N Y: State University of New York Press.

Aoki, M. (1983) 'Managerialism Revisited in the Light of Bargaining-Game Theory', *International Journal of Industrial Organisation* 1: 1–21.

Aoki, M. (1984) *The Cooperative Game Theory of the Firm*, Oxford: Oxford University Press.

Aoki, M., Gustafsson, B. and Williamson, O.E. (eds) (1990) *The Firm as a Nexus of Treaties*, London: Sage.

Aranson, P. H. (1990) 'Theories of Economic Regulation: from Clarity to Confusion', *Journal of Law and Politics* 6: 247–287.

Arbomeit, H. (1986) 'Privatisation in Great Britain', *Annals of Public and Cooperative Economy* 57: 153–179.

Argyris, C. and Schon, D. (1978) *Organizational Learning: A Theory of Action Perspective*, Reading, Mass.: Addison-Wesley.

Armstrong, M., Cowan, S. and Vickers, J. (1994) *Regulatory Reform: Economic Analysis and British Experience*, Cambridge, Mass.: MIT Press.

Arrow, K. J. (1963) *Social Choice and Individual Values*, New Haven, Conn.: Yale University Press.

223

THE IMPACT OF PRIVATISATION

Arrow, K. J. (1974) *The Limits of Organization*, New York: Norton.
Arrow, K. J. (1985) 'The Economics of Agency', in J.W. Pratt and R.J. Zeckhauser (eds) *Principals and Agents: the Structure of Business*, Boston, Mass.: Harvard University Press.
Arrow, K. (1987) 'Reflections on the Essays', in G. Feiwel (ed.) *Arrow and the Foundations of the Theory of Economic Policy*, New York: NYU Press.
Ashworth, M. and Forsyth, P. (1984) *Civil Aviation Policy and the Privatisation of British Airways*, IFS Report 12, London: Institute for Fiscal Studies.
Atkinson, S. E. and Halvorsen, R. (1986) 'The Relative Efficiency of Public and Private Firms in a Regulated Environment: the Case of US Electric Utilities', *Journal of Public Economics* 29: 281–294.
Averch, H. and Johnson, L. L. (1962) 'Behavior of the Firm under Regulatory Constraint', *American Economic Review* 52: 1052–1069.
Aylen, J. (1988) 'Privatisation of the British Steel Corporation', *Fiscal Studies* 9 (3): 1–25.
BA (1977) *Annual Report and Accounts 1976/77*, London: British Airways.
BA (1987) *Prospectus: British Airways plc*, London: British Airways.
BAA (1993) *Annual Report and Accounts*, London: British Airports Authority.
Bacon, N., Blyton, P. and Morris, J. (1991) 'Steel, State and Industry Relations: Restructuring Work and Employee Relations in the Steel Industry', paper presented to the International Privatisation: Strategies and Practices conference, University of St Andrews, 12–14 September 1991.
Bailey, E. E. (1973) *Economic Theory of Regulatory Constraint*, Lexington, DC: Heath.
Bain, J. S. (1951) 'Relation of Profit Rates to Industry Concentration: American Manufacturing, 1936–1940, *Quarterly Journal of Economics* 65: 293–324.
Ball, J. Sir (1991) 'Short Termism – Myth or Reality?', *National Westminster Bank Quarterly Review*, August, 20–30.
Banker, R. D., Charnes, A. and Cooper, W.W. (1984) 'Some Models for Estimating Technical and Scale Efficiencies in Data Envelopment Analysis', *Management Science* 30 (9): 1078–1092.
Banker, R. D. and Morey, R. C. (1986) 'The Use of Categorical Variables in Data Envelopment Analysis', *Management Science* 32: 1613–1627.
Banker, R. D. and Thrall, R.M. (1992) 'Estimation of Returns to Scale using Data Envelopment Analysis', *European Journal of Operational Research* 62: 74–84.
Barney, J. B. and Ouchi, W.G (eds) (1986) *Organizational Economics*, San Francisco: Jossey-Bass.
Barrett, P. (1990) 'The Contingency Approach – a Positive view', *Graduate Management Research* 5, (2): 3–10.
Barrow, M. and Wagstaff, A. (1989) 'Efficiency Measurement in the Public Sector: an Appraisal', *Fiscal Studies* 10 (1): 72–97.
Bartram, P. (1994) 'Re-engineering Revisited', *Management Today*, July: 61–63.
Bate, P. (1994) *Strategies for Cultural Change*, Oxford: Butterworth-Heinemann.
Batt, M. (1990) 'Putting a Brand on British Airways', *Marketing Business*, April, 14–15.
Baumol, W. J. (1959) *Business Behaviour, Value and Growth*, London: Macmillan.
Baumol, W. J. (1980) 'On the Implications of the Conference Discussions', in W. J. Baumol (ed.) *Public and Private Enterprise in a Mixed Economy*, London: Macmillan.
Baumol, W. J. (1990) 'Comment on the Paper by T. N. Srinivasan', in W.J. Baumol (ed.) *Public and Private Enterprise in a Mixed Economy*, London: Macmillan.
Baumol, W. J. and Bradford, D. (1970) 'Optimal Departures from Marginal Cost Pricing', *American Economic Review* 60: 265–283.

REFERENCES

Beaumont, P. (1991) 'Privatization, Contracting-out and Public Sector Industrial Relations: the Thatcher Years in Britain', *Journal of Collective Negotiations in the Public Sector* 20 (2): 89–100.

Becker, G. S. (1976). *The Economic Approach to Human Behaviour*, Chicago: University of Chicago Press.

Beer, J. and Davis, O. A. (1966) 'An Elementary Political and Economic Theory of Expenditure of Local Governments', *Southern Economic Journal* 33: 149–165.

Beesley, M. E. and Laidlaw, B. (1989) *The Future of Telecommunications*, Research Monograph 42, London: Institute of Economic Affairs.

Beesley, M. E. and Littlechild, S.C. (1983) 'Privatisation: Principles, Problems and Priorities', *Lloyds Bank Review* 149: 1–20.

Berglof, E. (1990) 'Capital Structure as a Mechanism of Control: a Comparison of Financial Systems', in M. Aoki, B. Gustafsson and O.E. Williamson (eds) *The Firm as a Nexus of Treaties*, London: Sage.

Berle, A. A. and Means, G. C. (1932) *The Modern Corporation and Private Property*, New York: Macmillan.

Bhagwati, J. (1982) 'Directly Unproductive Profit-Seeking Activities', *Journal of Political Economy* 90: 1069–1087.

Bhaskar, V. and Khan, M. (1995) 'Privatization and Employment: a Study of the Jute Industry in Bangladesh', *American Economic Review* 85 (1): 267–273.

Bibeault, D. B. (1982) *Corporate Turnaround*, New York: McGraw-Hill.

Bishop, M. And Green, M. (1995) *Privatisation and Recession – the Miracle Tested*, Centre for the Study of Regulated Industries, London: Chartered Institute of Public Finance and Accountancy.

Bishop, M. and Kay, J. (1989) 'Privatization in the United Kingdom: Lessons from Experience', *World Development* 17 (5): 643–657.

Bishop, M. and Kay, J. (1988) *Does Privatization Work? Lessons from the UK*, Centre for Business Strategy, London: London Business School.

Bishop, M. and Thompson, D. (1992) 'Regulatory Reform and Productivity Growth in the UK's Public Utilities', *Applied Economics* 24: 1181–1190.

Bishop, M. and Thompson, D. (1993) 'Privatization in the UK: Deregulatory Reform and Public Enterprise Performance', in V.V. Ramanadham (ed.) *Privatization: a Global Perspective*, London: Routledge.

Bishop, M. and Thompson, D. (1994) 'Privatisation in the UK: International Organization and Productive Efficiency', in M. Bishop, J. Kay and C. Mayer (eds) *Privatization and Economic Performance*, Oxford: Oxford University Press.

Blankart, C. B. (1983) 'The Contribution of Public Choice to Public Utility Economics: a Survey', in J. Finsinger (ed.) *Public Sector Economics*, London: Macmillan.

Blumenthal, J. M. (1983) 'Candid Reflections of a Businessman in Washington', in J. L. Perry and K. L. Kramer (eds) *Public Management*, Mountain View, Cal.: Mayfield.

Blyton, P. (1993) 'Steel', in A. Pendleton and J. Winterton (eds) *Public Enterprise in Transition: Industrial Relations in State and Privatized Corporations*, London: Routledge.

Boardman, A., Freedman, R. and Eckel, C. (1986) 'The Price of Government Ownership', *Journal of Public Economics* 31: 269–285.

Boardman, A. E. and Vining, A. R. (1989) 'Ownership and Performance in Competitive Environments: a Comparison of the Performance of Private, Mixed and State-Owned Enterprises', *Journal of Law and Economics* 32: 1–33.

Borcherding, T. (1977) 'The Sources of Growth in Public Expenditures', in T. Borcherding (ed.) *Budgets and Bureaucrats: the Sources of Government Growth*, Durham, NC.: Duke University Press.

Borcherding, T., Pommerehne, W. and Schneider, F. (1982) 'Comparing the Efficiency of Private and Public Production: the Evidence from Five Countries', *Zeitschrift für Nationalökonomie* 42, supplement 2: 127–136.

Bös, D. (1986) *Public Enterprise Economics: Theory and Application*, New York: North-Holland.

Bös, D. (1988) 'Privatization, Internal Control, and Internal Regulation', *Journal of Public Economics* 36: 231–258.

Bös, D. (1991) *Privatization: a Theoretical Treatment*, Oxford: Clarendon Press.

Bös, D. (1993) 'Privatization in Europe: A Comparison of Approaches', *Oxford Review of Economic Policy* 9 (1): 95–111.

Bös, D. and Peters, W. (1989) 'A Principal–Agent Approach on Manager Effort and Control in Privatized and Public Firms', University of Bonn, Discussion Paper A-252.

Bös, D. and Peters, W. (1991) 'Privatization of Public Enterprises: a Principal–Agent Approach. Comparing Efficiency in Private and Public Sectors', *Austrian Economic Papers* 18 (1): 5–16.

Boussofiane, A., Dyson, R. G. and Thanassoulis, E. (1991) 'Applied Data Envelopment Analysis', *European Journal of Operational Research* 52: 1–15.

Boycko, M., Shleifer, A. and Vishny, R. W. (1996) 'A Theory of Privatization', *Economic Journal* 106: 309–319.

Bozeman, B. (1987) *All Organizations are Public: Bridging Public and Private Organizational Theories*, San Francisco, Cal.: Josey-Bass.

Bozeman, B. and Straussman, J. D. (1990) *Public Management Strategies*, San Francisco, Cal.: Jossey-Bass.

Bradley, K. and Nejad, A. (1989) *Managing Owners: the National Freight Corporation in Perspective*, Cambridge: Cambridge University Press.

Bradley, M., Desai, A. and Kim, E. H. (1988) 'Synergistic Gains from Corporate Acquisitions and their Division Between the Stockholders of Target and Acquiring Firms', *Journal of Financial Economics* 21: 3–40.

Breton, A. (1974). *The Economic Theory of Representative Government*, London: Macmillan.

Breton, A. and Wintrobe, R. (1975). 'The Equilibrium Size of a Budget–Maximizing Bureau: A Note on Niskanen's Theory of Bureaucracy', *Journal of Political Economy* 83: 195–207.

Breton, A. and Wintrobe, R. (1982) *The Logic of Bureaucratic Control: an Economic Analysis of Competition, Exchange and Efficiency in Private and Public Organizations*, Cambridge: Cambridge University Press.

British Gas (1991) *Annual Report and Accounts* 1991, London: British Gas.

Bruggink, T.H. (1982) 'Public versus Regulated Private Enterprise in the Municipal Water Industry: a Comparison of Operating Costs', *Quarterly Review of Economics and Business* 22: 111–125.

Brunnen, D. (1989) 'Developing an Enterprise Culture at British Telecom', *Long Range Planning* 22 (2): 27–36.

Bryant, J. (1989) 'Assessing Company Strength Using Added Value', *Long Range Planning* 22 (3): 34–44.

BT (1987) *British Telecom in Operation*, London: British Telecom.

Buchanan, J. M (1968) *The Demand and Supply of Public Goods*, Chicago: Rand McNally.

Buchanan, J.M. (1972) *Theory of Public Choice*, Michigan: University of Michigan Press.

Buchanan, J. M. (1978) in *The Economics of Politics*, IEA Readings 18, London: Institute of Economic Affairs.

Buchanan, J. M. and Tullock, G. (1962). *The Calculus of Consent: Logical Foundations of Constitutional Democracy*, Ann Arbor: University of Michigan Press.

Buchanan, J. M. (1986). *Liberty, Market and State: Political Economy in the 1980s*, Brighton: Wheatsheaf.

Burns, P., Crawford, I. and Dilnot, A. (1995) 'Regulation and Redistribution in Utilities', *Fiscal Studies* 16 (4): 1–22.

Burns, P. and Weyman-Jones, T. (1994a) 'Regulatory Incentives, Privatisation and Productivity Growth in UK Electricity Distribution', CRI Technical Paper 1, Centre for the Study of Regulated Industries, London: Chartered Institute of Public Finance and Accountancy.

Burns, P. and Weyman-Jones, T. (1994b) 'Cost Drivers and Cost Efficiency in Electricity Distribution: a Stochastic Frontier Approach', CRI Technical Paper 2, Centre for the Study of Regulated Industries, London: Chartered Institute of Public Finance and Accountancy.

Burns, P. and Weyman-Jones, T. (1994c) 'Productive Efficiency and the Regulatory Review of Regional Electricity Companies in the UK', Regulatory Policy Research Centre Discussion Paper 1, Oxford: Hertford College.

Burns, T. and Stalker, G.M. (1961) *The Management of Innovation*, London: Tavistock Press.

Burton, R.M. and Obel, B. (1986) 'Implications of Deregulation: an Overview', in R.M. Burton and B. Obel (eds) *Innovation and Entrepreneurship in Organizations: Strategies for Competitiveness, Deregulation and Privatization*, Amsterdam: Elsevier.

Button, K. J. and Weyman-Jones, T. (1992) 'Ownership, Institutional Organization and Measured X-inefficiency', *American Economic Review* 82 (2): 439–445.

Button, K. and Weyman-Jones, T. (1994) 'Impacts of Privatization Policy in Europe', *Contemporary Economic Policy* 141 (4): 23–33.

Byatt, I. (1985) 'Market and Non-Market Alternatives in the Public Supply of Public Services: British Experience with Privatization', in F. Forte and A. Peacock (eds) *Public Expenditure and Government Growth*, Oxford: Blackwell.

Campbell, A., Devine, M. and Young, D. (1990) *A Sense of Mission*, London: Economist/Hutchinson.

Campbell-Smith, D. (1986) *Struggle for Take-Off: the British Airways Story*, London: Coronet.

Carroll, K. A. (1990) 'Bureau Competition and Inefficiency: a Re-evaluation of Theory and Evidence', *Journal of Economic Behaviour and Organization* 13: 21–40.

Carter Committee (1978) *The Post Office*, Cmd 7292, London: HMSO.

Caves, R. E. (1989) 'Mergers, Takeovers and Economic Efficiencies: Foresight vs. Hindsight', *International Journal of Industrial Organization* 7 (1): 151–174.

Caves, R. E. (1990) 'Lessons from Privatization in Britain: State Enterprise Behaviour, Public Choice and Corporate Governance', *Journal of Economic Behaviour and Organization* 13 (2): 145–169.

Caves, D. W. and Christensen, L.R. (1980) 'The Relative Efficiency of Public and Private Firms in a Competitive Environment: the case of Canadian Railroads', *Journal of Political Economy* 8: 958–976.

Caves, D. W., Christensen, L.R. and Diewert, W. E. (1982) 'Multilateral Comparisons of Output, Input and Productivity using Superlative Index Numbers', *Economic Journal* 92: 73–86.

Chapman, C. (1990) *Selling the State: Has Privatization Worked?*, London: Hutchinson Business Books.

Charnes, A., Clark, C. T., Cooper, W. W. and Golany, B. (1985) 'A Developmental Study of Data Envelopment Analysis in Measuring the Efficiency of Maintenance Units in the US Air Force', *Annals of Operations Research* 2: 95–112.

Charnes, A., Cooper, W.W. and Rhodes, E. (1978) 'Measuring the Efficiency of Decision-making Units', *European Journal of Operational Research* 2 (6): 429–444.

Christensen, L. R., Jorgenson, D. W. and Lau, L. J. (1973) 'Transcendental Logarithmic Production Functions', *Review of Economics and Statistics* 55: 28–45.

Clarkson, K.W. (1972) 'Some Implications of Property Rights in Hospital Management', *Journal of Law and Economics* 15: 363–384.

Cmnd 1337 (1961) *The Financial and Economic Obligations of the Nationalised Industries*, London: HM Treasury.

Coase, R. H. (1937) 'The Nature of the Firm', *Economica* 4: 386–405.

Cobb, C. W. and Douglas, P. H. (1928) 'A Theory of Production', *American Economic Review*, 23: 139–165.

Coffee, J. Jr. (1986) 'Shareholders versus Managers: the Strain in the Corporate Web', *Michigan Law Review* 85: 1–109.

Corby, M. (1979) *The Postal Business 1969–79*, London: Kogan Page.

Corzine, R. (1996) 'Start of Gas Competition Hit by Four–Week Delay', *Financial Times*, 28 February: 16

Cowling, K and Waterson, M. (1976) 'Price-Cost Margins and Market Structure', *Economica* 43: 267–274.

Crain, M. and Zardkoohi, A. (1978) 'A Test of the Property Rights Theory of the Firm: Water Utilities in the United States', *Journal of Law and Economics* 40: 395–408.

Crain, M. and Zardkoohi, A. (1980) 'X-inefficiency and Nonpecuniary Rewards in a Rent-Seeking Society: a Neglected Issue in the Property Rights Theory of the Firm', *American Economic Review* 70 (4): 784–792.

Crew, M. A. and Rowley, C. K. (1988) 'Toward a Public Choice Theory of Monopoly Regulation', *Public Choice* 57: 49–67.

Cullis, J. G. and Jones, P. R. (1987) *Microeconomics and the Public Economy: a Defence of Leviathan*, Oxford: Basil Blackwell.

Dahl, R. A. and Lindbolm, C. E. (1953) *Politics, Economics, and Welfare*, New York: Harper & Row.

Davies, D. G. (1971) 'The Efficiency of Public versus Private Firms: the case of Australia's Two Airlines', *Journal of Law and Economics* 14: 149–165.

Davies, D. G. (1977) 'Property Rights and Economic Efficiency – the Australian Airlines Revisited', *Journal of Law and Economics* 20: 223–226.

Davies, D. G. (1980) 'Property Rights in a Regulated Environment: a reply', *Economic Record* June: 186–189.

Davies, D. G. (1981) 'Property Rights and Economic Behaviour in Private and Government Enterprises: the Case of Australia's Banking System', in R.O. Zerbe (ed.) *Research in Law and Economics* 3, Greenwich Conn.: JAI Press.

Davis, E. and Kay, J. (1990) 'Assessing Corporate Performance', *Business Strategy Review* 1 (2): 1–16.

Davis, O. A., Dempster, M. A. H. and Wildavsky, A. (1966) 'On the Process of Budgeting: an Empirical Study of Congressional Appropriation', *Public Choice* 1: 63–132.

De Alessi, L. (1969) 'Implications of Property Rights for Government Investment Choices', *American Economic Review* 59: 13–24.

De Alessi, L. (1974a) 'Managerial Tenure under Private and Government Ownership in the Electric Power Industry', *Journal of Political Economy* 82: 645–653.

De Alessi, L. (1974b) 'An Economic analysis of Government Ownership and Regulation: Theory and Evidence from the Electric Power Industry', *Public Choice* Fall: 1–42.

De Alessi, L. (1977) ' Ownership and Peak-load Pricing in the Electric Power Industry', *Quarterly Review of Economics and Business* 17: 60–70.

De Alessi, L. (1980) 'The Economics of Property Rights: a Review of the Evidence', *Research in Law and Economics* 2: 1–47.

De Fraja, G. (1991) 'Efficiency and Privatisation in Imperfectly Competitive Industries', *Journal of Industrial Economics* 39 (3): 311–321.

De Fraja, G. (1993) 'Productive Efficiency in Public and Private Firms', *Journal of Public Economics* 50: 15–30.

DeGagné, A. J. and Goh, S.C. (1995) 'Transforming the Culture of a Public Sector Organization', in J. Prokopenko (ed.) *Management for Privatization: Lessons from Industry and Public Service*, Geneva: International Labour Office.

Demsetz, H. (1983) 'The Structure of Ownership and the Theory of the Firm', *Journal of Law and Economics* 26: 375–390.

Demsetz, H. and Lehn, K. (1985) 'The Structure of Corporate Ownership: Causes and Consequences', *Journal of Political Economy* 93: 1155–1177.

Dertouzos, M. L., Lester, R. K. and Solow, R. M. (the MIT Commission on Industrial Productivity) (1989) *Made in America: Regaining the Productive Edge*, Cambridge, Mass.: MIT Press.

Di Lorenzo, T. J. and Robinson, R. (1982) 'Managerial Objectives Subject to Political Market Constraints: Electric Utilities in the US', *Quarterly Review of Economics and Business* 22 (2): 113–125.

Diewart, W.E. (1976) 'Exact and Superlative Index Numbers', *Journal of Econometrics* 11: 5–45.

Doble, M. and Weyman-Jones, T. G. (1991) 'Measuring Productive Efficiency in the Area Electricity Boards of England and Wales using Data Envelopment Analysis: a Dynamic Approach', Public Sector Economics Research Centre, University of Leicester.

Dopson, S. and Stewart, R. (1990) 'Public and Private Sector Management: the Case for a Wider Debate', *Public Money and Management* 10 (1): 37–40.

Downs, A. (1957) *An Economic Theory of Democracy*, New York: Harper & Row.

Downs, A. (1967) *Inside Bureaucracy*, Boston, Mass.: Little Brown.

Doyle, J. and Green, R. (1994) 'Efficiency and Cross-Efficiency in DEA: Derivations, Meanings and Uses', *Journal of the Operational Research Society* 45 (5): 567–578.

Dror, Y (1971) *Ventures in Policy Sciences*, New York: Elsevier.

Duch, R.M. (1991) *Privatizing the Economy: Telecommunications Policy in Comparative Perspective*, Ann Arbor: University of Michigan Press.

Dunleavy, P. (1986) 'Explaining the Privatization Boom: Public Choice versus Radical Approaches', *Public Administration* 64 (2): 13–34.

Dunleavy, P. (1991) *Democracy, Bureaucracy and Public Choice: Economic Explanations in Political Science*, London: Harvester Wheatsheaf.

Dunsire, A. (1991) 'Organisational Structure: Status Change and Performance', in Hartley, K. and Ott, A. (eds) *Privatization and Economic Efficiency*, Aldershot: Edward Elgar.

Dunsire, A., Hartley, K. Parker, D. and Dimitriou, B. (1988) 'Organisational Status and Performance: a Conceptual Framework for Testing Public Choice Theories', *Public Administration* 66: 363–388.

Dunsire, A., Hartley, K. and Parker, D. (1991) 'Organisational Status and Performance: Summary of the Findings', *Public Administration* 69 (1): 21–40.

Dunsire, A., Hood, C. and Huby, M. (1989) *Cutback Management in Public Bureaucracies: Popular Theories and Observed Outcomes in Whitehall*, Cambridge: Cambridge University Press.

Dyer, G. (1995) 'ABP Accounting Policies Queried', *Financial Times*, 28 November: 23.

Edwards, J., Kay, J. and Mayer, C. P. (1987) *The Economic Analysis of Accounting Profitability*, Oxford: University Press.

Eggar, T. (1995) 'The Regulation of the Former Nationalised Utilities: a Government View', in D. Helm (ed.) *British Utility Regulation: Principles, Experience and Reform*, Oxford: Oxera Press.

Elcock, H. (1993) 'Strategic Management', in D. Farnham and S. Horton (eds) *Managing the New Public Services*, London: Macmillan.

Enderwick, P. (1994) 'Multinational Enterprises and Partial Privatisation of State-Owned Enterprises', *International Business Review* 3 (2): 135–147.

Estrin, S. and Perotin, V. (1991) 'Does Ownership Always Matter?', *International Journal of Industrial Organization* 9: 55–72.

Fama, E. F. (1980) 'Agency Problems and the Theory of the Firm', *Journal of Political Economy* 88: 288–307.

Fama, E. F. (1991) 'Efficient Capital Markets: II', *Journal of Finance* 46 (5): 1575–1617.

Fama, E. F. and Jensen, M. C. (1983) 'Separation of Ownership and Control', *Journal of Law and Economics* 26: 301–325.

Färe, R., Grosskopf, S. and Logan, J. (1985) 'The Relative Performance of Publicly-Owned and Privately-Owned Electric Utilities', *Journal of Public Economics* 26: 89–106.

Färe, R., Grosskopf, S., Yaisawarng, S., Li, S.K. and Wang, Z. (1990) 'Productivity Growth in Illinois Electric Utilities', *Resources and Energy* 12: 383–398.

Färe, R., Grosskopf, S. and Lovell, C.A.K. (1994) *Production Frontiers*, Cambridge: Cambridge University Press.

Farnham, D. and Horton, S. (eds) (1993) *Managing the New Public Services*, London: Macmillan.

Farrell, M. J. (1957) 'The Measurement of Productive Efficiency', *Journal of the Royal Statistical Society* Series A 120, part 3: 253–281.

Farrell, J. and Scotchmer, S. (1988) 'Partnerships', *Quarterly Journal of Economics* 103: 279–298.

Feigenbaum, S. and Teeples, R. (1983) 'Public versus Private Water Delivery: a Hedonic Cost Approach', *Review of Economics and Statistics* 65: 672–678.

Ferner, A. and Colling, T. (1991) 'Privatisation, Regulation and Industrial Relations', *British Journal of Industrial Relations* 29 (3): 391–409.

Ferner, A. and Colling, T. (1992) 'The Limits of Autonomy: Devolution, Line Managers and Industrial Relations in Privatized Companies', *Journal of Management Studies* 29 (2): 219–227.

Ferner, A. and Colling, T. (1993) 'Privatisation of the British Utilities: Regulation, Decentralization and Industrial Relations', in T. Clarke and C. Pitelis (eds) *The Political Economy of Privatization*, London: Routledge.

Fevre, R. (1986) 'Contract Work in the Recession', in K. Purcell, S. Wood, S. Walby, A. Waton and S. Allen (eds) *The Changing Experience of Employment: Restructuring and Recession*, London: Macmillan.

Finsinger, J. (1986) 'A State Controlled Market: the German Case', in J. Finsinger and M. V. Pauly (eds) *The Economics of Insurance Regulation a Cross-National Study*, London: Macmillan.

Fiorina, M. P. and Noll, R. G. (1978) 'Voters, Bureaucrats and Legislators: a Rational Choice Perspective on the Growth of Bureaucracy', *Journal of Public Economics* 9: 239–254.

Firth, M. (1979) 'The Profitability of Takeovers and Mergers', *Economic Journal* 89: 316–328.

Firth, M. (1980) 'Takeovers, Shareholder Returns and the Theory of the Firm', *Quarterly Journal of Economics* 94: 110–120.

Fisher, F. M. and McGowan, J. J. (1983) 'On the Misuse of Accounting Rates of Return to Infer Monopoly Profits', *American Economic Review* 73 (1): 82–97.

Flynn, N. (1988) 'Consumer-oriented Culture', *Public Money and Management* 8 (2): 27–31.

Foreman-Peck, J. (1985) 'Competition and Performance in the United Kingdom Telecommunications Industry', *Telecommunications Policy* 9: 215–228.

Foreman-Peck, J. (1989) 'Ownership, Competition and Productivity Growth: the Impact of Liberalisation and Privatisation upon British Telecom', *Warwick Economic Research Papers* 338, University of Warwick.

Foreman-Peck, J. and Manning, D. (1988) 'How Well is BT Performing? An International Comparison of Telecommunications Total Factor Productivity', *Fiscal Studies* 9, 3: 54–67.

Foreman-Peck, J. and Millward, R. (1994) *Public and Private Ownership of British Industry 1820–1990*, Oxford: Clarendon Press.

Foreman-Peck, J. and Waterson, M. (1984) 'The Comparative Efficiency of Public and Private Enterprise in Britain: Electricity Generation between the World Wars', *Economic Journal*, conference papers, supplement to 95: 83–95.

Førsund, F. R., Lovell, C. A. K. and Schmidt, P. (1980) 'A Survey of Frontier Production Functions and of their Relationship to Efficiency Measurement', *Journal of Econometrics* 13: 27–56.

Forsyth, P. J., Hill, R. D. and Trengove, C. D. (1986) 'Measuring Airline Efficiency', *Fiscal Studies* 7 (1): 61–81.

Forsyth, P. J. and Hocking, R. D. (1980) 'Property Rights and Efficiency in a Regulated Environment: the case of Australian Airlines', *Economic Record* 56, June: 182–185.

Foster, C. D. (1992) *Privatisation, Public Ownership and the Regulation of Natural Monopoly*, Oxford: Blackwell.

Franks, J. R. and Harris, R. S. (1989) 'Shareholder Wealth Effects of Corporate Takeovers: the UK Experience 1955–1985', *Journal of Financial Economics* 23: 225–249.

Franks, J. R. and Mayer, C. (1990) 'Capital Markets and Corporate Control: a Study of France, Germany and the UK', *Economic Policy* 10: 189–231.

Frech III, H. E. (1980) 'Property Rights, the Theory of the Firm and Competitive Markets for Top Decision-Makers', *Research in Law and Economics* 2: 49–63.

Funkhouser, R. and MacAvoy, P.W. (1979) 'A Sample of Observations on Comparative Prices in Public and Private Enterprise', *Journal of Public Economics* 11: 353–368.

Furubotn, E. G. and Pejovich, S. (1972) 'Property Rights and Economic Theory: a Survey of the Recent Literature', *Journal of Economic Literature* 10: 1137–1162.

Furubotn, E. G. and Pejovich, S. (1974) *The Economics of Property Rights*, Cambridge, Mass.: Ballinger.

Galal, A., Jones, L., Tandon, P. and Vogelsang, I. (1992) *Welfare Consequences of Selling Public Enterprises*, Washington, DC.: World Bank.

Ganley, J. A. and Cubbin, J. S. (1992) *Public Sector Efficiency Measurement: Applications of Data Envelopment analysis*, Amsterdam: North Holland.

Gantt, A. H. and Dutto, G. (1968) 'Financial Performance of Government-Owned Corporations in Less Developed Countries', *IMF Staff Papers* 15 (1): 102–140.

Gao, X. M. and Reynolds, A. (1994) 'A Structural Equation Approach to Measuring Technical Change: an Application to Southeastern US Agriculture', *The Journal of Productivity Analysis* 5: 123–139.

Gemini Consulting (1995) *Privatisation in Practice: Mobilising Middle Management*, London: Gemini.

Gibbard, A. and Varian, H. (1978) 'Economic Models', *Journal of Philosophy* 75: 665–667.

Goodsell, C. T. (1985) *The Case for Bureaucracy: a Public Administration Polemic*, New Jersey: Chatham House.

Graham, R. (1983) 'British Airways and Government: a Disastrous and Ineffectual Relationship', *Public Money* 3 (1): 29–34.

Graham, C. and Prosser, T. (1988) 'Golden Shares: Industrial Policy by Stealth', *Public Law*: 413–431.

Gravelle, H. S. (1984) 'Bargaining and Efficiency in Public and Private Sector Firms', in M. Marchand, P. Pestieau and H. Tulkens (eds) *The Performance of Public Enterprises*, Amsterdam: North-Holland.

Gravelle, H. S. (1982) 'Incentives, Efficiency and Control in Public Firms', *Journal of Economics*, supplement 2: 79–104.

Green, D. P. and Shapiro, I. (1994). *Pathologies of Rational Choice Theory: a Critique of Applications in Political Science*, Yale: Yale University Press.

Green, R. and Vogelsang, I. (1994) 'British Airways: a Turn-Around Anticipating Privatization', in M. Bishop, J. Kay and C. Mayer (eds) *Privatization and Economic Performance*, Oxford: Oxford University Press.

Greenwood, R. and Hinings, C. R. (1988) 'Organizational Design Types, Tracks and the Dynamics of Strategic Change', *Organization Studies* 9 (3): 293–316.

Grinyer, P.H., McKiernan, P. and Yasai-Ardekani, M. (1988) 'Market Organizational and Managerial Correlates of Economic Performance in the UK Electrical Engineering Industry', *Strategic Management Journal* 9: 297–318.

Grossman, S. and Hart, O. (1980) 'Takeover Bids, the Free-Rider Problem and the Theory of the Corporation, *Bell Journal of Economics* 11: 42–64.

Grossman, S. and Hart, O. (1986) 'The Costs and Benefits of Ownership: a Theory of Vertical and Lateral Integration', *Journal of Political Economy* 94: 691–719.

Haas, J. E., Hall, R. H. and Johnson, N. J. (1966) 'Toward an Empirically Derived Taxonomy of Organizations', in R. V. Bowers (ed.) *Studies of Behaviour in Organizations*, Athens, Gpo.: University of Georgia Press.

Hamilton, N. M. (1971) *Pricking Pryke: the Facts on State Industry*, London: Aims of Industry.

Hammer, M. and Champy, J. (1993) *Re-engineering the Corporation: A Manifesto for Business Revolution*, London: Nicholas Brealey.

Hampden-Turner, C. (1990) *Corporate Culture: from Vicious to Virtuous Circles*, London: Economist/Hutchinson.

Hancock, R. and Price, C.W. (1995) 'Competition in the British Domestic Gas Market: Efficiency and Equity', *Fiscal Studies* 16 (3): 81–105.

Handy, C. (1986) *Understanding Organizations*, Harmondsworth: Penguin.

Hanke, S. (ed.) (1987) *Prospects for Privatization*, New York: Academy of Political Science.

Harper, J. M. (1989) *Telecommunications Policy and Management*, London: Pinter Publishers.

Hart, O. D. (1993) 'Incomplete Contracts and the Theory of the Firm', in O. E. Williamson and S. G. Winter (eds) *The Nature of the Firm: Origins, Evolution and Development*, Oxford: Oxford University Press.

Hart, O. D. (1995) *Firms, Contracts and Financial Structure*, Oxford: Oxford University Press.

Hart, O.D. and Holmstrom, B. (1987) 'The Theory of Contracts', in T.F. Bewley (ed.) *Advances in Economic Theory*, Cambridge: Cambridge University Press.

Hartley, K. and Lynk, E. (1983) 'Labour Demand and Allocation in UK Engineering Industry', *Scottish Journal of Political Economy* 30: 42–53.

REFERENCES

Hartley, K. and Ott, A. (eds) (1991) *Privatization and Economic Efficiency: a Comparative Analysis of Developed and Developing Countries*, Aldershot: Edward Elgar.

Hartley, K. and Parker, D. (1991) 'Privatization: a Conceptual Framework', in K. Hartley and A. Ott (eds) *Privatization and Economic Efficiency: a Comparative Analysis of Developed and Developing Countries*, Aldershot: Edward Elgar.

Hartley, K., Parker, D. and Martin, S. (1990) 'Privatisation and Performance in the UK Energy Industry', *International Journal of Global Energy Issues* 2 (3): 167–176.

Hartley, K., Parker, D. and Martin, S. (1991) 'Organisational Status, Ownership and Productivity', *Fiscal Studies* 12 (2): 46–60.

Haskel, J. (1994) 'The Winners and Losers from UK Privatisation', Department of Economics Working Paper No. 308, London: Queen Mary and Westfield College.

Haskel, J. and Szymanski, S. (1990) 'A Bargaining Theory of Privatisation', Centre for Business Strategy Working Paper Series 91, London: London Business School.

Haskel, J. and Szymanski, S. (1991) 'Privatisation, Jobs and Wages', *Employment Institute Economic Report* 6: 7.

Haskel, J. and Szymanski, S. (1992) 'A Bargaining Theory of Privatisation', *Annals of Public and Cooperative Economy* 63: 207–227.

Haskel, J. and Szymanski, S. (1993a) 'Privatization, Liberalization, Wages and Employment: Theory and Evidence from the UK', *Economica* 60: 161–182.

Haskel, J. and Szymanski, S. (1993b) 'The Effects of Privatisation, Restructuring and Competition on Productivity Growth in UK Public Corporations', Department of Economics Working Paper No. 286, London: Queen Mary and Westfield College.

Heath, J. (1988) 'Privatisation: the Case of BAA plc', in V. Ramanadham (ed.) *Privatization in the UK*, London: Routledge.

Heathfield, D. F. and Wibe, S. (1987) *An Introduction to Cost and Production Functions*, London: Macmillan.

Heller, R. (1995) 'British Steel', *Management Today*, June: 44–46.

Helm, D. and Powell, A. (1992) 'Pool Prices, Contracts and Regulation in the British Electricity Supply Industry', *Fiscal Studies* 13 (1): 89–105.

Helm, D. and Thompson, D. (1991) 'Privatised Transport Infrastructure and Incentives to Invest', *Journal of Transport Economics and Policy* 25: 231–246.

Hemming, R. and Mansoor, A. M. (1988) *Privatization and Public Enterprises*, Occasional Paper 56, Washington, DC.: International Monetary Fund.

Herzberg, F. (1966) *Work and the Nature of Man*, New York: World Publishing.

Hickson, D. J., Butler, R. J., Cray, D., Mallory, G. and Wilson, D. C. (1986) *Top Decisions: Strategic Decision Making in Organizations*, Oxford: Blackwell.

Hindley, B. (1970) 'Separation of Ownership and Control in the Modern Corporation', *Journal of Law and Economics* 13: 185–222.

Hirschman, A. O. (1970) *Exit, Voice and Loyalty: Responses to Decline in Firms, Organizations and States*, Cambridge, Mass.: Harvard University Press.

Hjalmarsson, L. and Veiderpass, A. (1992) 'Productivity in Swedish Electricity Retail Distribution', *Scandinavian Journal of Economics*, Special Issue, October: 193–206.

Hofstede, G. (1981) 'Management control of public and not-for-profit activities', *Accounting, Organizations and Society* 6(3): 193–211.

Holmes, A. (1990) *Electricity in Europe: Power and Profit*, London: Financial Times Management Report.

Holmstrom, B. and Tirole, J. (1989) 'The Theory of the Firm', in R. Schmalensee and R. Willig (eds) *Handbook of Industrial Organization*, Amsterdam: North-Holland.

233

Hood, C., Huby, M. and Dunsire, A. (1984) 'Bureaucrats and Budgeting Benefits: How Do British Central Departments Measure Up?', *Journal of Public Policy* 4 (3): 163–179.

Hughes, A. (1989) 'The Impact of Merger: a Survey of Empirical Evidence for the UK', in J. Fairburn and J. A. Kay (eds) *Mergers and Merger Policy*, Oxford: Oxford University Press.

Hughes, A. and Singh, A. (1987) 'Takeover and the Stock Market', *Contributions to Political Economy* 6: 73–85.

Hutchinson, G. (1991) 'Efficiency Gains through Privatization of UK Industries', in K. Hartley and A. F. Ott (eds) *Privatization and Economic Efficiency: a Comparative Analysis of Developed and Developing Countries*, Aldershot: Edward Elgar.

Hyman, H. (1989) 'Privatisation: the Facts', in C. Veljanovski (ed.) *Privatisation and Competition*, Hobart Paperback 28, London: IEA.

Jackson, P. M. (1982) *The Political Economy of Bureaucracy*, Oxford: Philip Allan.

Jackson, P. M. (1985) 'Economy, Democracy and Bureaucracy', in R. C. O. Matthews (ed.) *Economy and Democracy*, London: Macmillan.

Jackson, P. M. (ed.) (1995) *Measures for Success in the Public Sector*, Public Finance Foundation, London: CIPFA.

Jacobs, M. T. (1991) *Short-term America: the Causes and Cures of our Business Myopia*, Harvard, Mass.: Harvard Business School.

Jarrel, G., Brickley, J. and Netter, J (1988) 'The Market for Corporate Control: the Empirical Evidence since 1980', *Journal of Economic Perspectives* 2: 49–68.

Jenkinson, T. and Mayer, C. (1994) *Hostile Takeovers: Defence, Attack and Corporate Governance*, London: McGraw-Hill.

Jensen, M. C. (ed.) (1983) 'Symposium on the Market for Corporate Control', *Journal of Financial Economics* 11.

Jensen, M. C. (1986) 'Agency Costs of Free Cash Flows, Corporate Finance and Takeovers', *American Economic Review* 76: 323–329.

Jensen, M. C. and Meckling, W.H. (1976) 'Theory of the Firm: Managerial Behaviour, Agency Costs and Ownership Structure', *Journal of Financial Economics* 3 (4): 305–60.

Jensen, M. C. and Ruback, R. (1983) 'The Market for Corporate Control: the Scientific Evidence', *Journal of Financial Economics* 11: 5–50.

Jones, L. P., Tandon, P. and Vogelsang, I. (1990) *Selling Public Enterprises: a Cost Benefit Methodology*, Cambridge, Mass.: MIT Press.

Jones, L. P., Tandon, P. and Vogelsang, I. (1991) 'Net Benefits from Privatization of Public Enterprises', in K. Hartley and A.F. Ott (eds) *Privatization and Economic Efficiency: a Comparative Analysis of Developed and Developing Countries*, Aldershot: Edward Elgar.

Joubert, C. (1988) 'Strategy in the Public Sector', *Public Money and Management*, Autumn: 17–20.

Kay, J. A. (1976) 'Accountants Too Could be Happy in a Golden Age: the Accountant's Rate of Profit and Internal Rate of Return', *Oxford Economic Papers* 28: 447–460.

Kay, J. A. and Mayer, C. P. (1986) 'On the Application of Accounting Rates of Return', *Economic Journal* 96: 199–207.

Kay, J. A. and Thompson, D. J. (1986) 'Privatisation: a Policy in Search of a Rationale', *Economic Journal* 96: 18–32.

Keen, P. (1988) *Competing in Time*, Cambridge, Mass.: Ballinger.

REFERENCES

Kesner, I. F. (1987) 'Directors Stock Ownership and Organizational Performance: an Investigation of Fortune 500 Companies', *Journal of Management* 13 (3): 499–507.

Kettl, D. F. (1988) *Government by Proxy*, Washington, DC.: CQ Press.

Kikeri, S., Nellis, J. and Shirley, M. (1992) *Privatisation: the Lessons of Experience*, Washington, DC.: World Bank.

Kim, K. S. (1981) 'Enterprise Performance in the Public and Private Sectors Tanzanian Experience, 1970–75', *Journal of Development Areas* 15: 471–484.

Kim, W. S., Lee, L. W. and Francis, J.C. (1988) 'Investment Performance of Common Stocks in Relation to Inside Ownership', *Financial Review* 23 (1): 53–64.

King, J. (1986) 'The British Telecom Experience – Transformation of a Public Corporation to a Public Limited Company', *International Journal of Technology Management*, 1 (1/2): 77–84.

King, Lord J. L. (1987) 'Lessons of Privatization', *Long Range Planning*, 20 (6): 18–22.

Kopp, R. J. (1981) 'The Measurement of Productive Efficiency: a Reconsideration', *Quarterly Journal of Economics* 97: 477–503.

Kotter, J. P. and Hesketh, S. J. L. (1992) *Corporate Culture and Performance*, New York: Free Press.

Kristensen, O. P. (1980) 'The Logic of Political-bureaucratic Decision Making as a Cause of Government Growth', *European Journal of Political Research* 8: 249–264.

Kuehn, D. (1975) *Takeovers and the Theory of the Firm*, London: Macmillan.

Labich, K. (1988) 'The Big Comeback at British Airways', *Fortune* 118 (13): 163–174.

Laffont, J. J. (1989) *The Economics of Uncertainty and Information*, Cambridge, Mass.: MIT Press.

Laffont, J. J. and Tirole, J. (1990) *Privatization and Incentives*, Cambridge, Mass.: MIT Press.

Laffont, J. J. and Tirole, J. (1993) *A Theory of Incentives in Procurement and Regulation*, Cambridge, Mass.: MIT Press.

Lamming, R. (1993) *Beyond Partnership: Strategies for Innovation and Lean Supply*, London: Prentice Hall.

Langley, A. (1988) 'The Roles of Formal Strategic Planning', *Long Range Planning* 21 (3): 40–50.

Lawrence, P. R. and Lorsch, J. W. (1967) *Organization and the Environment*, Boston, Mass.: Harvard University Press.

Lawriwsky, M.L. (1984) *Corporate Structure and Performance*, London: Croom Helm.

Lawson, C. (1994) 'The Theory of State-owned Enterprises in Market Economies', *Journal of Economic Surveys* 8 (3): 283–309.

Leech, D. (1987) 'Ownership Concentration and the Theory of the Firm: a Simple Game Theoretic Approach', *Journal of Industrial Economics* 35 (3): 225–240.

Leech, D. and Leahy, J. (1991) 'Ownership Structure, Control Type Classifications and the Performance of Large Companies', *Economic Journal* 101: 1418–1437.

Lewin, L.(1991). *Self-Interest and Public Interest in Western Politics*, Oxford: Oxford University Press.

Lindblom, C. E. (1977) *Politics and Markets: The World's Political-Economic Systems*, New York: Basic Books.

Lindsay, C. M. (1976) 'A Theory of Government Enterprise', *Journal of Political Economy* 87: 1061–1077.

Lipsey, R. and Lancaster, K. (1956) 'The General Theory of Second Best', *Review of Economic Studies* 24 (1): 11–32.

Littlechild, S. C. (1981) 'Ten Steps to Denationalisation', *Journal of Economic Affairs* 2 (1): 11–19.

Littlechild, S. C. (1983) *Regulation of British Telecommunications' Profitability*, London: HMSO.

Lloyd, W. P., Jahera, J. S. and Goldstein, S.J. (1986) 'The Relationship between Returns, Ownership Structure and Market Value', *Journal of Financial Research* 9 (2): 171–177.

Long, W. F. and Ravenscraft, D. L. (1984) 'The Misuse of Accounting Rates of Return', *American Economic Review* 74 (3): 494–500.

Lovell, C. A. K. (1993) 'Production Frontiers and Productive Efficiency', in H.O. Fried, C. A. K. Lovell and S.S. Schmidt (eds) *The Measurement of Productive Efficiency*, Oxford: Oxford University Press.

Lutter, R. (1992) *Behaviour of State-owned and Private Enterprises in Imperfectly Competitive Markets: Evidence from Air Transport*, Washington, DC.: Office of Management and Budget.

Lynk, E. L. (1991) 'Telecommunications Divestiture in the UK: a Crossed Line', *Applied Economics* 23 (2): 379–384.

Lynk, E. L. (1993) 'Privatisation, Joint Production and the Comparative Efficiencies of Private and Public Ownership: the UK Water Industry Case', *Fiscal Studies* 14 (2): 98–116.

Mackenzie, K. D. (1986) 'Environmental Change and the Search for Organizational Congruency in the Financial Services Industry' in R. M. Burton and B. Obel (eds) *Innovation and Entrepreneurship in Organizations: Strategies for Competitiveness, Deregulation and Privatization*, Amsterdam Elsevier.

Madden, G. P. (1981) 'Potential Corporate Takeovers and Market Efficiency: a Note', *Journal of Finance* 36: 1191–1198.

Mann, P. and Mikesell, J. (1976) 'Ownership and Water Systems Operation', *Water Works Bulletin*, October.

Manne, H. G. (1965) 'Mergers and the Market for Corporate Control', *Journal of Political Economy* 73: 110–120.

Mansfield, R. and Poole, M. (1991) 'Advancing the Horizons: the Central Role of the Manager', paper presented to the British Academy of Management Conference, University of Bath.

Marchand, M., Pestieau, P. and Tulkens, H. (1984) *The Performance of Public Enterprises: Concepts and Measurements*, Amsterdam: North-Holland.

Marris, R. (1964) *The Economic Theory of 'Managerial' Capitalism*, New York: Free Press.

Marschak, J. and Radner, R. (1972) *Economic Theory of Teams*, New Haven: Yale University Press.

Marshall, C. (1988) 'British Airways', in R. Nelson (ed.) *Turnaround: How Twenty Well-known Companies Came Back from the Brink*, London: Mercury Books.

Maslow, A. H. (1964) *Motivation and Personality*, New York: Harper & Row.

McCormick, R. E. and Meiners, R. E. (1988) 'University Governance: a Property Rights Perspective', *Journal of Law and Economics* 31: 423–442.

McDonald, K. R. (1993) 'Why Privatization is Not Enough', *Harvard Business Review*, May–June: 49–59.

McGuire, R. A. and Ohsfeldt, R. (1986) 'Public versus Private Water Delivery: a Critical Analysis of a Hedonic Approach', *Public Finance Quarterly* 14 (3): 339–350.

McKelvey, B. (1982) *Organizational Systematics*, Berkeley, Cal.: University of California.

REFERENCES

Meeks, G. (1977) *Disappointing Marriage: a Study of the Gains from Mergers*, Occasional Paper 51, Cambridge: Cambridge University Press.

Megginson, W. L., Nash, R. C. and Randenborgh, M. Van (1994) 'The Financial and Operating Performance of Newly Privatized Firms: an International Empirical Analysis', *Journal of Finance* 49 (2): 403–452.

Mellon, E. (1993) 'Executive Agencies: leading Change from the Outside-in', *Public Money and Management* 13 (2): 25–31.

Metcalfe, L. and Richards, S. (1990) *Improving Public Sector Management*, London: Sage.

Meyer, R. A. (1975) 'Publicly Owned versus Privately Owned Utilities: a Policy Choice', *Review of Economics and Statistics* 57: 391–399.

Migue, J. L. and Belanger, C. (1974) 'Towards a General Theory of Managerial Discretion', *Public Choice* 17: 27–43.

Miles, R. H. (1982) *Coffin Nails and Corporate Strategies*, Englewood Cliffs, NJ.: Prentice Hall.

Miles, R. E. and Snow, C. C. (1984) 'Fit, Failure and the Hall of Fame', *California Management Review* 26 (3): 10–28.

Millward, R. (1988) 'Measuring Sources of Inefficiency in the Performance of Private and Public Enterprises in LDCs', in P. Cook and C. Kirkpatrick (eds) *Privatization in Less Developed Countries*, Brighton: Wheatsheaf.

Millward, R. (1990) 'Productivity in the UK Services Sector: Historical Trends 1956–1985 and Comparisons with the USA 1950–85', *Oxford Bulletin of Economics and Statistics* 52 (4): 423–435.

Millward, R. (1991) 'The Nationalized Industries', in M. Artis and D. Cobham (eds) *Labour's Economic Policies 1974–79*, Manchester: Manchester University Press.

Millward, R. and Parker, D. (1983) 'Public and Private Enterprise: Comparative Behaviour and Relative Efficiency', in R. Millward, D. Parker, L. Rosenthal, M.T. Sumner and N. Topham (eds) *Public Sector Economics*, London: Longman.

Millward, R. and Singleton, J. (1995) *The Political Economy of Nationalisation in Britain 1920–1950*, Cambridge: Cambridge University Press.

Millward, R. and Ward, R. (1987) 'The Costs of Public and Private Gas Enterprises in late 19th Century Britain', *Oxford Economic Papers* 39: 719–737.

Milward, H. B. and Rainey, H. G. (1983) 'Don't Blame the Bureaucracy', *Journal of Public Policy* 2: 1949–1968.

Mintzberg, H. (1979) *The Structuring of Organizations*, New Jersey: Prentice Hall.

Mintzberg, H. (1994) *The Rise and Fall of Strategic Planning*, London: PrenticeHall.

Mitchell, W.C. (1983) 'Fiscal Behaviour of the Modern Fiscal State: Public Choice Perspectives and Contributions', in L. Wade (ed.) *Political Economy: Recent Reviews*, Boston, Mass.: Kluwer-Nijhoff.

Mitchell, W.C. (1988) *Government As It Is*, Hobart Paper 109, London: Institute of Economic Affairs.

Mitnick, B. (1980) *The Political Economy of Regulation*, New York: Columbia University Press.

MMC (1980) *The Inner London Letter Post: a Report on the Letter Post Service in the Area Comprising the Numbered London Postal Districts*, HC 515, London: HMSO.

MMC (1981) *Central Electricity Generating Board: a Report on the Operation by the Board of its System for the Generation and Supply of Electricity in Bulk*, HC 315, London: HMSO.

MMC (1983) *National Coal Board: a Report on the Efficiency and Costs in the Development, Production and Supply of Coal by the NCB*, Cmnd 8920, London: HMSO.

MMC (1988) *British Steel Corporation*, Cm. 437, London: HMSO.

MMC (1993) *Gas and British Gas plc*, Cm. 2314–17, London: HMSO.

Molyneux, R. and Thompson, D.J. (1987) 'Nationalised Industry Performance: Still Third Rate?', *Fiscal Studies* 8 (7): 48–82.

Monsen, R. J. and Walters, K. D. (1983) *Nationalized Companies: a Threat to American Business*, New York: McGraw-Hill.

Moore, J. (1970) 'The Effectiveness of Regulation of Electric Utility Prices', *Southern Economic Journal* 36: 365–375.

Moore, J. (1983) *Why Privatise?*, Press Release, London: HM Treasury.

Moore, J. (1992) 'British Privatization: Taking Capitalism to the People', *Harvard Business Review*, January-February: 115–24.

Morck, R., Shleifer, A. and Vishny, R. W. (1990) 'Do Managerial Objectives Drive Bad Acquisitions?', *Journal of Finance* 45 (1): 31–48.

Morley, W. (1986) 'The Privatization of British Telecom – its Impact on Management', *Long Range Planning* 19 (6): 124–129.

Muellbauer, J. (1986) 'The Assessment: Productivity and Competitiveness in British Manufacturing', *Oxford Review of Economic Policy* 2 (3): 1–25.

Mueller, D. C. (1980) *The Determinants and Effects of Mergers: an International Comparative Study*, Cambridge, Mass.: Oclgeschlager Gunn & Hain.

Mueller, D. C. (ed.) (1989) *Public Choice II*, Cambridge: Cambridge University Press.

National Economic Development Office (NEDO) (1976) *A Study of UK Nationalised Industries: their Role in the Economy and Control in the Future*, London: HMSO.

Navajas, F. H. (1984) *Managerial Incentives and Control in Public Enterprises*, unpublished D.Phil thesis, University of Oxford.

Neuberg, L. G. (1977) 'Two Issues in the Municipal Ownership of Electric Power Distribution Systems', *Bell Journal of Economic and Management Science* 8: 303–323.

Newman, K. (1986) *The Selling of British Telecom*, London: Rinehart & Winston, Holt.

Nichols, T. and O'Connell Davidson, J. (1992) 'Employee Shareholders in Two Privatised Utilities', *Industrial Relations Journal* 23 (2): 107–119.

Nickell, J. (1993) 'Competition and Corporate Performance', Applied Economics Discussion Paper Series 155, Institute of Economics and Statistics, University of Oxford.

Niskanen, W. A. Jr. (1971) *Bureaucracy and Representative Government*, Chicago: Aldine.

Niskanen, W. A. Jr. (1973) *Bureaucracy, Servant or Master?* London: Institute of Economic Affairs.

Niskanen, W. A. Jr. (1987) 'Bureaucracy', in C. K. Rowley (ed.) *Democracy and Public Choice*, Oxford: Basil Blackwell.

Nove, A. (1973) *Efficiency Criteria for Nationalised Industries*, London: Allen & Unwin.

Nutt, P.C. and Backoff, R. W. (1992) *Strategic Management of Public and Third Sector Organizations: a Handbook for Leaders*, San Francisco, Cal.: Jossey-Bass.

O'Connell Davidson, J. (1993) *Privatization and Employment Relations: the Case of the Water Industry*, London: Mansell.

Oelert, W. (1976) 'Reprivatisierung des Offentlichen Personalverkehrs', *Der Personenverkehr* 4.

Ohmae, K. (1989) 'The Global Logic of Strategic Alliances', *Harvard Business Review* March-April: 143–154.

Okun, A. M. (1975) *Equality and Efficiency: the Big Tradeoff*, Washington, DC.: The Brookings Institution.

Olson, M. (1965) *The Logic of Collective Action*, Cambridge, Mass.: Harvard University Press.

Orzechowski, W. (1977) 'Economic Models of Bureaucracy: Survey, Extensions and Evidence', in T. Borcherding (ed.) *Budgets and Bureaucrats: the Sources of Government Growth*, Durham, NC.: Duke University Press.

Oswald, S. L. and Jahera, J.S. Jr. (1991) 'The Influence of Ownership on Performance: an Empirical Study', *Strategic Management Journal* 12: 321–326.

Pack, J. R. (1987) 'Privatization of Public Sector Services in Theory and Practice', *Journal of Policy Analysis and Management* 6 (4): 523–540.

Palmer, J. P., Quinn, J. and Ray, R. (1983) 'A Case Study of Public Enterprise: Gray Coach Lines Ltd', in J. R. S. Pritchard (ed.) *Crown Corporations in Canada: the Calculus of Instrument Choice*, Toronto: Butterworths.

Parker, D. (1985) 'Is the Private Sector More Efficient? A Study in the Public v Private Debate', *Public Administration Bulletin* 48: 2–23.

Parker, D. (1986) 'Public Sector Efficiency: an Enigma', *Public Enterprise* 38: 7–10.

Parker, D. (1990) 'The 1988 Local Government Act and Compulsory Competitive Tendering', *Urban Studies* 27(5): 653–67

Parker, D. (1991) 'Measuring Changes in Organisational Performance', *Graduate Management Research* 5 (4): 8–29.

Parker, D. (1993) 'Ownership, Organizational Changes and Performance', in T. Clarke and C. Pitelis (eds) *The Political Economy of Privatization*, London: Routledge.

Parker, D. (1994a) 'Privatisation and Business Restructuring: Change and Continuity in the Privatised Industries', *The Review of Policy Issues* 1 (2): 3–27.

Parker, D. (1994b) 'A Decade of Privatisation: the Effect of Ownership Change and Competition on British Telecom', *British Review of Economic Issues* 16 (40): 87–113.

Parker, D. (1995a) 'Privatisation and Agency Status: Identifying the Critical Factors for Performance Improvement', *British Journal of Management* 6: 29–43.

Parker, D. (1995b) 'Privatization and the Internal Environment: Developing our Knowledge of the Adjustment Process', *International Journal of Public Sector Management* 8 (2): 44–62.

Parker, D. and Hartley, K. (1991a) 'Organisational Status and Performance: the Effects on Employment', *Applied Economics* 23 (2): 403–416.

Parker, D. and Hartley, K. (1991b) 'Do Changes in Organisational Status affect Financial Performance?', *Strategic Management Journal* 12: 631–641.

Peltzman, S. (1971) 'Pricing in Public and Private Enterprises and Electric Utilities in the United States', *Journal of Law and Economics* 14: 109–147.

Peltzman, S. (1990) 'How Efficient is the Voting Market', *Journal of Law and Economics* 33: 27–63.

Peltzman, S. (1992) 'Voters as Fiscal Conservatives', *Quarterly Journal of Economics* 57 (2): 327–361.

Pendleton, A. and Winterton, J. (eds) (1993) *Public Enterprise in Transition: Industrial Relations in State and Privatized Companies*, London: Routledge.

Pera, A. (1989) 'Deregulation and Privatization in an Economy-Wide Context', *OECD Economic Studies* 22 (Spring): 159–204.

Perelman, S. and Pestieau, P. (1987) *The Performance of Public Enterprises: a Comparative Efficiency Study of Railways and Postal Services*, Sonderförschungsbereich 303, Bonn: Rheinische Friedrich-Wilhelms-Universitat.

Perry, J. L. and Rainey, H. G. (1988) 'The Public–Private Distinction in Organization Theory: a Critique and Research Agenda', *Academy of Management Review* 3 (2): 182–201.

Pescatrice, D. R. and Trapani, J. M. III (1980) 'The Performance and Objectives of Public and Private Utilities Operating in the US', *Journal of Public Economics* 13: 259–275.

Pestieau, P. (1989) 'Measuring the Performance of Public Enterprises: a Must in Times of Privatization', *Annals of Public and Cooperative Economy* 60 (3): 293–305.

Peters, B. G. (1989) *Comparing Public Bureaucracies: Problems of Theories and Methods*, Tuscaloosa, Ala.: University of Alabama Press.

Picot, A. and Kaulman, T. (1989) 'Comparative Performance of Government-owned and Privately-owned Industrial Corporations – Empirical Results from Six Countries', *Journal of Industrial and Theoretical Economics* 145: 298–316.

Pint, E. (1991) 'Nationalization vs. Regulation of Monopolies: the Effects of Ownership on Efficiency', *Journal of Public Economics* 44: 131–164.

Pirie, M. (1988) *Privatization in Theory and Practice*, Aldershot: Wildwood House.

Pitt, D. (1990) 'An Essentially Contestable Organisation: British Telecom and the Privatisation Debate', in J. J. Richardson (ed.) *Privatisation and Deregulation in Canada and Britain*, Aldershot: Dartmouth Press.

Plane, P. (1992) 'Production Efficiency of Public Enterprises: a Macroeconomic Analysis based on a Cross-section Estimation of a Neoclassical Production Function', *Applied Economics* 24: 833–844.

Polanyi, G. (1968) *Comparative Returns from Investment in Nationalised Industries*, London: Institute of Economic Affairs.

Polanyi, G. and Polanyi, P. (1972) 'The Efficiency of Nationalised Industries', *Moorgate and Wall Street Review*, Spring: 17–49.

Polanyi, G. and Polanyi, P. (1974) *Failing the Nation: the Record of the Nationalised Industries*, London: Fraser Ansbacher.

Pollitt, M. G. (1994) 'Productive Efficiency in Electricity Transmission and Distribution Systems', Applied Economics Discussion Paper Series, University of Oxford: Institute of Economics and Statistics.

Pollitt, M. G. (1995) *Ownership and Performance in Electric Utilities: the International Evidence on Privatization and Efficiency*, Oxford: Oxford University Press.

Posner, M (1984) 'Privatisation: the Frontier between Public and Private', *Policy Studies* 5 (1): 22–32.

Powell, V. (1987) *Improving Public Enterprise Performance: Concepts and Techniques*, Geneva: International Labour Office.

Price, C. and Weyman-Jones, T. G. (1993) 'Malmquist Indices of Productivity Change in the UK Gas Industry before and after Privatisation', Economic Research Paper 93/12, Loughborough University of Technology: Department of Economics.

Prokopenko, J. (1995) 'Future Management Strategies', in J. Prokopenko (ed.) *Management for Privatization: Lessons from Industry and Public Service*, Management Development Series 32, Geneva: International Labour Office.

Pryke, R. (1971) *Public Enterprise in Practice*, London: MacGibbon & Kee.

Pryke, R. (1981) *The Nationalised Industries: Policies and Performance since 1968*, Oxford: Martin Robertson.

Pryke, R. (1982) 'The Comparative Performance of Public and Private Enterprise', *Fiscal Studies* 3(2): 68–81.

Pugh, D. S. and Hickson D. J. (1976) *Organisational Structure in its Context: the Aston Programme*, Farnborough: Saxon House.

Pugh, D. S., Hickson, D. J. and Hinings, C. R. (1969) 'An Empirical Taxonomy of Work Organizations', *Administrative Science Quarterly* 14: 115–126.

Rainey, H. G. (1989) 'Public Management: Recent Research on the Political Context and Managerial Roles, Structures and Behaviours', *Journal of Management* 15 (2): 229–250.

Rainey, H. G. (1991) *Understanding and Managing Public Organizations*, San Francisco, CA.: Jossey-Bass.

REFERENCES

Rainey, H. G., Backoff, R. W. and Levine, C.L. (1976) 'Comparing Public and Private Organizations', *Public Administration Review* 36: 233–246.

Ravenscraft, D. and Scherer, F. (1987) *Mergers, Sell-Offs and Economic Efficiency*, Washington, DC.: The Brookings Institution.

Rees, R. (1984) 'A Positive Theory of Public Enterprises', in M. Marchand, P. Pestieau and H. Tulkens (eds) *The Performance of Public Enterprises: Concepts and Measurement*, Amsterdam: New Holland.

Rees, R. (1985) 'The Theory of Principal and Agent: Parts 1 and 2', *Bulletin of Economic Research* 37 (1): 46–69 and 37 (2): 70–90.

Rees, R. (1989) 'Modelling Public Enterprise Performance', in D. Helm, J. Kay and D. Thompson (eds) *The Market for Energy*, Oxford: Oxford University Press.

Reidy, M. (1995) 'Privatisation, Regulation and the Electricity Market', in D. Helm (ed.) *British Utility Regulation: Principles, Experience and Reform*, Oxford: Oxera Press.

Richardson, J. J. (1993) 'Public Utilities management', in K. A. Eliassen and J. Kooliman (eds) *Managing Public Organizations: Lessons from Contemporary European Experience*, second edition, London: Sage.

Ring, P. S. and Perry, J. L. (1985) 'Strategic Management in Public and Private Organizations: Implications of Distinctive Contexts and Constraints', *Academy of Management Review* 10: 276–286.

Robson, W. A. (1969) 'Ministerial Control of the Nationalised Industries', *Political Quarterly*, January: 103–112.

Roethlisberger, F. J. and Dickson, W. J. (1939) *Management and the Worker*, Cambridge, Mass.: Harvard University Press.

Roll, R. (1986) 'The Hubris Hypothesis of Corporate Takeovers', *Journal of Business* 59: 197–216.

Ross, S. A. (1973) 'The Economic Theory of Agency: the Principal's Problem', *American Economic Review* 62: 134–139.

Roth, G. (1987) 'Airport Privatisation', *Proceedings of the Academy of Political Science* 36 (3): 74–82.

Rowley, C. K. and Yarrow, G. K. (1981) 'Property Rights, Regulation and Public Enterprise: the Case of the British Steel Industry 1957–1975', *International Review of Law and Economics* 1: 63–96.

Rumelt, R.P. (1974) *Structure, and Economic Performance*, Boston, Mass.: Harvard University Press.

Salamon, G. L. and Smith, E. D. (1979) 'Corporate Control and Management Misrepresentation of Firm Performance', *Bell Journal of Economics* 10 (1): 319–328.

Sampson, C. I. (1995) 'Privatizing Banking Services in Jamaica', J. Prokopenko (ed.) *Management for Privatization: Lessons from Industry and Public Service*, Management Development Series 32, Geneva: International Labour Office.

Sappington, D. and Stiglitz, J. E. (1987) 'Information and Regulation', in E.E. Bailey (ed.) *Public Regulation: New Perspectives on Institutions and Policies*, Cambridge, Mass.: MIT Press.

Schellenger, M. H., Wood, D. D., and Tashakori, A. (1989) 'Board of Directors Composition, Shareholder Wealth and Dividend Policy', *Journal of Management* 15 (3): 457–467.

Scherer, F. M. (1980) *Industrial Market Structure and Economic Performance*, second edition, Chicago: Rand McNally.

Schmidt, P. and Lovell, C. A. K. (1979) 'Estimating Technical and Allocative Inefficiency Relative to Stochastic Production and Cost Frontiers', *Journal of Econometrics* 9: 343–366.

Schotter, A. (1985) *Free Market Economics: a Critical Appraisal*, New York: St Martins Press.

Seiford, L. M. and Thrall, R. M. (1990) 'Recent Developments in DEA: the Mathematical Approach to Frontier Analysis', *Journal of Econometrics* 46 (1/2): 7–38.

Select Committee on Nationalised Industries (1968) *Report and Proceedings of the Committee*, volume 1, London: HMSO.

Shapiro, C. and Willig, R. D. (1990) 'Economic Rationales for the Scope of Privatization', in E.N. Suleiman and J. Waterbury (eds) *The Political Economy of Public Sector Reform and Privatization*, Boulder: Westview Press.

Shleifer, A. (1985) 'A Theory of Yardstick Competition', *Rand Journal of Economics* 16: 319–27.

Shleifer, A. and Summers, L. (1991) 'Breach of Trust in Hostile Takeovers', in A. Auerbach (ed.) *Corporate Takeovers: Causes and Consequences*, Chicago: Chicago University Press.

Shleifer, A. and Vishny, R. W. (1986) 'Large Shareholders and Corporate Control', *Journal of Political Economy* 94: 461–488.

Siegel, S. (1956) *Nonparametric Statistics*, Tokyo: McGraw-Hill Kogakusha.

Singh, A. (1971) *Takeovers, their Relevance to the Stock Market and the Theory of the Firm*, Cambridge: Cambridge University Press.

Singh, A. (1975) 'Takeovers, Economic Natural Selection and the Theory of the Firm: Evidence from the Post-war UK Experience', *Economic Journal* 85: 497–515.

Skapinker, M. (1995) 'Ayling Takes the Controls', *Financial Times*, 13 November: 12.

Slatter, S. (1984) *Corporate Recovery*, Harmondsworth: Penguin.

Smith, P. (1990) 'The Use of Performance Indicators in the Public Sector', *Journal of the Royal Statistical Society* Series A 153 (1): 53–72.

Smith, P. (1993) 'Outcome-related Performance Indicators and Organizational Control in the Public Sector', *British Journal of Management* 4: 135–151.

Smith, P. E., Barnard, J. M. and Smith, G. (1986) 'Privatisation and Cultural Change: a Case Study of Management Development in British Telecom', *Journal of Management Development* 5 (2): 51–61.

Smith, P. E., Barnard, J. M. and Smith, G. (1988) 'When Public Becomes Private', *Management Decision* 26 (1): 11–15.

Sorensen, R. J. (1993) 'The Efficiency of Public Service Provision', in K.A. Eliassen and J. Koolman (eds) *Managing Public Organizations: Lessons from Contemporary European Experience* second edition, London: Sage.

Souter, D. (1995) 'A Stakeholder Approach to Regulation', in D. Helm (ed.) *British Utility Regulation: Principles, Experience and Reform*, Oxford: Oxera Press.

Spackman, M. (1991) *Discount Rates and Rates of Return in the Public Sector: Economic Issues*, Government Economic Service Working Paper 113, London.

Sterne, G. (1993) 'Company Profitability and Finance', *Bank of England Quarterly Bulletin* 33 (3): 361–371.

Stevens, B. (1992) 'Prospects for Privatisation in OECD Countries', *National Westminster Bank Quarterly Review*, August: 2–22.

Stewart, J. and Ranson, S. (1988) 'Management in the Public Domain', *Public Money and Management*, Summer: 13–19.

Stewart, J. and Walsh, K. (1994) 'Performance Measurement: When Performance can Never be Defined', *Public Money and Management* 14 (2): 45–49.

Thompson, J. D. (1967) *Organizations in Action*, New York: McGraw-Hill.

REFERENCES

Thompson, P. (1991) *Sharing the Success: the Story of NFC*, London: Fontana/ Collins.

Torbert, W. R. (1989) 'Leading Organizational Transformation', in R.W. Woodman and W.A. Pasmore (eds) *Research in Organization Change and Development*, Greenwich, Conn.: JAI Press.

TUC (1986) *Bargaining in Privatised Companies*, London: Trades Union Congress.

Tullock, G. (1965) *The Politics of Bureaucracy*, Washington, DC.: Public Affairs Press.

Tullock, G. (1976) *The Vote Motive*, London: Institute of Economic Affairs.

Tullock, G. (1979) 'Bureaucracy and the Growth of Government', in *The Taming of Government*, London: Institute of Economic Affairs.

Turnbull, P. (1991) 'Labour Market Deregulation and Economic Performance – the Case of Britain's Docks', *Work, Employment and Society* 5 (1): 17–35.

Turnbull, P. (1993) 'Docks', in A. Pendleton and J. Winterton (eds) *Public Enterprise in Transition: Industrial Relations in State and Privatized Corporations*, London: Routledge.

Turnbull, P. and Weston, S. (1993) 'Cooperation or Control? Capital Restructuring and Labour Relations on the Docks', *British Journal of Industrial Relations* 31 (1): 115–134.

Tyler, W. G. (1979) 'Technical Efficiency in Production in a Developing Country: an Empirical Examiniation of the Brazilian Plastics and Steel Industries', *Oxford Economic Papers* 31 (3): 477–495.

Udehn, L. (1996) *The Limits of Public Choice: a Sociological Critique of the Economic Theory of Politics*, London: Routledge.

United Research (1990) *Privatization: Implications for Cultural Change*, Morristown, NJ.: United Research.

Vacha, S. (1995) 'Privatization in Three Large Manufacturing Companies in the Czech Republic and Slovakia', in J. Prokopenko (ed.) *Management for Privatization: Lessons from Industry and Public Service*, Management Development Series 32, Geneva: International Labour Office.

Veljanovski, C. (1987) *Selling the State*, London: Weidenfeld & Nicolson.

Vernon, R. (1989) 'Conceptual Aspects of Privatization', *CEPAL Review* 37: 143–149.

Vickers, J. and Yarrow, G. (1988) *Privatization: An Economic Analysis*, Cambridge, Mass.: MIT Press.

Vining, A. R. and Boardman, A. E. (1990) 'Ownership versus Competition: Efficiency in Public Enterprise', mimeo., Simon Fraser University.

Wallace, R. L. and Junk, P. E. (1970) 'Economic Inefficiency of Small Municipal Electric Generating Systems', *Land Economics*, February: 98–104.

Waterson, M. (1995) 'Developing Utility Regulation in the UK', in D. Helm (ed.) *British Utility Regulation: Principles, Experience and Reform*, Oxford: Oxera Press.

Weber, M. (1912: 1964) *The Theory of Social and Economic Organization* (translated by A.M. Henderson and T. Parsons), New York: Free Press.

Weiss, H. L. (1974) 'Why Business and Government Exchange Executives', *Harvard Business Review*, July-August: 129–140.

Wheatley, J. J. (1986) 'Competition, Privatization and Change at British Telecom', in R. M. Burton and B. Obel (eds), *Innovation and Entrepreneurship in Organizations: Strategies for Competitiveness, Deregulation and Privatization*, Amsterdam and Oxford: Elsevier.

Wildavsky, A. (1979) *The Politics of the Budgetary Process*, Boston, Mass.: Little Brown.

Williamson, O. E. (1964) *The Economics of Discretionary Behaviour: Managerial Objectives in a Theory of the Firm*, Englewood Cliffs, NJ.: Prentice Hall.

Williamson, O. E. (1970) *Corporate Control and Business Behaviour*, Englewood Cliffs, NJ.: Prentice Hall.

Williamson, O. E. (1975) *Markets and Hierarchies: Analysis and Antitrust Implications: a Study in the Economics of Internal Organisation*, London: Free Press.

Williamson, O. E. (1991) 'The Firm as a Nexus of Treaties: an Introduction', in M. Aoki, M. B. Gustafsson and O. E. Williamson (eds) *The Firm as a Nexus of Treaties*, London: Sage.

Wilson, J. Q. (1989) *Bureaucracy: What Government Agencies Do and Why They Do It*, New York: Basic Books.

Windle, R. J. (1991) 'The World's Airlines: a Cost and Productivity Comparison', *Journal of Transport Economics and Policy* 25: 31–49.

Wintrobe, R. (1987) 'The Market for Corporate Control and the Market for Political Control', *Journal of Law, Economics and Organization* 3: 435–448.

Winward, J. (1994) 'Privatization and Domestic Consumers' in M. Bishop, J. Kay and C. Mayer (eds) *Privatization and Economic Performance*, Oxford: Oxford University Press.

Wittmer, D. (1991) 'Serving the People or Serving for Pay: Reward Preferences Amongst Government, Hybrid Sector and Business Managers', *Public Productivity and Management Review* 14: 369–383.

Wood, E. G. (1975) *Comparative Performance of British Industries*, London: Graham & Trotman.

Woodward, N. (1988) 'Managing Cultural Change on Privatisation', in V.V. Ramanadham (ed.) *Privatisation in the UK*, London: Routledge.

Woodward N. (1990) 'Public Enterprise, Privatization, and Cultural Adaptation', in J. Heath (ed.) *Public Enterprise at the Crossroads*, London: Routledge.

World Bank (1983) *World Development Report 1983*, Washington, DC.: World Bank.

World Bank (1995) *Bureaucrats in Business: the Economics and Politics of Government Ownership*, Washington, DC.: Oxford University Press/World Bank.

Wright, M. (1987) 'Government Divestments and the Regulation of Natural Monopolies in the UK', *Energy Policy* 15 (3): 193–216.

Yarrow, G. (1986) 'Privatization in Theory and Practice', *Economic Policy* 2: 319–378.

Yarrow, G. (1989) 'Privatisation and Economic Performance in Britain', *Carnegie-Rochester Conference Series on Public Policy* 31: 303–344.

Yunker, J. A. (1975) 'The Economic Performance of Public and Private Enterprise: the Case of US Electric Utilities', *Journal of Economics and Business* 28: 60–67.

Zahra, S. A. and Pearce, J.A. II (1989) 'Boards of Directors and Corporate Financial Performance: a Review and Integrative Model', *Journal of Management* 15 (2): 291–334.

Zeckhauser, R. J. and Horn, M. (1989) 'The Control and Performance of State-owned Enterprises', in P. W. MacAvoy, W. T. Stanbury, G. Yarrow and R. J. Zeckhauser (eds) *Privatization and State-owned Enterprises: Lessons from the United States, Great Britain and Canada*, Boston: Kluwer.

INDEX

Note: page numbers in italics refer to figures or tables where these are separated from their textual reference.